A VISION FOR AMERICA'S F·U·T·U·R·E

AN AGENDA FOR THE 1990S:
A CHILDREN'S DEFENSE BUDGET

CHILDREN'S DEFENSE FUND

DEAR LORD
BE GOOD TO ME
THE SEA IS SO
WIDE AND SO
MY BOAT IS
SO SMALL

ISBN: 938008-67-6
Library of Congress 88-063421

DEDICATION

In memory of

M. Carl Holman

Gentle, caring friend and brother, teacher, poet, civil rights leader, friend of children and the poor whose constancy and presence we miss so much.

Wiley Branton

Joyful, effective civil rights lawyer whose commitment to serving others touched so many lives.

John Doe, alias "Willie" or "Wolfman"

Homeless American who died in November 1988 on a grate across from the State Department in our nation's capital which he inhabited for over a decade—a daily symbol of America's unfinished business. He left a legacy to be emulated by the rest of us. "He had a dignity to himself," a Catholic caseworker said. "Never once did I see him raise his voice. If someone took his food from him, he'd walk away. He was unfailingly wonderful."

Lisa Steinberg

Battered and murdered child whose life and death should remind us that suffering and violence and neglect are no respecters of race and class. Child of a teen mother; illegal adoptee of professional, privileged white parents; ward of a negligent, understaffed child welfare system; Lisa, like Willie, challenges each of us to see, to hear, and to act.

The thousands of invisible starving children of Somalia and the 38,000 children of the world who die each day from hunger and malnutrition.

ACKNOWLEDGMENTS

The following CDF staff wrote the chapters indicated. Please address any specific questions to them: Sara Rosenbaum, Kay Johnson, Dana Hughes, and Joseph Liu (Health); Nancy Ebb, Cliff Johnson, and MaryLee Allen (Family Income); Lisa Mihaly (Homelessness and Housing); Karen Pittman (Education); Cliff Johnson (Young Families and Youth Employment); Karen Pittman, Gina Adams, and Sharon Adams-Taylor (Adolescent Pregnancy Prevention); Helen Blank (Child Care); MaryLee Allen (Vulnerable Children and Families). Mary Bourdette and Camille Fountain prepared CDF's Nonpartisan Congressional Voting Record of 1988.

Bob Greenstein of the Center on Budget and Policy Priorities made a major contribution to the chapter on Food Assistance. Any questions about food stamps or other programs discussed in that chapter should be directed to him at the Center, 236 Massachusetts Avenue, N.E., Suite 305, Washington, D.C., 20002, (202) 544-0591.

James D. Weill directed overall work on this book. Virginia Witt and Belva Finlay edited the material, and Donna M. Jablonski coordinated production. Paul Smith oversaw the research and Janet Simons assisted with research and produced many of the charts and tables. David Heffernan and Janis Johnston provided editorial and production assistance.

Sharie Brown, Pamela Cary, Kathy Douglas, Melva Edmondson, Chiquita Edwards, Camille Fountain, Beverley Gallimore, Kymberly Sykes, Perlia Smith, and Michele Thompson helped prepare the manuscript. Janice Euell and Orlando Bugarin assisted in assuring smooth production and distribution, and Tommy Golen and Darrick Weaver provided other production assistance.

All press inquiries should be directed to Claude Duncan.

The New York Community Trust and the Rockfeller Family Fund have generously supported the analysis for this book, and the Revson Foundation gives general support to CDF publications.

Typesetting, design, and layout by Lexicon Graphics. Printing by District Lithograph Company, Inc.

CONTENTS

THE STATUS OF AMERICA'S CHILDREN

"AND A LITTLE CHILD SHALL LEAD THEM ALL"

FOREWORD

Woe to those who are at ease in Zion ... but are not grieved over the ruin of Joseph!

Amos 6:1-6

I do not trust my weapons. They could not save me.

King David, Psalm 44

The American people are infected with racism—that is the peril. Paradoxically, they are also infected with democratic ideals—that is the hope. While doing wrong, they have the potential to do right. But they do not have a millennium to make changes. Nor have they a choice of continuing in the old way. The future they are asked to inaugurate is not so unpalatable that it justifies the evils that beset the nation. To end poverty, to extirpate prejudice, to free a tormented conscience, to make a tomorrow of justice, fair play, and creativity—all these are worthy of the American ideal.

We have ... an opportunity to avoid a national disaster and create a new spirit of class and racial harmony. We can write another luminous moral chapter in American history. All of us are on trial in this troubled hour, but time still permits us to meet the future with a clear conscience.

Martin Luther King, Jr.
"Showdown for Nonviolence,"
published in *Look* magazine
after his assassination on April 4, 1968

This book, *A Vision for America's Future*, is a picture of the lives of American children and families today and a projected picture of the year 2000 and beyond, if current trends persist. It provides the most recent national, state, city, and international data about America's children; outlines an immediate preventive and ameliorative investment agenda for the federal government, states, and private sector; and suggests some ways to pay for it. It describes what children need both from their parents and from extended community parents; and also describes some of the successful and promising policies, programs, and actions occurring around the country to prevent and reduce child poverty and its offsprings (hunger, homelessness, infant and child mortality and sickness, unsafe day care, teen pregnancies, and school dropouts). Finally, it calls for greater commitment to service by all Americans and shows you how your Senators and Representatives voted on key children's issues in 1988.

Like all CDF publications, this book is the collective effort of an extraordinarily dedicated and skilled CDF staff. We will continue to inundate you with reports and information in every form we can manage until the nation sees, hears, and responds to the needs of our children and our future. I also hope I give adequate voice and thanks to the millions of hands of compassion all over

America that have been sticking increasingly numbed fingers in the dikes to staunch their community's tides of child and family need. Millions more must join them—starting at the top and working down (from the White House and Congress, State Houses and legislatures, city halls and councils, corporate board rooms, pulpits, and professional associations) and from the bottom up (from grassroots networks, rural poverty pockets, ghettos, and barrios).

I am not running for anything, take no government money, seek no government or other job, share all the foibles and frustrations I decry here, and am as scared as any parent about my lack of control over my children's futures. And I am almost as concerned about the many disconnected, drifting children of privilege, who have too many things but too little purposeful challenge, as I am about the victims of spiraling child poverty, who are time bombs of misery and despair waiting to explode in communities all over America. As a result, this Foreword is both blunt and personal. I alone am responsible for any errors in judgment.

Lisa, Jessica, Shamal, and "Jason"

Americans are mesmerized by Lisa Steinberg's tragic death, a child whose illegal adoption was not detected by our overburdened, inadequate child welfare system. We cheered when Jessica McClure was rescued from an open well shaft at an unregulated family day care home she should not have fallen into in the first place. When eight-month-old Shamal Jackson died in New York City from poverty complicated by low birthweight, poor nutrition, viral infection, and homelessness, we did not hear much about him. But during his short life he never slept in an apartment or house. He had slept in shelters with strangers, in hospitals, in welfare hotels, in the welfare office, and in the subways which he and his mother rode late at night when there was no place else to go. Nor have we heard about two-pound, six-ounce "Jason," fighting for his life at the District of Columbia's Children's Hospital Neonatal Intensive Care Ward, like thousands of other babies in similar wards all over America. At birth—three months before he was due—Jason weighed just over one pound. Jason lives because tubes connect his lungs and every available vein to the many machines that are needed to feed him, keep him warm, and help him take his next breath. He has a heart problem. And he has already suffered seizures because of damage to his nervous system caused by bleeding into his head. Jason may face life with mental handicaps because of the bleeding, his nurse says.

Prematurity like Jason's can result from a number of complex medical and social problems that affect a mother's health and her pregnancy. What exactly led to Jason's premature birth will never be known. We do know, however, that unless a mother receives early and adequate prenatal care, conditions that can lead to prematurity cannot be detected or treated. And Jason's mother, like almost one-third of American mothers, did not.

Remember these children. They are the small human tragedies all over America behind the statistics you are about to read.

The 1988 Election Year: A Bipartisan Consensus On Early Childhood Investment

CDF's goal is to make preventive investment in children and families a cornerstone of national domestic policy over the next four years, in order to make sure that current and future Lisas, Jessicas, Shamals, and "Jasons" are born and grow up healthy, have quality child care, are well-educated, have a decent home with a family and community strong enough to meet their needs, and have a chance to contribute to our nation.

During 1988 children's needs took a bipartisan leap toward the center of the political marketplace. The election of 1988 rang out with campaign promises for America's children. Child care centers replaced factory sites as the preferred backdrop for television news coverage. Presidential candidates issued position papers on children and both party platforms, competing for ownership of the future, pledged to invest in children. And Congress took a few important incremental steps to improve child health, child support, and child care (for welfare recipients).

At least 10 senatorial candidates featured children's ads in their campaigns (seven won) and 34 governors, Republicans and Democrats, prominently featured investment in children in their state of the state addresses. Virginia Gov. Gerald Baliles, chairman of the National Governors' Association (NGA), has set the needs of children as a top NGA priority. A new NGA task force to identify steps states can take to reduce infant mortality, provide health services for children, address the needs of dropouts, and meet working parents' needs for child care, has been organized and is being chaired by Arkansas Gov. Bill Clinton. Republican governors like Oklahoma's Henry Bellmon, Illinois' James Thompson, and New Jersey's Thomas Kean are emphasizing investing in children in their states.

The National League of Cities published a 1988 report on children and families, and the Conference of Mayors issued a study on the status of children in cities.

A national bipartisan consensus has been achieved on the importance of early childhood investment. It is long overdue. Now we have got to *do* it. The debate over the next four to eight years will be on the form, level, and timetable of that investment. The recent *American Agenda* report, cochaired by former Presidents Ford and Carter, put investing in at-risk children among the top six immediate national priorities. The study, given to President Bush in November, calls for a $2 billion increase in investment in each of the next eight years to ensure full funding for these successful children's programs: Head Start; the Supplemental Food Program for Women, Infants, and Children (WIC); prenatal care, immunizations, and preventive health care; and Chapter 1 of the Elementary and Secondary Education Act education supplements. This list is very similar to CDF's immediate priorities, which also include prompt enactment of the Act for Better Child Care (ABC) bill to provide available, affordable, quality child care; an increase in the minimum wage and other income supplements to help working poor families; and measures to prevent growing child homelessness. We also seek a national commitment to providing service opportunities for all youths and increased investments in the survival and protection of children all around the world, especially Third World children.

President Bush's campaign position paper, *Invest in Our Children*, overlaps significantly with the Ford-Carter and CDF immediate investment agenda. Although there are differences on the form of federal child care assistance, he and a critical mass within both parties agree on the need for a federal role and a significant investment in child care for working parents.

President Bush's campaign proposal for a $1.5 billion children's tax credit is a welcome supplement to but not substitute for the ABC bill: Its maximum $1,000 tax break will not address the inadequate supply, or quality, or cost of child care (a national average of $3,000 per child per year) for a low- or moderate-income working family. And poor parents have a cash flow problem and cannot wait a year for a refund through the Internal Revenue Service (IRS). Poor parents need both the place and the upfront means to have their children cared for each day and week.

If families are to have real choices about a parent's staying home with the children, our nation must provide them with the economic supports they need to make those choices and still provide for their children. Those supports would include adequate employment opportunities, the chance to earn a decent family wage, parental leave and flexible work schedules, and more family income support policies similar to the children's tax credit President Bush espouses. But we must deal right now with a child care crisis that demands an immediate response like the ABC bill.

A Bill of Hope for America's Children

CDF's immediate preventive investment goals are to:

1. Ensure a health floor under every low-income mother and child in the nation by 1992.

2. Ensure that the nutrition program for pregnant women, infants, and children (WIC) reaches all rather than just half of the women and children needing nutrition supplements.

3. Ensure that every eligible child will be able to enroll in a Head Start program by 1992.

4. Ensure that American children are fully immunized.

5. Ensure that every low-income child with a mother in the labor force has available, affordable, quality child care through immediate enactment of the Act for Better Child Care.

6. Ensure that every child eligible for the compensatory education services of Chapter 1 of the Elementary and Secondary Education Act will receive them by 1992—a goal already set by Congress.

7. Increase the minimum wage and other family income supplements and ensure decent, affordable housing for every child and parent.

We believe these first-tier survival goals are achievable over the next four or five years and should be pursued as fast as the delivery systems of these already successful and proposed new programs can effectively serve more children. The longer we wait the more children we will lose. State and local governments do not have to wait for the federal government to act, but should be providing supplemental funding for as many of these programs as they can. For we are at a point in national life when we no longer have the luxury of time nor the unchallenged myth of a guaranteed tomorrow.

To these seven minimum survival goals we add three more:

8. A commitment to national service for all youths. We support the Wingspread Conference Resolution of the Coalition for National Service that states, "with appropriate leadership and support from the federal government, the best of existing youth service programs will be expanded, new initiatives will be developed, many more young people will be involved, and citizen service can become an integral part of every young American's experience."

9. Generous investment in the child survival campaigns of UNICEF and others to prevent the 38,000 daily unnecessary poverty-related child deaths around the world, which are a rebuke to God and to humankind (see UNICEF's *State of the World's Children 1989*).

10. Strong U.S. support for adoption of the United Nations Convention on the Rights of the Child to assure an internationally accepted moral and legal framework for the world's children.

President Bush's Promises to Children

I applaud President Bush's repeated campaign promises to invest in children (see p. xxxvii). As every parent knows, it is very important not to break a promise to a child. I have confidence that he will keep his word. I thank him for his campaign pledge in Littleton, Colorado, to "talk and talk and talk until our country is working together to reach children." I look forward, on many occasions, beginning with his inaugural address and annual State of the Union addresses, to his fulfilling it.

Only two presidents in the twentieth century have sent messages to the Congress of the United States devoted solely to children. I urge President Bush to be the third. Beginning in 1989, I also hope he will not only "talk and talk and talk" but act and act and act—in his legislative proposals; in his budgets; in his effective implementation of new child care, child support, employment and training, child health, and fair housing protections enacted by the Congress in 1988; and in using the White House, like President Theodore Roosevelt, as a bully pulpit to reverse the child and family deficits I am about to describe.

Why America May Go to Hell

A few days before his assassination on April 4, 1968, Dr. Martin Luther King, Jr., called his mother to give her his sermon title for the next Sunday bulletin at Ebenezer Baptist Church. It was "Why America May Go to Hell."

The facts and trends I am about to recite may take us there unless we open our eyes and ears and hearts and see and hear and respond to our children, families, and neighbors in need with a sense of urgency and action.

This is truth and consequences time in America. The election year is over and the chickens of child neglect are coming home to roost. Our national facade of general prosperity is pitted by pockets of depression in many rural and urban areas and among some groups of Americans, including young families of all races. And it hides intolerable extremes of wealth and need exemplified by Donald Trump's luxurious yacht and homeless "John Doe's" November 1988 death on a grate across from the State Department. Our national security teeters atop an overstocked, overpriced suicide arsenal in which we have invested $1.9 trillion since 1980 while cutting $40 billion from programs for poor children and families. Yet today we cannot even ensure the safety of our children, or of any of us, on the streets of America.

Each day in the United States in 1986, an average of five youths under 18 were murdered. In our nation's capital, an average of two children a month died of knife and gunshot wounds during the first eight months of 1988. A child is safer in Northern Ireland than in America.

Our children are growing poorer while our nation is growing richer. All groups of children are poorer today than they were at the beginning of the decade—especially white children, whose poverty rates have increased by almost a third. If present trends persist, white children may eventually face the same savage levels of poverty in the future that now afflict black and Hispanic children. Today nearly one in two black and one in three Hispanic children is poor.

If we do not rise off our national rear end and mobilize to prevent and reduce child poverty, between now and the year 2000 *all* of the growth in our child population will consist of poor children and our children in the next century will be poorer than today.

• In the year 2000, one in four of all American children, 16 million children, will be poor—3 million more than in 1987.

• By the year 2030, one in three, or 25 million American children, will be poor—about double the number today.

And these projections assume that the nation's economy remains stable, with typical cycles of recession and boom, for children are the first to suffer during recession and the last to benefit from recovery. An unusually severe economic setback could push the child poverty rate even higher.

A Growing Proportion of America's Children Are Not Only Poor but Black and Brown

Not only will American children be poorer at the turn of the century, a larger proportion of those on the train carrying both an aging America and a multitrillion dollar federal debt-ridden economy into the next century will be black and brown children. Unless America heals its racial divisions, the chickens of continuing racism also will come home to roost in declining economic competitiveness and quality of life.

• By the year 2000, the total number of minority children will increase by more than 25 percent and will constitute one-third of all children; the number of white, non-Hispanic children will increase by only two-tenths of 1 percent.

• By the year 2030, minority children will increase by more than 52 percent and constitute 41 percent of our child population; 45 percent by the year 2080. There will be 6 million fewer white, non-Hispanic children in 2030 than today.

• In the twenty-second century, America may become a majority nonwhite (black or Hispanic) nation more closely resembling today's world, which is two-thirds nonwhite.

The darker hands of America's more distant future are already shaping our present and our immediate tomorrow. The number of young adults 18 to 24 years old who are our college students, labor force, military recruits, and parents will continue to decline between 1985 and 2030, and all of the growth after 2000 will be minority. Between now and the year 2000, only one in four new labor force entrants will be white males; in 2000, the Hudson Institute estimates, only 15 percent of all new labor force entrants will be white males born in the United States.

Demographics do not dictate destiny. Attitudes, leadership, and values do. It is the set of the national sails and not the gales that will determine the safety and quality of the American future. This is, for all its shadows, *not* a gloom and doom book. It is a "work hard together and go fetch our future" book.

We cannot go back and change the last decade's birth rates. But we can prevent and reduce our rising child, family, and human deficits. In the waning years of the twentieth century, doing what is right and doing what is necessary to save our national skins have converged. I see the 1990s as a marvelous opportunity to revitalize and strengthen our democracy.

In 11 years, when the new century dawns with new global economic and military challenges, America will be ready to compete economically and lead morally only if we:

• Stop cheating and neglecting our children for selfish, short-sighted, personal and political gain.

• Stop clinging to our racial past and recognize that America's ideals, future, and fate are as inextricably intertwined with the fate of its poor and nonwhite children as with its privileged and white ones.

- Love our children more than we fear each other and our perceived or real external enemies.

- Acquire the discipline to invest preventively and systematically in all of our children *now* in order to reap a better trained work force and more stable families *tomorrow*.

- Curb the desires of the overprivileged so that the survival needs of the less privileged may be met, and spend less on weapons of death and more on lifelines of constructive development for our citizens.

- Set clear national, state, city, community, and personal goals for child survival and development, and invest whatever leadership, commitment, time, money, and sustained effort are needed to achieve them.

- Begin to live our lives in less selfish and more purposeful ways, redefining success by national and individual character and service rather than by national consumption and the superficial barriers of race and class.

The cost of repairing our crumbling national foundation will be expensive in leadership, effort, time, and money. The cost of not repairing it, or patching cosmetically, may be fatal.

The Vision of America in the Year 2000 and Beyond

Now is the time for us to begin the shoring up of our national foundation together with leadership from a new president and Congress. Unless the entire nation mobilizes for children and the future, and unless rich, democratic America with the world's most sophisticated health technology somehow cannot do a better job in saving and producing healthy babies than some Communist and poor Third World countries already do, key child and maternal health indicators which have stagnated for all babies and eroded for others will persist or worsen by the year 2000.

- Today we rank eighteenth in the world, behind Spain and Singapore, in overall infant mortality. American black infant mortality rates place us twenty-eighth in the world, behind the overall rates of Cuba and Bulgaria.

- A black baby born in Indianapolis, Detroit, or in the shadow of the White House and Capitol was more likely to die in the first year of life in 1986 than a baby born in Jamaica, Trinidad and Tobago, Chile, Panama, Romania, or the Soviet Union. Black infant mortality rates in 1986 were equivalent to white infant mortality rates in 1970.

- If recent trends continue, in the year 2000, one out of every five births and more than a third of all black births will be to a mother who did not receive early prenatal care. Babies born without prenatal care are three times more likely to die in their first year. At current rates of progress, the nation will not meet the Surgeon General's 1990 prenatal care goal for all women until the year 2094 and for black women until 2153. This is bad budget as well as human policy. It costs $600 to provide a mother adequate prenatal care. It costs about $1,000 a day to try to save premature babies in intensive care units.

- If recent trends continue, the Surgeon General's 1990 goal for reducing the percentage of low-birthweight births will not be met for all infants until 2031 and for black infants until 2055.

- Based on the 1980-1985 trends, the United States will never meet the Surgeon General's 1990 goal for immunizing our youngest children. While we correctly spend billions to combat the new pestilence of AIDS, for which there is no cure, we need to invest the modest millions to save our children from diseases we do know how to prevent (diphtheria, tetanus, pertussis, and polio). It costs about $1 to immunize a child and saves $10 in remedial costs.

- AIDS will take an increasing toll on families and children in the next decade. The Centers for Disease Control estimate that within two years at least 10,000 children will be infected by the AIDS virus. The majority will be poor.

Children's family status also will become more tenuous as families change or fail to form.

- Today one in five of all American children has a single parent and one child in five is poor. By the year 2000, one in four will have a single parent and one in four will be poor.

- In the year 2000 one in every five 20-year-old women will be a mother and more than four out of five of them will not be married. Only six in 10 will have high school diplomas, compared with nine of 10 of their peers who are not parents, at a time when businesses require better work and basic skills. Basic skills levels and poverty are the primary predictors of teen parenthood.

- Two-parent young families will continue to have difficulty forming. If the proportion of young families headed by single parents continues to rise at the pace of the past two decades, only three of every five young families will be headed by a married couple.

- More young children will have mothers in the labor force and, unless we act, too few of them will have available, safe, and affordable child care. Today half of all children younger than two have mothers in the labor force and by the year 2000 seven out of 10 preschool children will have mothers in the labor force.

- The fastest growing segment of the homeless population in America is families with children. According to the National Academy of Sciences, an estimated 100,000 children are homeless each night. We must build housing for low- and moderate-income families. Streets and shelters are no places to raise children.

- The quarter of a million children who are living apart from their families in foster care, group homes, residential treatment centers, and other institutions will increase. A disproportionate number, as today, will be minority, very young children, and teenagers, and will have increasingly severe medical and emotional problems.

- More children will run away from home. About 1.5 million children and adolescents run away from home each year or are thrown out.

- The number of abused children in 1986—675,000—will grow, as will their emotional problems and dependency on society. As of February 1987 there were 53,503 young people in public juvenile facilities—many of which are criminal training schools. The number of youths held for alcohol and drug offenses increased by 56 percent between 1985 and 1987.

- Between 7.5 million and 9.5 million children and adolescents in this country need help from mental health professionals. No more than 30 percent of that number are getting the attention they need. Even among the 3 million children who are severely emotionally disturbed, a majority do not receive appropriate treatment.

The rage and pain of these homeless, hopeless, abused, alienated children will continue to explode in our faces in communities all over America.

Eliminating Poverty—Too Expensive?

At a time of massive budget and trade deficits, America cannot afford to waste resources by failing to prevent and curb the human deficits that cripple our children and cost billions in later remedial and custodial dollars. At a time when future demographic trends guarantee a shortage of young adults who will be workers, soldiers, leaders, and parents, America cannot afford to waste a single child, not even the poorest, blackest one. At a time of unprecedented economic competition from abroad and of changing patterns of production at home which demand higher basic educational skills, America cannot wait another minute to do whatever is needed to ensure that today's and tomorrow's work forces are well prepared rather than useless—whatever their color.

The federal government counts the number of poor people in the country and the amount by which their incomes fall below the poverty line. So we know what it would cost to eliminate poverty.

Based on 1987 figures, the cost of:

- Eliminating child poverty is $17.22 billion.

- Eliminating poverty in families with children is $26.874 billion.

- Eliminating poverty among all persons is $51.646 billion.

These numbers sound like a lot of money. And they are. But this is also a large and wealthy country. The cost of eliminating all poverty ($51.646 billion) is equivalent to only 1 percent of our gross national product. Eliminating poverty in families with children ($26.874 billion) would cost about 1.5 percent of what federal, state, and local governments spend.

We *can* save our children—and our future—but only by making hard national choices and reordering our national investment priorities. The issue is not money but national will and values.

If the U.S. Energy Department can ask for $50 billion to increase our nuclear weapon capacity; if proponents of the Strategic Defense Initiative (SDI) can ask for $5 billion a year just to plan a potentially $100 billion space war; if the Pentagon does not hesitate to ask for $50 billion to $70 billion to build a new Stealth B-2 bomber before it can figure out how to make the old B-1 bombers we've already invested $30 billion in work; if bankers can call for a proposed $80 billion to $100 billion to bail out deregulated, imprudent savings and loans; if we can afford to leave untaxed the $5 billion in tax breaks for inherited capital gains for the wealthy and add $6 billion to $10 billion more in capital gains tax reductions, as President Bush has suggested, do not tell me that this nation is unable to afford to lift its 13 million children out of poverty. (See suggestions for funding children's programs and helping reduce the federal deficit, p. xlvi.)

Until enough citizens and child advocates are working together to reorder our national goals and to exterminate the "termites" eating away at the foundations of our national life, our political leaders will continue present investment priorities at the expense of our children and of all of our future.

TEN TERMITES EATING AWAY AT THE FOUNDATION OF AMERICAN LIFE THAT WE MUST EXTERMINATE TOGETHER

One: The "It's not my problem" termite. Children are a special interest group. But they are a *very* special interest group in which every American has a share and stake. They are at least as critical to our national security as the Pentagon. Focusing the political marketplace on children has been traditionally very difficult

1989 Children's Preventive Investment Agenda

Medicaid for All Pregnant Women and Children to Age 8 with Incomes Below Twice the Poverty Line	$500,000,000
Special Supplemental Food Program for Women, Infants, and Children (WIC) (first year down payment)	$200,000,000
Immunization	$20,000,000
Act for Better Child Care	$2,500,000,000
Head Start (first year down payment)	$400,000,000
Chapter 1 Compensatory Education (first year down payment)	$700,000,000
Minimum Wage, Adjustment for Inflation	No federal cost
Total	$4,320,000,000

To raise this $4.3 billion per year we could:

• Reduce the allowable tax deduction for business entertainment, meals, sporting events, and social dues from 80 percent to 50 percent, with reasonable maximums on each type of expenditure.

or

• Stop "forgiving" loans we make to foreign governments to purchase weapons from us.

The cost of CDF's Preventive Investment Agenda in 1992 would be about $9.1 billion, or $4.8 billion more than in 1989. This increase is because it will cost: about $1.5 billion more to extend Medicaid to all children (regardless of age) with family incomes below twice the poverty line, $1.2 billion more to fully fund Head Start, $1.3 billion more to fully fund Chapter 1, and $800 million more to fully fund WIC.

To raise the extra $4.8 billion we could:

• Triple the cigarette excise tax and index it for inflation.

or

• Eliminate the tax break for the well-to-do that lets those who inherit not pay taxes on capital gains when they sell assets from an estate.

or

• Raise the liquor, wine, and beer excise taxes up to the levels we had in the early 1950s (adjusted for inflation).

because children do not vote, lobby, make campaign contributions, or write letters to the editor. But a crop of healthy, well cared for, and educated children is the best growth stock in which any American can invest.

If you are a white, middle-class parent you already know that many of the economic and social uncertainties and stresses that poor families have struggled with from time immemorial have invaded your home. Many middle-class parents who used to cry when their children left home for college, job, or marriage are now crying because their children may never leave home. They cannot afford to. Escalating college, health insurance, housing, and child care costs as well as elderly dependents are stretching the middle-class purse and psyche to the limits. And young families of all races and incomes are losing ground as they struggle to afford both a house and a child on declining wages. Increasingly, the lines grow thinner between the nonpoor, near poor, and truly poor. The wolves of plant closing, foreclosure, divorce, loss of child support, serious illness, and drug or alcohol addiction lurk behind every American door.

If you are a business person, a more productive work force today and a well trained, competitive one tomorrow rests on good child care for today's workers and a quality early childhood foundation for their children and your future workers. A 1988 *Fortune* magazine study concluded that child care problems are the most reliable predictors of workers' absenteeism and unproductive work time. That is why Marriott, IBM, American Express, Campbell Soup, and other corporations are beginning to grapple with the child care needs of their employees and why more business people are becoming interested in ensuring that all children get a Head Start. I look forward to your strong, positive, and sustained support of the early childhood investments backed by members of the Committee for Economic Development (CED) in its report, *Children in Need: Investment Strategies for the Educationally Disadvantaged.* I also applaud growing corporate efforts like Aetna's Saturday Academy, Time Inc.'s literacy corps, Eugene Lang's "I Have A Dream" foundation and the Los Angeles Coalition of 100 Black Men's efforts to help disadvantaged youths stay in school and attend college, and the Robin Hood Foundation started by young Wall Street entrepreneurs to help the hungry and homeless by tithing a portion of their profits. All of these activities need to become the rule rather than examples. We need community learning centers all over America to keep children constructively involved in the afternoons, on weekends, and during arid, idle summer months in order to supplement parent and school efforts to bolster basic skills and help minority children understand their own history and culture. The Japanese have a huge supplemental learning system called *juku.* Retired, privileged, and not so privileged individuals as well as corporate and organizational volunteers can all tutor children and help forge a new community ethic of learning and service throughout America. Examples abound, which CDF is more than happy to share with you.

If you are an elderly person or nearing retirement age, the declining size and high poverty rates of the young working-age population is of direct concern to you. The child in first grade will graduate from high school, *if* you help give her enough supports and services and encouragement to keep her in school that long, and will enter the work force in the year 2000. If you are 60 today, you will be 71 then; if you are 50, you'll be 61. If that child gets pregnant, and drops out of school, she becomes a dependent rather than a productive person and her earning power decreases. Today it takes 2.6 white males to support the retirement of one white male, but 3.6 black females. That is one of the reasons why AARP (the American Association of Retired Persons) and other elderly groups are beginning to work more closely with children's groups. All elderly Americans need to recognize that their own grandchildren are an endangered species and that they share with children the common perils of crime and fear as the quality of life in our streets, parks, and neighborhoods deteriorates. Moreover, if the elderly don't support funding for good child care and schools, industry won't move into their communities and their own children will have to move away to find decent jobs.

If you are an American in your thirties or forties the babies born in the next few years will graduate from college when you retire or are thinking about retirement. If one in every five of today's children is missing from the work force that year because of the barriers you refuse to help eliminate for them today, your future security will be more fragile than the present.

If you are concerned about America's military preparedness you should join some of those farsighted leaders in and out of the armed forces who have begun to focus more on the need for preventive health care, child care, family support services, and education, not only for the children of military personnel, but for all children. Admiral James D. Watkins, former chief of Naval Operations and former head of President Reagan's AIDS commission (Commission on the Human Immunodeficiency Virus Epidemic) has become an eloquent voice on the relationship between national security and children's basic skills levels. And it is noteworthy that the first major federal program for education in this century—the National Defense Education Act—was passed in 1958 in response to the Soviet Sputnik launch and the perceived threat to national security.

If you are a college or university president worried about the declining representation of minorities in your student bodies, administrations, and faculties and the inadequate basic skills of entering freshman, it is time for you to join a growing cadre of higher education leaders in helping bolster early childhood investment as well as elementary and secondary education. You need to recognize that getting children ready for college and graduate and professional school does not begin in high school or even in first grade, but at birth.

If you are interested in America's world leadership role and diplomatic success as well as our ability to compete in the new markets of today's predominantly nonwhite world, you have a self-interest in building strong, educated brown and black, as well as white, future ambassadors to sell the American dream abroad. If we can't make it work at home we're not going to sell it to foreigners. And all of our children need to be better prepared to communicate and compete in a multiracial, multicultural, and multilingual world. Students of all income groups, even our most advanced twelfth-grade mathematics students, ranked next to last in an international test of mathematical skills. Our children's language preparation lags behind that of our chief competitors for world leadership.

If you are one of those Americans I have heard from who chose not to have children or have enough money to support those you do have and resent supporting "other people's" children, especially those who are black and brown, you ought to know that even if you don't like them and resent their poor parents (who in reality do not have more babies than the rest of us) it is nevertheless in your own and the nation's self-interest to prevent as many of their problems as possible at the cheapest cost. That way your tax dollars will not pay more later for welfare, for sickness, for ignorance, and for alienation that increase your stress and fear as well as strain your pocketbook.

If you are just sick and tired of government taxes, deficits, and perceived or real government failures, even you have a self-interest in investing in the children's programs that work and save more money later. A penny to immunize saves a dime of sickness. A penny of quality child care saves about a nickel in later dependency. And I urge you to take more time—and make those you vote for take more care—in distinguishing between specific programs and policies that work and that don't work. I am sick and tired of indiscriminate journalistic and political pronouncements that all social programs are failures. All Pentagon programs are not failures just because the DIVAD is a dud.

Two: The "Do what I say and not what I do" termite. We hear a whole lot of talk about young people's values today. But it is adult and national values (deed not creed) that need improving. We tell our children not to lie. And we lie in public life, in corporate board rooms, in television ministries, in our private dealings with each other, at home, and to our children.

We tell our children not to take drugs, while adults in high and low places all over America are using drugs. A neighbor recounted her recent stint of jury duty during which a 19-year-old youth was acquitted on three counts of possessing cocaine. Although the jury felt he was guilty, they did not feel they should punish him for doing what high public and private officials are doing with impunity all over our nation's capital and land. Conservatively, Americans spent an estimated $16 billion in 1987 on cocaine. While massive and much more effective interdiction of drugs flooding our borders, cities, and rural areas is essential, more massive attention is needed to exterminate the virus of demand and the spiritual poverty that feeds it. Why should our children say no to drugs when adults are saying yes to drugs in every nook and cranny of our national house? Why should they respect us? They are following us.

We tell them smoking is bad for their health and lack the courage to stop North Carolina Sen. Jesse Helms' taxpayer subsidies to tobacco growers or the mass marketing of killer cigarettes to our young through billboards and print ads. Cigarette and tobacco companies spend hundreds of millions of dollars each year hawking their dangerous wares. Blacks, whose life expectancy is sliding backward, are inundated by tobacco advertising and organizational event sponsorship. They need to weigh as carefully as possible the human cost benefits. When R. J. Reynolds, Inc., a former very small contributor to CDF, ceased doing so after we advocated, as we still do, a significant increase in the cigarette tax, it provoked us to look at and change our own policy about taking such money. I regret that they rather than we initiated it. Corporate and community leaders need to seek a better balance between protecting adult choices and seducing and influencing youths who may not be able to weigh all the consequences of their actions.

Similarly, we tell our children that drinking and driving is dangerous. We do not tell them enough that drinking without driving also can be dangerous if not done in moderation and after maturity. And we tolerate mass marketing of beer and liquor by sports and entertainment figures who are role models to many of our youths. Parents and children and those who participate in such ads need to weigh these glamorous messages against the consequences. The American investment of $26 billion a year in intoxicating beverages has contributed to the spread of alcoholism to millions of Americans in my family and yours. Alcoholism decreases the economic productivity and increases business costs many times more than would granting parents leave to take care of their newborn or ill children or elderly parents—costs many businesses have opposed vociferously.

We tell our children that out-of-wedlock sex is not appropriate behavior while adult women—white and black, rich and poor—have two-thirds of all out-of-wedlock babies each year. And if she is a movie star, we may even put an unwed mother on the cover of *People* magazine. If she is a 15-year-old black teen in Newark, we disparage her values. We tell our girls to stay chaste while we encourage boys to "score," and we let too many males off the hook after they do and if pregnancy results.

We tell our children that work is the American way, yet we tolerate too many schools that are factories of illiteracy which fail to prepare millions of our young for our changing job market. And we do not ensure a higher education to many youths when they do stay in high school, or provide a job at a wage that will enable them to adequately support a family. One in four black high school students and one in eight college graduates are unemployed today. Only one in four black men between the ages of 20 and 24 earned enough to support a family of three above the poverty level in 1986.

We tell our children to live on what they earn and have dug ourselves a potential grave of national debt. In 1980 we were spending $6 million an hour on interest on the national debt. In 1988 we spent $17 million an hour on interest on the national debt. A December 1988 *Yale Weekly Bulletin* reported a new Yale-Tokyo University study estimating that by the year 2010, 30 percent of America's capital stock will be owned by the Japanese and Germans. Millions of our individual households resemble our national and world economic house of cards. Poor American children and parents cannot pay off the the $2.6 trillion debt they did not cause any more than developing world children can move the estimated $1.2 trillion debt their governments owe developed world bankers and governments.

We tell our children that fairness is the American way yet tolerate the daily robbery of the poor by the rich. In the last decade, profligate tax breaks were provided to nonneedy individuals and corporations by the Administration and Congress, hidden under what Dr. King labeled "sophisticated nomenclatures such as parity, subsidies, tax incentives to industry," while already inadequate aid to needy children and families was slashed $40 billion under the guise of deficit reduction. If we simply reduce the business meal and entertainment tax write-off from 80 percent to 50 percent, we could raise about $3 billion in Fiscal Year 1990 and more than $4 billion annually thereafter to prevent child deficits. This business welfare money alone is more than enough to pay for the Act for Better Child Care (ABC) bill or the full funding of Head Start. Which investment is more important to America's future? Whose welfare should the federal government be subsidizing?

We tell our children to believe in peace and have squandered our national purse on swords rather than plowshares during a time of escalating child and family suffering and poverty. In 1980 we were spending $15 million an hour on the military. In 1988 we spent $33 million an hour. And although Pentagon officials have simply delayed rather than cut out-year weapons systems spending, some of our national leaders have the temerity to ask for more for the military while others are too timid to really curb the greedy military termite or demand the same standards of merit, performance, and strategic planning and testing they correctly demand for domestic programs serving the poor. This accountability should be extended to all programs for the nonpoor and for Pentagon brass and defense contractors.

Three: The "Quick fix" termite. Our children live in an environment where instant sex without consequence or responsibility, instant gratification without effort, instant solutions without struggle, instant answers without thought, instant profits without concern for future costs are the too-frequent signals of our economic, political, mass media, and popular culture.

There are no simple or single answers to the complex problems of child and family poverty any more than there are to proliferating nuclear and conventional arms and pollution of the air we breathe, water we drink, and food we eat. But there are answers, many described in chapters throughout this book and elsewhere. Hands of mercy and minds with vision and commitment are translating answers in communities all around the country into improved child lives. Their individual and combined efforts will take years, many ups and downs, small victories and big setbacks, before they yield a critical mass of positive results. But they will, sooner, if they are joined by millions more citizen hands and by supportive government and sensitive private sector leaders at all levels.

Building strong children, families, and communities does not happen overnight but by chipping away year after year until the tough barriers they face fall or are overcome. Our national goal-setting, planning, and implementation strategies must incorporate the understanding that poverty is the child of many causes which affect different children in different families, income, racial, and cultural groups and geographic areas for different reasons at different times with different consequences requiring different remedies. Most poor people are not in an underclass and go in and out of poverty for different reasons. All teens at risk of pregnancy share a common need for responsible adult communication, but poor teens also need good basic skills and hope that a future ahead is worth delaying parenthood. Careful homework and analysis coupled with boundless persistence by all of us who seek to protect the future are preconditions to successful outcomes. An anonymous sage hit the nail on the head: "Nothing in the world can take the place of persistence. Talent will not; nothing is more common than unsuccessful men with talent. Genius will not; unrewarded genius is almost a proverb. Education alone will not; the world is full of educated derelicts. Persistence and determination alone are omnipotent."

Four: The "Too little, too late" termite. Some poor children only need a Head Start program to make it. Let's give it to as many of them as fast as we can. Thousands more babies could start life crying lustily rather than at low birthweight if we simply reached out to their mothers with cost-effective prenatal care, nutrition supplements, and sensitive counseling. But we must also recognize that some poor children, youths, and parents are so damaged that we have to both urgently and patiently develop a comprehensive, seamless web of prevention and remediation measures first to keep them afloat, then to get them back up on their feet, and finally to keep them there. Even if we provided every child and family enough money through jobs and income supports to lift them out of poverty right now, as I hope we will, this alone would not cure immediately the deeply embedded psychic as well as physical deficits wrought by years of deprivation. That is why the preventive investment agenda we advocate throughout this book and in all of our work, as well as an agenda that goes beyond survival to optimal development, must go hand in hand with necessary jobs and income supplements.

In July 1988, after a visit to the only day shelter for homeless families and children in Atlanta, I visited the neonatal intensive care nursery at Grady Memorial Hospital and watched wonderful doctors and nurses perform extraordinarily expensive, technology-aided miracles saving the lives of premature infants and seeing and learning about the mothers of some of these babies—many teens, some addicted to crack, others out of school and out of hope. The unit was like a scene from a surrealistic battlefield hospital where lives are saved only to be returned to the trenches for new brushes with death and suffering. For once these infants and their teen and older mothers leave the hospital, they, for the most part, leave the system, leave our community, leave our sight and caring—lost until some new tragedy disrupts their or our lives.

Scenes like those I witnessed at Grady are being played out in city hospitals throughout the country and efforts to root out the underlying problems will take years and perhaps generations. Lasting change must have at its core a strong cadre of professionals and citizens at the local, state, and national levels who understand the multiple needs of at-risk children and have the vision and knowledge to initiate, integrate carefully and humanely, and implement a continuum of programs and policies that both prevent and reduce child deficits before birth, in the earliest years, and throughout the school and teen years to adulthood. Linkages between all child-serving systems and support services must be made. Policy makers and professional service deliverers must recognize, as the chapter in this book on Vulnerable Children and Families shows, that child welfare, mental health, and juvenile justice labels are often meaningless because many multiple-needs children fit two or more of the labels.

The national consensus on early childhood investment must not only be funded and implemented now but also be extended to older children, youths, and young families. No good parents would choose between food, shelter, child care, and education for their children after birth any more than they would stop providing these things when their children reach school age or the teen years. Why should good social policy be any different?

Five: The "Convenient ignorance" termite. This termite is a more deadly threat to America than AIDS. It tells us that the racial problem is solved; that the poor are all black and brown and on welfare; that they alone, not economic and social shifts, are culpable for their misery; that government can do no right and that the private sector can do no wrong; and that individuals and families in America can make it alone if they simply try hard enough.

Poor white Americans far outnumber poor black and brown Americans. The working poor far outnumber the welfare poor and are waging valiant war against declining wages, job shifts from the manufacturing to the service sector, and foreign competition.

Indiscriminate government-bashing is no more productive than indiscriminate bashing of poor people. In a democratic society, what government does well or badly generally reflects what a society and its members do well or badly, whether in public or private life. Was the Challenger tragedy the fault of the Morton Thiokol Company or of NASA? Are the cost overruns and malfunctions of major defense systems the fault of the Pentagon or of the major defense contractors? The public may identify these as failed government programs, but they failed as much because of private performance and are really reflections of broader social failures (in the defense case) or perhaps simply the imperfections of human efforts (in the Challenger case).

Medicaid's passage in 1965 is an example of successful public-private efforts (tainted occasionally by *provider* fraud) which enabled many poor people to gain access to the predominantly private health delivery system through public insurance payments. Fifteen years after Medicaid began, black infant mortality dropped 49 percent, more than nine times the rate of decline of the 15 years before Medicaid.

National problems cannot be solved until they are recognized, honestly analyzed, and broken down into manageable pieces for action—each of us doing our part. Lech Walesa, in a message which Harvard University's President Derek Bok read at the 1983 Commencement, praised his countrymen for "small, daily acts of courage" that have forged a new consciousness among young Poles. "This consciousness," he said, "is my great hope ... and has great impact on reality. This is why we do not have to overthrow the system. It is weaker than the national self-awareness. It either shrinks before it or absorbs it."

The more we as citizens open our eyes and begin to see and respond to the suffering all around us, the less we will tolerate the slogans of political and media leaders who extol the prosperity of too few at the expense of too many. The more we read carefully about and visit El Salvador and Nicaragua and Ethiopia and South Africa and Harlem and Watts and Anacostia, the more we will be able to judge for ourselves the pronouncements of political officials that are too seldom matched by deed or funding. The more we go across town and volunteer at soup kitchens or homeless shelters or nursing homes and take our members of Congress and media friends with us, the sooner we will cut through the politics of misery, illusion, and moral blindness that characterize too much of our national life today.

No person or politician is wise enough for you to delegate your thinking and conscience to him or her. Most politicians follow rather than lead: "The politician," Buckminster Fuller said, "is someone who deals in man's problems of adjustment. To ask a politician to lead us is to ask the tail of a dog to lead the dog."

Six: The "I didn't contribute to the problem" termite. It is time for every one of us in every sector of American life to exercise more care for our nation's children and future. Finger-pointing at the expense of our common good and children is foolish and solves nothing. Dwelling on what we don't have or can't do while not using what we do have and doing what we can do is abnegating our responsibility in whatever role we play.

If you are carelessly or willfully polluting the air and water, you are not helping America's children.

If you are in the food business but are more interested in a few extra pennies of profit than in the nutritional content of the food our children eat, then you are not doing your best to help produce healthy children and prevent costly crippling diseases.

If you are in the entertainment industry but are not creative enough to produce television and radio programs, films, and songs that entertain *and* carry positive and not just negative messages about and to families and children, nonviolent as well as violent ones, then you are not working hard enough to protect America's children and future.

If you are a professional or bureaucrat or simple laborer whose standard of job performance is doing as little as you can or getting by rather than doing as well as you can do or excelling, then you are eroding the quality and service of American life.

If you are a teacher who does not help every child feel good about himself or herself, or expect and help every child to succeed, then you are undermining one of the most important missions in America today.

If you cannot take the time to vote or follow how your representatives at all levels vote, then you are not doing your part for children and America's future. Please examine CDF's Nonpartisan Congressional Voting Record of 1988 on page 119. If those representing you have a rating of 80 or above thank them; if less, prod them to do better.

If you cannot take the time to write a letter to the editor, to the media, to political leaders telling them what you like and don't like about the policies and programs for children, then you need to try harder.

If you are a professional who forgets that your clients' narrow interest and the public's interest may not always be the same and do not quietly seek to balance both, or if you are a doctor or lawyer who won't help poor clients, you are not pulling your weight in protecting America's children and future.

Seven: The "Me and my organization" termite. All of us have to remind ourselves daily of what our goals are and keep our eye on the child—the Children's Defense Fund staff and I, as much as anybody else. Winning for children is more important than CDF. Winning for children *is* winning for CDF and for all of us—regardless of who gets the credit. Providing good child care and education for all of our children is more important than any education or single-issue group. The nation's future is more important than political parties and presidential politics. Child health is more important than professional medical groups and providers. Children with emotional problems need help as much as those with physical or developmental problems and do not need competition among advocates for special needs children. God is more important than the church or synagogue or mosque and denominational or sectarian bickering. Good publicity must take second place to good policy for children and families. Being famous is not synonymous with being effective. If we do not work together and put aside our selfish turf and personal jockeying, all of us, along with our children, are going to lose. And while we are combating the "Me and my organization" termite, we should swat its brother, the "Reinvent the wheel" termite, and tell it to "Put its shoulder to the political wheel for children and get it moving."

Eight: The "Nothing works" termite. As in any area, there are programs for children that work and that do not work. We must build on the ones that do and weed out and modify the ones that do not. We know a lot about what works, as we indicate throughout this book. Lisbeth and Daniel Schorr's book, *Within our Reach,* documents many local community successes, as do other organizational reports. Read them and curb this termite who garnered headlines and spread heat but not light on urgent problems we could have alleviated this past decade. We have to regain the desire to try to help more children and to go out and actually do it. And we have to identify, share, and demonstrate more approaches that work.

Nine: The "I did it all by myself" termite. Americans correctly prize independence. But we also fantasize absolute self-sufficiency as the only correct way of life. Throughout our history we have given government help to our people and then forgotten that fact when it came time to celebrate our people's achievements. Two hundred years ago, Congress granted federal lands to the states to help maintain public schools. One hundred and twenty-seven years ago, President Lincoln signed the Morrill Act, granting land for colleges. The first food voucher and energy assistance programs came not during the New Deal or the War on Poverty but at the end of the Civil War, when Congress and President Lincoln created the Freedmen's Bureau. Federal help for vaccinations, vocational education, and maternal health began not with Kennedy, Johnson, and Carter, but under Madison, Wilson, and Harding, respectively.

Our parents, grandparents, and great-grandparents benefited from this government help just as we all do today. Only the blindest economists could doubt that American prosperity, like Japan's, is built on the synergistic relations between government and private initiative. But it is some of the blindest economists, political scientists, and "moral philosophers" who have the ear of many of our leaders or are themselves political leaders.

One such leader was born in Fort Benning, Georgia, in 1942, where his father was living on a federal veterans disability pension. He attended the University of Georgia, a public university, where his tuition and expenses were paid by the federal War Orphans Act. He had planned to go into physics; but learning that physics postdoctoral fellows got low pay, he did graduate work in economics, paid for by a federal National Defense Education Act fellowship. He started his career teaching at Texas A&M, a federal land-grant college.

Today he is United States Sen. Phil Gramm, a conservative who seeks to do away with most federal domestic programs. In 1981 he was one of the prime authors of the law that sought to decimate almost every federal program for low-income children—a law referred to as Gramm-Latta. And he is one of the prime authors of the Gramm-Rudman-Hollings balanced budget amendment, which threatens to wreak even greater, indiscriminate havoc on federal programs for needy children and families.

Sen. Gramm seems to suffer from the peculiarly American amnesia or hypocrisy that wants us to think that poor families must be wholly self-sufficient; that makes us forget how government helps us all, regardless of class; and that makes us believe that the government is simply wasting its billions supporting a wholly dependent, self-perpetuating class of poor people, while doing nothing but taxing the rest of us.

Chrysler and Lee Iacocca didn't do it alone. Defense contractors don't do it alone. Nor can most families and children, especially poor ones. In tackling the deficit, Congress must take the time and have the courage to make specific choices and not wield a leveling budget axe or hide behind uniform but unjust freezes of current inequalities.

Ten: The "I can't make a difference" termite. This is the most dangerous termite of all and unless each individual American battles it within himself or herself, we will not be able to kill the rest of the termites eating away at America's future.

Dr. Martin Luther King, Jr., reminded us what countless lives, known and unknown, have shown us. He said: "Everybody can be great. Because anybody can serve. You don't have to have a college degree to serve. You don't have to make your subject and your verb agree to serve. You don't have to know Einstein's theory of relativity to serve. You don't have to know the second theory of thermodynamics in physics to serve. You only need a heart full of grace. A soul generated by love."

In his fine book, *Servant Leadership*, Robert Greenleaf tells the stories of a number of servant-leaders, like John Woolman, who, as a young man, set a goal to rid the members of the Society of Friends (Quakers) of owning slaves. He spent 30 of his adult years, traveling by foot and horseback, visiting Quaker slaveholders one on one and quietly encouraging them to stop this unjust practice. As a result of this one, not very physically strong man, Greenleaf said, almost 100 years before the Civil War, no Quakers owned slaves. Greenleaf described many individuals who catalyzed massive social changes through different styles of leadership. What they all had in common, though, was a commitment to serving others.

Unsung heroines and heroes abound and we can each add to their numbers in the future. Legal segregation in America fell not primarily through the leadership of powerful white institutions or political leaders, but by the vision and dogged hard work of a very small band of black lawyers whose partners in courage were a handful of black parents who sought a better life for their children. They did not think about or get paralyzed by the fact that every card in the national deck, from the interpretation of the Constitution by the Supreme Court, to state laws, customs, and attitudes, was stacked against them. They did not try to tear down the thick wall of legal segregation all at once but chiseled away at it a little at a time. They did not have much money, many friends, or a lot of allies. But they had enough. They had a just goal and unwavering determination to reach it. And they did.

Today you and I must pick up where they left off—each of us chiseling away at the unjust social and economic underpinnings that continue to deny millions of black, brown, and white children a fair chance. At stake is America's economic bottom line, future, and every American family's safety and quality of life. Countless middle-class and privileged youths today are suffering the same broken families, drug and alcohol addiction, too-early pregnancies, and emotional disconnectedness as countless poor children. Mrs. Mary O. Ross, an important black church leader, succinctly stated the antidote. "Our children need," she said, "a faith fit to live by, a self fit to live with, and a work fit to live for." Like the rest of us.

Too many children today—white, black, and brown, privileged and underprivileged—are not getting these anchors from enough adults—parents, "extended parents," teachers and other professionals, religious and public leaders, or anybody. As a result, they lack buffers against some of the termites of contemporary culture I've just described. Parents and "extended community parents"—while pushing and waiting for American leaders and society to provide a fairer and safer environment for children, must simultaneously buffer our children from the external assaults which dry up their dreams and compete for their minds and hearts by teaching children the difference between shadow and substance.

SELLING THE SHADOW FOR THE SUBSTANCE: WHAT PARENTS AND COMMUNITY PARENTS MUST DO FOR CHILDREN

The wisdom of an illiterate slave woman, Sojourner Truth, has frequently guided me as I have struggled and continue to struggle to see, hear, understand, feel, and heal in my life. American parents, citizens, and leaders need to follow Sojourner's advice "to sell the shadow to support the substance"; to be able to know the difference between them; and to pass on that understanding to our children. My parents, many other "ordinary" black adults, and black leaders taught these lessons to my generation of black children.

As the granddaughter, daughter, and sister of Baptist ministers, service was as essential a part of my upbringing as eating and sleeping and going to school. The church was a hub of black children's social existence and caring black adults were buffers against the segregated prison of the outside world that told us we were inferior and unimportant. But our parents said it wasn't so. Our teachers said it wasn't so. And our preachers said it wasn't so. So the message I internalized, despite the ugly racism of my childhood, was to let no man or woman look down on you and to look down on no man or woman.

Children were taught, not by sermonizing but by personal example, that nothing was too lowly to do and that the work of our hands and the work of our minds were of equal dignity and value. I remember a debate my parents had about whether I was too young to go with an older brother to help clean the bed and bedsores of a very sick, poor woman. I went. And I'm grateful. I learned early how much even the smallest helping hand can mean to a lonely, suffering person.

I also was taught not to ask in the face of need "why doesn't *somebody* do something" but rather "why don't *I* do something." As black children, we couldn't play in public playgrounds or sit at drugstore lunch counters and order a Coke, so my Daddy built a playground and canteen behind the church. Whenever he saw a need, he tried to respond. There were no homes for the black aged in South Carolina so he began one across the street and he and my mother and we children cooked and served and cleaned. I resented it sometimes, but I learned that it was my responsibility to take care of elderly family members and neighbors, and that everybody was my neighbor. My mother carried on "the old folks home" after my father died and one of my brothers has carried it on since our mother died in 1984.

Finding another child in my room or a pair of my shoes gone was far from unusual, and 12 foster children followed my sister and me and my three brothers as we left home. When my mother died, an old white man in my town asked me what I did. In a flash I realized I do exactly what my parents did—just on a different scale.

The ugly external voices of assault of my rural segregated childhood (as a very young child I remember standing and hearing former South Carolina Sen. James Byrnes railing on the local courthouse lawn about how black and white children would never go to school together) were tempered by the internal voices of parental and community expectation and pride. My father and I waited anxiously for the *Brown v. Board of Education* decision. We talked about it and what it would mean for my future and the future of millions of other black children. He died the week before *Brown* was decided. But I and other children lucky enough to have caring and courageous parents were able, in later years, to walk through the new but heavy doors that *Brown* slowly and painfully opened. I remember Langston Hughes coming to my small town, reading poetry and signing a book of poems I still treasure. And I remember having dinner at Benedict College in Columbia, South Carolina, with Mary McLeod Bethune, founder of the National Council of Negro Women, and hearing her boast, "the blacker the berry the sweeter the juice!" and her stories about going into segregated shops to buy hats and overwhelming flabbergasted white sales clerks with: "Do you know who I am? I am Mary McLeod Bethune!"

Caring black adults at all levels, within and without my family, countered the constant negative messages of the outside world. Child-rearing and parental work were inseparable. I went everywhere with my parents and was under the watchful eyes of members of the congregation and community who were my extended parents. They kept me when my parents went out of town, they reported on and chided me when I strayed from the straight and narrow of community expectations, and they basked in and supported my achievements when I did well. Doing well meant high academic achievement, playing the piano for Sunday school or singing and participating in church activities, being helpful to somebody, displaying good manners (which is nothing more than consideration toward others), and reading. I was reminded recently that the only time my Daddy would not give us a chore ("Can't you find something constructive to do?" was his favorite refrain and he always made sure we *did* have something constructive to do) was when we were reading. So we read *a lot* and were clear early on about what our parents and extended community parents valued.

My brother, Harry, at a 1981 tribute to our mother by the Mothers Club of the Shiloh Baptist Church (which she founded), thanked her for providing us three things that he thought were instrumental in helping all of us set and reach individual goals: "(1) elementary courtesy, character, and respect; (2) inspiring us to dream; and (3) leading us to an awareness of the reality of God."

"Throughout our lives," he said, "we shall reflect your teaching and you shall live as long as we shall live." And I hope as long as our children and their children and their children's children shall live.

Black adults in our churches and community made children feel valued and valuable. They took time and paid attention to us. They struggled to find ways to keep us busy. And while life often was very hard and resources very scarce, as it is for so many today, we always knew who we were and that the measure of our worth was inside our heads and hearts and not on our backs or in other people's minds. We were told that the world had a lot of problems; that black people had extra problems, but that we were able and obligated to struggle and change them; that being poor or black was no excuse for not achieving; and that extra intellectual and material gifts brought with them the privilege and responsibility of sharing with others less fortunate. As a result, we never lost hope, like so many children today have. We learned that service is the rent we pay for living. It is the very purpose of life and not something you do in your spare time. And nobody ever promised that it would be simple or easy.

The legacies my parents and preachers and teachers left to my generation of black children were priceless but not material: a living faith reflected in daily service, the discipline of hard work and stick-to-it-ness, and a capacity to struggle in the face of adversity (giving up and burnout were not part of the language of my elders—you got up every morning and you did what you had to do and you got up every time you fell down and tried as many times as you had to until you got it done right). They had grit. They valued family life, family rituals, and tried to be and expose us to good role models.

Role models were of two kinds: those who achieved in the outside world like Marian Anderson, my namesake; former Morehouse College president and Martin Luther King Jr.'s mentor Benjamin Mays; and former Howard University President Mordecai Johnson, whose three- and four-hour speeches I sat through once a year (my parents believed in osmosis!) even before I could understand or stay awake through them; and those who didn't have a whole lot of education or fancy clothes but who taught us, by the special grace of their lives, and without ever opening a book on philosophy or theology other than the Bible, that the Kingdom of God is within—in what you are and not in what you have or look like. And I still hope I can be half as good as Miz Lucy McQueen, Miz Tee Kelly, Miz Kate Winston, and Miz Amie Byers (who helped me raise my three sons), "uneducated" but very wise and smart women, who were kind and patient and loving with children and with others. When I went to Spelman College Miz Tee sent me shoe boxes with chicken and biscuits and greasy dollar bills. And I think you and I owe our children and their children the same kind of loving support as these and so many others like them of every race and class in America on whose shoulders of sacrifice and care we all stand today.

It never occurred to any Wright child that we were not going to college or were not expected to share what we learned with the less fortunate. I was 40 years old before I figured out that when my Daddy often responded to my requests for money by saying he didn't have any change that he *really* didn't have any, rather than nothing smaller than a $20 bill. When he died in 1954, he had holes in his shoes but two children out of college, a child in college, and another in divinity school. He knew the difference between substance and shadow. By example, he, my mother, and community leaders taught children to seek, work for, and find a better America. And we did. But I fear we are losing it.

Can You Be Counted In?

Each year in December, millions of Americans celebrate the birth of the most famous poor child in history. Yet more of us are celebrating rather than following Him because we are not making room in our national inn for millions of poor children like Him. Children all over America are being deprived of their basic childhood necessities and happiness. One child's letter reflects the spirit of leadership and commitment every American needs to follow.

"Dear Mr. God,

My Sunday school teacher told me yesterday that you lost your Son. I'm sorry to hear that you lost your Son. Mommy and Daddy have one son too— that's me. I'm six years old. I'm not very strong. I don't have any money. But I'm writing this letter to you to say to you. I don't really understand what you're doing in the world. But whatever it is that you're doing in the world, count me in on it.

(Signed)
Your friend,
Herbie."[1]

I hope every American will say to children, to the nation, and to God, count me in in ensuring that the least and most vulnerable and increasingly precious Americans among us will have a fair chance to live, grow, and serve America and the world.

Marian Wright Edelman
President
Children's Defense Fund

[1]Stuart Hample and Eric Marshall, *Children's Letters to God*, Pocket Books, New York, 1966

TOOLS TO HELP YOU HELP CHILDREN

. . . Today

STEVE SHAMES, VISIONS

. . circa 1912

LEWIS HINES

To be effective, we need facts and figures to back up our arguments on behalf of children. We also need language to awaken and nurture the humane and caring impulses in each of us. What follows is a brief compilation of key facts, presidential promises and statements, and other quotations you may find helpful and inspiring in your work to improve the lives of America's children.

ONE DAY IN THE LIVES OF AMERICAN CHILDREN

16,833 women get pregnant
2,740 of them are teenagers

1,105 teenagers have abortions
369 teenagers miscarry
1,293 teenagers give birth

676 babies are born to women who have had inadequate prenatal care
700 babies are born at low birthweight (less than 5 lbs., 8 oz.)
125 babies are born at very low birthweight (less than 3 lbs., 5 oz.)
69 babies die before one month of life
107 babies die before their first birthday

27 children die because of poverty
9 children die from guns
6 teens commit suicide

7,742 teens become sexually active
623 teenagers get syphilis or gonorrhea

1,375 teenagers drop out of high school

1,849 children are abused
3,288 children run away from home
1,629 children are in adult jails

2,407 children are born out of wedlock
2,989 children see their parents divorced

31,003 people lose jobs

PROMISES TO REMEMBER

Statements by President George Bush

Children

I think when I talk about investing in our kids, in the many proposals I've made in that area, that would be an indication of how I will pursue this objective of a "kinder and gentler" nation.

First postelection press conference,
November 9, 1988

One thing I'm going to do is raise the level of public debate on how best to help our children. I'm going to talk and talk and talk until our country is working together to reach our children.

Littleton, Colorado,
October 5, 1988

This nation's children represent our future—and our responsibility. Good health care and nutrition, sound education, and access to safe child care should be a concern to all of us.

Statement on Child Care

George Bush believes that our national character can be measured by how we care for our children—all of the nation's children—how we invest in them, how they grow, and what we convey to them.... George Bush will lead a national commitment to invest in our children.

George Bush believes our children—especially those at risk—require a more intensely focused effort by all of us....

Investment: this means a community where quality education is available to enable all children, whether rich or poor, to participate fully in the American dream, an education that must begin long before the first year of formal schooling.

Investment: this means a community where the houses they live in and the schools they attend are protected from radon, free of lead paint or asbestos contamination; where the air our children breathe is pure and the water they drink is clean.

Investment: this means a community where parents can find affordable day care to fit their unique needs, where expectant mothers—especially adolescent mothers—learn how to help their babies grow healthy and how to care, nurture, and teach those babies as they grow in the world....

George Bush will lead the effort toward a national commitment to community investment in children....

He believes in all of us investing in all of our children. George Bush will be a leader for children.

Campaign position paper,
Invest in Our Children
October 1988

Health

George Bush will see that quality health services so critical for improving maternal and infant health will be available to the pregnant women and young children in our nation.

Infant mortality is unacceptably high in this country. . . .

The costs are enormous, in human and economic terms. Every low birthweight, the major cause of infant mortality, that can be prevented would save $14,000 to $30,000 in medical costs. Lower incidence of teen pregnancies, access to prenatal care, basic nutrition, and health education are the keys to reducing infant mortality.

The rising cost of health care has put affordable insurance beyond the reach of some young families. . . . George Bush will work to ensure that families have affordable public or private insurance for their children.

He will provide the leadership to focus on these needs, and will:

Improve the Reach and Effectiveness of Medicaid—George Bush supports proper health care through mandatory Medicaid coverage for all children with family incomes below 100 percent of the federal poverty level, working with those at highest risk as a first priority. In addition, he supports measures to phase in affordable coverage for pregnant women and infants up to 185 percent of poverty. He will work to phase in affordable coverage for older children as well. . . .

Decrease Infant Mortality—He proposes that the Maternal and Child Health Block Grant be expanded for an extensive education effort which would provide all pregnant women . . . with health education materials and information about Medicaid and the availability of community prenatal services if the mother is uninsured. In addition, he proposes that case management be provided as an essential component for high-risk and teenage pregnancies that are likely to result in low birthweight babies.

Assure Adequate Immunization for All Children—George Bush supports funding the Childhood Immunization Program to pay for vaccines. . . .

Provide Proper Nutrition—George Bush will request sufficient funding for important programs designed to reach young children—such as the school lunch program, and the Women, Infant, and Children's program.

Provide Catastrophic Protection For Very Sick and Chronically Ill Children—George Bush will work to ensure that families—often young families with few resources—are protected against the potentially devastating costs of a very sick or chronically ill child.

Invest in Our Children,
October 1988

Child Care and Early Childhood Development

The issues in child care are simple: how to provide a nurturing, safe and affordable environment. . . .

America's working couples, America's single parents, and most importantly—America's children—deserve our attention.

Statement on Child Care

The single most important issue arising from the changes in our work force is child care. . . . Today, child care is nothing short of a family necessity. . . . We must find a way to put a greater range of choices in the hands of low-income parents—because they face the greatest difficulty in meeting the demands of work and family.... I would maintain the existing dependent care tax credit, and take an additional important step to make it refundable. Too many low-income families go without the assistance we have made available to upper income families because they do not earn enough to pay taxes....

The states and the federal government ought to provide additional resources ... for a broader range of choices and higher quality child care.

> National Federation of Business
> and Professional Women's Clubs,
> Albuquerque, New Mexico,
> July 24, 1988

The first years of our children's lives are crucial to the success or failure of their education. Head Start is a successful, federally-funded program which provides educational, medical, nutritional, and social services to low-income preschool children.

- In 1970, George Bush co-sponsored the Comprehensive Head Start Child Development Act as a Congressman from Texas. He will maintain his commitment to this successful program by phasing in Head Start to reach all eligible four-year-old children. Head Start provides comprehensive development services for pre-school children from low-income families. This program works; George Bush will sharply increase its funding.

> Fact Sheet on Education

Homelessness

I've seen the urban children who play amidst the shattered glass and shattered lives.

> National Convention,
> August 18, 1988

I have great compassion for those who are homeless and live on the margin of society.... Contrary to the common view of who is homeless, a significant number are ... families seeking shelter—and about one in five homeless works full or part time. We must do more to ... understand and eliminate the causes of homelessness.

> Statement on Social Issues/Homeless

We need to continue the 50-year federal commitment to providing housing assistance to low-income families....

The task for the next decade is to see that all Americans, especially young Americans, can find the homes and stable communities they need to build their lives and families.

> Statement on Housing

Child Support Enforcement

George Bush believes we must tighten the existing loopholes in current child support enforcement procedures.

Invest in Our Children,
October 1988

Education

The real challenge of the future will not be finding jobs for the people, but people for the jobs. That's why education is so important. I am committed to improving the education system in this country so that kids aren't handicapped by inadequate schools. I am committed to improving financial access to college through Pell grants, student aid, and the college work-study program. . . .

We should provide more support for Head Start, and more assistance to the disadvantaged. . . . Will this be expensive? . . . The chairman of Xerox estimates that businesses spend $25 billion each year to train workers who "can't read, can't write, and can't count." The best investment we can make is in our children. . . .

It's in the interest of America to help economically empower all.

Central State University,
Wilberforce, Ohio,
June 12, 1988

Education is our most powerful economic program, our most important trade program, and our most effective anti-poverty program. This year, the class of 2000 enters first grade. When these students graduate from high school, George Bush wants them to be the best prepared young people in the world. . . .

The role of the federal government is to keep education on the national agenda and to target its resources to ensure access to a high quality education for those traditionally denied access, especially the disadvantaged and the disabled. . . .

George Bush will assure that no student is deprived of a higher education for financial reasons. . . .

Our children are our most valuable resource. The Education President, George Bush, will make America a world leader, not only in jobs and technology, but also in the fight against illiteracy. With the leadership of George Bush and the involvement of students, parents, communities, and employers, real educational reform will happen student-by-student, classroom-by-classroom, and school-by-school. George Bush will make sure that our children are offered the best education in the world.

Fact Sheet on Education

All our hopes for our children will mean little if we don't make sure that the education they're given is outstanding. If we provide special attention to those with special needs, then we can wipe out illiteracy the way we wiped out polio.

Statement on Social Issues/Education

We need to spend more on education. Providing excellent education is an investment in America's future—and it is one of the most basic roles of government.

Statement on Education

Civil Rights

We must take specific steps to include those who have been excluded, whether from government itself or from the opportunity to succeed in a free society.

To me, this is not just a matter of social policy, but of fundamental right. . . .

We must have a positive civil rights agenda, one that protects the civil rights of every American. . . .

But just protecting civil rights does not assure equality of economic opportunity. We must also knock down the walls of indifference and other barriers that result in economic exclusion.

Central State University,
Wilberforce, Ohio,
June 12, 1988

SOME FORMER PRESIDENTS TO QUOTE

Each of these children represents either a potential addition to the productive capacity and the enlightened citizenship of the nation, or, if allowed to suffer from neglect, a potential addition to the destructive forces of the community. The ranks of criminals and other enemies of society are recruited in an altogether undue proportion from children bereft of their natural homes and left without sufficient care.

The interests of the nation are involved in the welfare of this army of children no less than in our great material affairs.

Theodore Roosevelt,
Special Message to Congress,
February 15, 1909

. . . The test of our progress is not whether we add more to the abundance of those who have much; it is whether we provide enough for those who have too little.

Franklin Delano Roosevelt,
Second Inaugural Address,
January 20, 1937

Every gun that is made, every warship launched, every rocket fired signifies . . . a theft from those who hunger and are not fed, those who are cold and are not clothed.

This world in arms is not spending money alone.

It is spending the sweat of its laborers, the genius of its scientists, the hopes of its children.

> Dwight David Eisenhower,
> "The Chance for Peace," delivered before
> the American Society of Newspaper Editors,
> April 16, 1953

... In education, in health, in all of human development, the early years are the critical years. Ignorance, ill health, personality disorder—these are destructions often contracted in childhood: afflictions which linger to cripple the man and damage the next generation.

Our nation must rid itself of this bitter inheritance. Our goal must be clear—to give every child the chance to fulfill his promise.

> Lyndon B. Johnson,
> Special Message to Congress Recommending
> a 12-Part Program for
> American Children and Youth

All the evidence available suggests that helping a poor child is a good public investment. The Committee on Economic Development estimates that $1 spent in early intervention saves $5 in the cost of remedial education, welfare, and crime control.

There is no easy answer to the problem of ingrained poverty. But early intervention in the lives of poor children offers the best opportunity to break the cycle of poverty. There is solid evidence that Federal programs such as Head Start, prenatal care, immunization, the [WIC] program and compensatory education do work, and offer one of the best investments the country can make in its own people. To cover all eligible children with these programs would cost from $9 to $13 billion yearly. Because of the lack of funds, only about 20 percent of eligible children can participate now in Head Start.

Spending public funds for these young Americans is not wasteful; it is wasteful *not* to invest in the medical attention, the education and the job training that will provide poor children with a share in the American opportunity.

We understand the budget constraints on any expansion of Federal spending programs; but we believe that it would be imprudent to delay any longer on taking Federal action to begin the long process of assisting these children of poverty.

We recommend that you:

- set a goal of full Federal funding for Head Start, WIC, Compensatory Education, prenatal care, immunization and preventive health care programs for all eligible disadvantaged children within eight years, and

- move toward that goal by recommending in your Fiscal 1990 budget ... annual increases of $2 billion until the goal is reached.

We also urge you to publicly encourage successful state, local and voluntary initiatives, and to provide funding for selected model demonstration projects focused on good parenting and child support.

To pay for these investments in our children we suggest reductions in less essential domestic programs, such as Amtrak subsidies and the Economic Development Administration, savings which we believe will occur in farm subsidies from the market-oriented agricultural policy our Domestic Policy Panel recommends, and, if necessary, part of the revenues from higher cigarette and alcohol taxes.

> Jimmy Carter and Gerald Ford,
> *American Agenda: Report to the*
> *Forty-first President of the*
> *United States*, November 1988

SOME ALLIES TO CALL UPON

Governors

... There are no quick or easy solutions to the needs of our children and families, but there are effective and affordable ways to save millions of children before the dawning of the next century. We need the political will to make investment in our children and families a national priority.

In this time of transition, the Governors' support for children's issues is critical.

> Gov. Gerald L. Baliles of Virginia,
> excerpted from *America in Transition:*
> *The International Frontier—1988-89*
> *Chairman's Agenda*, National Governors'
> Association

Mayors

The United States Conference of Mayors and the United States Conference of City Human Services Officials recognize the critical importance of investing in this nation's children. They are our country's future, yet the problems which too many of our children face have been increasing in recent years.... [This report] is intended to help this nation set a course for the future which will lead us toward critically needed investments in our children's future and, consequently, in our country's future.

> Thomas J. Cochran,
> Executive Director, U.S. Conference of Mayors,
> U.S. Conference of City Human Services Officials,
> from the Foreword to *A Status Report*
> *on Children in America's Cities*,
> October 1988

Cities and towns have a vital stake in the welfare of the children and youth in their communities. City elected leaders know firsthand the problems associated with poverty, infant mortality, adolescent pregnancy, hunger, child abuse, high school dropout rates, and teenage unemployment. From Phoenix, Arizona, to Portland, Maine, to Miami, Florida, city officials are playing new roles as catalysts for change. It is time now for government, at all levels, to work together to protect and nurture our most precious resource, our children and youth.

> Statement by Mayor Terry Goddard,
> President, National League of Cities,
> to the Board of Directors,
> December 3, 1988

Private Sector Leaders

This nation cannot continue to compete and prosper in the global arena when more than one-fifth of our children live in poverty and a third grow up in ignorance. And if the nation cannot compete, it cannot lead. If we continue to squander the talents of millions of our children, America will become a nation of limited human potential. It would be tragic if we allow this to happen. America must become a land of opportunity—for every child. . . .

. . . Children born into poverty often suffer from debilitating deprivations that seriously impair their ability to learn. Yet, most recent reforms have been targeted at the education system; rarely have they addressed the pressing needs of at-risk infants and toddlers and their families. We contend that reform strategies for the educationally disadvantaged that focus on the school system alone are doomed to continue to fail a substantial portion of these youths. Effective strategies must address the broader needs of these children from their earliest years.

Effective solutions to the problems of the educationally disadvantaged must include a fundamental restructuring of the school system. But they must also reach beyond the traditional boundaries of schooling to improve the environment of the child. An early and sustained intervention in the lives of disadvantaged children, both in school and out, is our only hope for breaking the cycle of disaffection and despair.

> Excerpted from *Children in Need: Investment Strategies for the Educationally Disadvantaged*, a statement by the Research and Policy Committee of the Committee for Economic Development, 1987

A Few Facts To Learn

(For answers see below.)

1. How many Americans are poor? _____

2. How many American children are poor? _____

3. Who makes up the poorest age group in America? _____

4. Are the majority of the poor white or black? _____

5. Are the majority of the poor working or on welfare? _____

6. What is the average welfare payment in America today? _____

7. Does a minimum wage job lift a family above the federal poverty line? _____

8. How many Americans lack health insurance? _____

9. What proportion of preschool children have mothers in the work force? _____

10. How many American teens gave birth in 1986? _____

11. Were the majority of these teens black or white? _____

12. What proportion of these teens live in cities with populations of 200,000 and less? _____

13. Which group of families is most likely to be poor? Young families (ages 18 to 24)? Those over 65? Those 40 to 50? ____

1. 32.5 million
2. 12.4 million
3. Children
4. White
5. Working
6. $4.16 per day
7. No. For a family of three, a full-time, year-round minimum wage job equals 69 percent of the poverty line; for a family of four, 58 percent
8. 37 million
9. More than half
10. 472,000
11. White
12. Approximately two-thirds
13. Young families

An American Child's Chances of Being Poor

If white	1 in 6
If black	4 in 9
If Hispanic	2 in 5
If younger than 3	1 in 4
If 3 to 5	2 in 9
If 6 to 17	1 in 5
If family head is younger than 25	1 in 2
If family head is younger than 30	1 in 3

SPENDING CHOICES TO PONDER

Eliminate the National Board for the Promotion of Rifle Practice:

This portion of the military budget no longer serves a military purpose and has become identified with handgun peddlers. Savings, $4 million a year—enough to buy nearly 10 million mid-afternoon snacks for hungry preschoolers in child care.

Reinstitute the Federal Excise Tax on Luxury Items:

The federal excise taxes on expensive jewelry, gems, and furs was repealed in 1965. We could reinstitute a 10 percent federal excise tax on those luxuries with a retail price of more than $100 to raise about $200 million the first year and $400 million a year thereafter—with which we could purchase 12.2 million monthly WIC packages for infants and pregnant women.

Raise the Federal Excise Tax on Distilled Spirits to Truman-Era Levels:

In 1951 the excise tax on distilled spirits was set at $10.50 per proof gallon. It is now $12.50 per proof gallon. If the rate were returned to the 1951 level, adjusted for inflation ($46.50 per proof gallon), even with substantial reduction in consumption, this proposal would raise about $3 billion the first year and $3.5 billion annually thereafter. With $3.5 billion we could provide Chapter 1 remedial education services to an additional 5.7 million children each year.

Raise Beer and Wine Excise Taxes to Eisenhower-Era Levels:

In 1955 the federal excise tax on beer was set at $9 per barrel ($7 for certain small brewers) and the tax on wine was set at 17 cents per wine gallon. These have not been raised since. All rates could be adjusted for inflation since 1955—to $40 per barrel of beer, and 75 cents per wine gallon—and the inflation adjustment could be made annually thereafter. Even with fairly drastic reductions in consumption, this proposal would raise about $2 billion in the first year, and $2.5 billion annually thereafter—enough to pay for the desperately needed services of the Act for Better Child Care.

Triple the Cigarette Excise Tax, and Index for Inflation:

If the federal excise tax on a pack of cigarettes equaled the same proportion of the retail price today as it did in 1951, it would be 68 cents a pack. Instead it is only 16 cents a pack. It could be tripled to 48 cents a pack and adjusted for twice the rate of inflation thereafter, until it reaches its 1951 level. Corresponding increases would be imposed on all other tobacco products. This proposal would raise about $5.5 billion per year—equal to the cost of free school lunches *and* breakfasts, 200 days per year, for 11.4 million children.

Reduce the Business Meal/Entertainment Write-off to 50 Percent:

Today an individual may deduct 80 percent of an expenditure for a meal, entertainment, sporting event, or social dues as a business expense. The deduction could be reduced to 50 percent, and a maximum placed on each type of expenditure (such as the median price of a meal away from home, a general admissions ticket to a professional sporting event). This proposal would raise about $3 billion in FY 1990, and more than $4 billion annually thereafter— enough to cover the cost of the maximum monthly food stamp allotment for 17 million families for a year.

Tax Ozone-Depleting Chemicals:

A tax of $5 a pound for chlorofluorocarbons (CFC-11) or equivalents would help a little to postpone the greenhouse effect and would raise $1 billion per year. Providing child care lunches five days a week, 52 weeks a year, costs $1 billion for 2.6 million children.

Tax Hazardous Wastes:

Many states impose taxes on hazardous wastes, yet the federal government must absorb most of the expenses of clean-up and human injuries. A tax of $100 a ton (of which $90 is forgiven if the waste is identified and disposed of in accordance with EPA standards) should raise about $1 billion the first year and $1.5 billion annually thereafter—or the full cost of child care for 500,000 children.

Eliminate the Capital Gains Tax Break for Inherited Wealth:

When a person sells an inherited asset he or she does not pay any tax on the capital gains made before it was inherited. We propose that all capital gains be taxed as income at the time of death, and before the asset is transferred to heirs. This should raise about $4.5 billion the first year and almost $5 billion annually thereafter—more than twice the amount needed to expand Medicaid to cover every child and pregnant woman with a family income of less than twice the poverty level.

Lower the Tax Break for Pension Contributions to the Social Security Wage Base:

Income diverted to pension plan contributions is not taxable up to the equivalent of a pension level of $100,000 current dollars per year. Very few workers have earnings high enough to benefit from such high levels. Lowering the limit to the Social Security wage base—the amount on which we all pay FICA tax—would save more than $2 billion in its first full year, and more than $2.5 billion annually thereafter—enough to provide complete maternity care for over 800,000 pregnant women.

Cancel the Army's FAAD C2I System:

Having wasted $1 billion each on the DIVAD anti-aircraft gun and the Aquila remote controlled model airplane, the Army has combined substitutes for both of them into a packaged anti-aircraft system called FAAD C2I. The Army estimates total program costs as $3.5 billion (an increase of $800 million in the last two years), and GAO estimates that as much as $2.6 billion in additional costs have been excluded. Eliminating the whole thing would raise at least $4 billion over the next several years—enough to provide aid to more than 300,000 poor college students each year for four years.

Stop Forgiving Loans for Foreign Military Sales:

Each year we "forgive" about $4 billion in loans made to foreign governments to cover their purchase of weapons from us. Exporting "forgiveness" does not reduce the trade deficit. Stopping this would save about $4 billion a year—enough to provide Head Start for every poor three- and four-year-old child.

SOME POLLS TO CITE

- When polled, parents say they will pay more taxes to support pro-family public programs, such as improving public schools (84 percent), making health care more available (76 percent), improving child care (69 percent), and making affordable housing more available (69 percent). (Gallup Poll for Family Resource Coalition, September 1988)

- Three of four voters (75 percent) want federal spending on aid to the homeless increased. By nearly two to one (51 percent to 29 percent), voters would be willing to pay $100 a year more in taxes to aid the homeless and hungry. (Millman & Lazarus Research for The National Campaign to End Hunger and Homelessness, January 1988)

- Sixty percent of voters favor government aid to help working parents pay for day care. Sixty-nine percent favor more government assistance to the poor. (*Washington Post* Poll, 1988)

- Eighty-three percent of working mothers and 63 percent of all voters believe the federal government should develop policies to make child care more available and affordable. Seventy-five percent of voters say the federal government should set minimum standards for health, safety, and quality of child care services. (Martilla & Kiley for American Federation of State, County and Municipal Employees and Children's Defense Fund, June 1988)

- Sixty percent of voters say that despite the deficit, the government should fully fund programs dealing with early childhood health and education because they save money in the long run. (Peter D. Hart Research Associates for KIDSPAC, July 1988)

STEPS *YOU* CAN TAKE IN 1989 TO HELP CHILDREN

1. Write House Speaker Jim Wright (U.S. House of Representatives, Washington, D.C. 20515), Senate Majority Leader George Mitchell (U.S. Senate, Washington, D.C. 20510), and President Bush (Washington, D.C. 20500) and tell them to place preventive investments in children at the top of their priorities.

2. Write letters to your congressional representative (Washington, D.C. 20515) and U.S. senators (Washington, D.C. 20510) supporting the investments in children outlined here. Watch how they vote and hold them accountable.

3. Write your governor, state senator, and representative urging them to support well-conceived state initiatives for children. Do your part in making sure they are well-conceived and well-implemented.

4. Invite newly elected and incumbent local officials to a postelection forum to hear about the problems of children in your community and to talk about how they intend to work with you to address those problems.

5. Get personally involved with one young person as a tutor or mentor, or get involved in an organization that serves needy children and families.

6. Visit a successful children's program in your community—such as a day care or Head Start program, health clinic, or school—to be able to talk knowledgeably about services for children.

7. Visit a neonatal intensive care nursery and a homeless shelter in your community so you can see, hear, and understand the needless suffering of children. Take a friend and a leader from the public or private sector with you. Together, work hard to alleviate and prevent child suffering.

8. Conduct an educational program for your club, religious organization, or other group about programs serving low-income youngsters and families. Spend less time meeting and more time helping. Spend less money on social functions and contribute more money to local groups helping children in need.

9. Pray that we and those we elect into positions of power will be guided by justice and compassion. Pray that, in this time ripe with opportunity for children, leaders and citizens will work together to provide a safe, healthy, nurturing world for our children.

STEPS CDF WILL TAKE IN 1989 TO HELP CHILDREN

1. Defining and refining a clear, substantive agenda with immediate and longer term federal, state, and local governmental, private sector, community, and parental responsibilities.

2. Continuing massive public education and consciousness-raising activities to create an informed and positive national climate of concern for children.

3. Making sure that all those holding public office at all levels and important private sector positions have a common set of facts and are aware of our proposed remedies for children.

4. Identifying, analyzing, and publicizing policies, programs, and approaches that work or appear promising.

5. Providing extensive, high-quality, substantive technical and information assistance to state and local officials and community leaders. Local leadership development and skills training will be a leading CDF priority over the next five years.

6. Launching three to five comprehensive local community involvement efforts to demonstrate and document a record of success in preventing first and second teenage pregnancies and their negative health and education outcomes.

7. Ensuring and strengthening CDF's institutional capacity and effectiveness and sharing what we learn with others.

A FEW WORDS TO THINK ABOUT

"Every wall is a door," Emerson correctly said. Let us not look for a door, and the way out, anywhere but in the wall against which we are living. . . . Let us seek the respite where it is—in the very thick of battle. . . . Great ideas, it has been said, come into the world as gently as doves. Perhaps, then, if we listen attentively, we shall hear, amid the uproar of empires and nations, a faint flutter of wings, the gentle stirring of life and hope. Some will say that this hope lies in a nation; others, in a man. I believe rather that it is awakened, revived, nourished by millions of solitary individuals whose deeds and works every day negate frontiers and the crudest implications of history. As a result, there shines forth fleetingly the ever threatened truth that each and every man, on the foundations of his own sufferings and joys, builds for them all.

Albert Camus,
from his lecture,
"Create Dangerously"

Prophets grow in stature as people respond to their message. If their early attempts are ignored or spurned, their talent may wither away.
It is *seekers*, then, who make prophets, and the initiative of any one of us in searching for and responding to the voice of contemporary prophets may mark the turning points in their growth and service.

Robert K. Greenleaf,
Servant Leadership: A Journey into the
Nature of Legitimate Power and Greatness,
Paulist Press, New York, 1977

I brought food to the hungry, and people called me a saint; I asked why people were hungry, and people called me a communist.

Bishop Dom Helder Camara,
quoted in Arthur Simon's *Christian*
Faith and Public Policy: No Grounds
for Divorce, William B. Eerdmans
Publishing Company, Grand Rapids, 1987

What is the explanation of "A little child shall lead them"? Simply this. A little child, under all circumstances, is its simple pure, sweet self; never appearing big when it is little; never appearing learned when it is ignorant; never appearing wealthy when it is in poverty; never appearing important when it is unimportant. In a word, the life of the child is founded upon the great and immutable, and yet simple, tender and delicate laws of nature. There is no pretence. There is no mockery.

> Booker T. Washington,
> *Character Building*, Manhattan Press,
> New York, 1902, p. 252

A man cannot have much character unless he has something to wear, and something to eat three hundred sixty-five days a year. He cannot have any religion either. You will find at the bottom of each crime the fact that the criminals have not had the common necessities of life supplied them.

> Ibid, pp. 130-131

Fools abound. Try not to add to their number . . . and remember that the world loves talent but pays off on character.

> John Gardner,
> 1986 Commencement Address,
> Sidwell Friends School

It must be borne in mind that the tragedy of life doesn't lie in not reaching your goal. The tragedy lies in having no goal to reach. It isn't a calamity to die with dreams unfulfilled, but it is a calamity not to dream. It is not a disaster to be unable to capture your ideal, but it is a disaster to have no ideal to capture. It is not a disgrace not to reach the stars, but it is a disgrace to have no stars to reach for. Not failure, but low aim is sin.

> Benjamin E. Mays,
> *Quotable Quotes of Benjamin E. Mays*,
> Vantage Press, New York, 1983

Our scientific power has outrun our spiritual power. We have guided missiles and misguided men.

> Martin Luther King, Jr.

[The GNP] does not include the beauty of our poetry or the strength of our marriages, the intelligence of our public debate or the integrity of our public officials. It allows neither for the justice in our courts, nor for the justness of our dealings with each other.
    The gross national product measures neither our wit nor our courage, neither our wisdom nor our learning, neither our compassion nor our devotion to country. It measures everything, in short, except the things that make life worthwhile. . . .

> Robert F. Kennedy,
> Schenectady, New York,
> October 6, 1967

SOME SUCCESSFUL CHILDREN'S PROGRAMS TO SHARE

Programs	Benefits for Children
Special Supplemental Food Program for Women, Infants, and Children (WIC) provides nutritional help to the needy.	Reduces infant mortality and number of births at low birthweight, improves nutritional outcomes for children in the first six years of life, including reduced anemia rates and better growth rates.
Medicaid, with Early and Periodic Screening, Diagnosis, and Treatment (EPSDT) services for children, puts health care within reach of the uninsured poor.	Results in earlier prenatal care, increased birthweight, decreased neonatal and postneonatal infant mortality and morbidity, and fewer abnormalities among children receiving comprehensive preventive services under EPSDT.
Childhood immunization program protects our children against preventable diseases.	Brought about dramatic declines in the incidence of rubella, mumps, measles, polio, diphtheria, tetanus, and pertussis; reduction in consequent impairments and institutionalization.
Child care help that enables low-income families to pay their child care bills.	Provides more supportive child care and increases safety of child care for children who otherwise would be left untended or in potentially harmful arrangements. Increases well-being of children through higher parental earnings and self-sufficiency.
Head Start gives disadvantaged youngsters a range of crucial services.	Increases school success and eventual employability.
Chapter 1 Compensatory Education gives extra educational help to disadvantaged children.	Linked to achievement gains and maintenance of gains in reading and mathematics while in the program.
Education for All Handicapped Children opens doors to learning for disabled youngsters.	Increases the number of students receiving services, increases availability of appropriate services and less restrictive settings in which services are provided.
Minimum wage increase (a proposal to restore the minimum wage to its levels of the 1970s).	Increases parental earnings and financial incentives to work.
Youth employment and training and the Job Corps help prepare disadvantaged young people for the world of work.	Brings about gains in future employability and earnings for teenagers and young adults.

Note: Based in part on data from the House Select Committee on Children, Youth and Families.

Cost Savings

$1 invested in the prenatal component of WIC has saved as much as $3 in short-term hospital costs. Improved early nutrition has been shown to be effective in preventing retardation.

$1 spent on comprehensive prenatal care saves $3.38; 10 percent lower annual health care costs for children receiving EPSDT services.

$1 spent on the childhood immunization program saves $10 in later medical costs.

Child care reimbursements cost the public a small fraction of what monthly welfare payments to a family without a working parent cost. In addition, employers and parents report less absenteeism and greater productivity if there is adequate child care.

$1 invested in quality preschool education returns $4.75 because of lower costs of special education, public assistance, and crime.

Investment of $600 for a child for one year of compensatory education can save $4,000 in the cost of a single repeated grade.

Early educational intervention has saved school districts $1,560 per disabled pupil.

Reduced expenditures for income support programs targeted on low-income families; increased personal income and payroll tax revenues associated with increased employment and earnings.

Every $1 invested Job Corps yields $1.45 in benefits to American society. Other youth employment and training programs have raised post-program employment rates by nearly a fourth and annual earnings by more than $1,300 per participant.

National Goals

Full participation of all eligible low-income mothers, infants, and children. (As of 1987, only 40 percent of those potentially eligible for WIC were served.)

Routine prenatal and pediatric care for all low-income women and and children. (As of 1987, less than half of America's poor pregnant women and children were covered by Medicaid.)

Immunization of 90 percent of American children by 1990. (In 1985, fewer children younger than two had been immunized than in 1980. For several groups immunization rates were below 80 percent.)

Safe and affordable child care for America's families. Enactment in 1989 of the Act for Better Child Care. (Today, the only federal form of child care help—Title XX—serves fewer than half a million children of the nearly 5 million children younger than 6 who are poor.)

Extend Head Start to at least half of the poor three- to five-year-olds by 1992. (The program now serves fewer than one in five eligible youngsters.)

Fully fund the Chapter 1 program to reach all eligible educationally disadvantaged children by 1992. (Today, the program serves only about one-half of the children who need it.)

A free and appropriate education for every child, regardless of disability. (The federal government is not living up to the commitment it made to share the costs.)

Preservation of a "family wage" that allows parents to earn enough to keep their children out of poverty. (Today's minimum wage, unchanged since 1981, now provides a full-time, full-year worker wages that leave a family of three at 71 percent of poverty.)

Provide every young person not going on to college a training opportunity that leads to a stable job with adequate wages. (Youth employment and training and the Job Corps together currently serve only 3 percent of the 1.4 million teenagers officially counted as unemployed.)

THE STATUS OF
AMERICAN CHILDREN

HEALTH

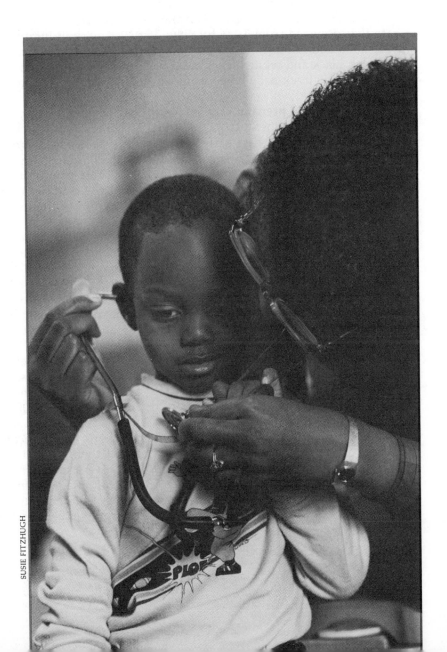

O ur nation's progress in the area of maternal and child health, which moved steadily forward during the late 1960s and 1970s, has faltered during the 1980s. On many key indicators progress has slowed or stopped. On several others this nation actually is losing ground. These alarming trends, if permitted to persist, will take a devastating toll on the health of America's mothers, infants, and children.

Lagging success at reducing infant deaths: The United States' infant mortality rate (10.4 deaths per 1,000 live births as of 1986, the most recent year for which final data are available) placed it eighteenth in the world, behind such nations as Spain, Singapore, and Hong Kong. The rate among black infants alone (18.0 deaths per 1,000 live births) would have ranked the United States twenty-eighth, behind such nations as Cuba and Bulgaria.

Unless the nation speeds up the pace of decline in the infant mortality rate that occurred from 1978 to 1986, 15,029 American infants will die in the year 2000 before reaching their first birthday. And if the infant death gap between black and white babies continues to grow at the rate it grew during that period, a black baby born in the year 2000 will be 2.2 times as likely to die as a white baby.

Inadequate prenatal care for mothers: Following a 10-year period of continuous improvement, from 1970 to 1980, the percentage of births to women who received prenatal care early in pregnancy has dropped three times in this decade—most recently between 1985 and 1986. This latest dip was from 76.2 percent to 75.9 percent. If the very slow overall rate of progress made during the 1978-1986 period continues until the year 2000, one out of every five births (and more than one-third of black births) will be to a woman who failed to receive this crucial care early in pregnancy.

High rates of preventable low-birthweight births: The nation made very little progress from 1978 to 1986 in reducing a very costly and painful problem—the proportion of babies born at less than 5.5 pounds. (The nation failed to move forward at all between 1980 and 1986.) At the 1978-1986 rate of improvement, in the year 2000, 6.3 percent of all infants, and 11.8 percent of all black infants, will be born at low birthweight. This would mean more than 3.6 million low-birthweight births would occur between 1986 and the year 2000. Of these, 790,000 babies would not have been born at low birthweight if the nation had made sufficient progress and met the Surgeon General's objective for tackling and reducing this problem by 1990 and merely maintained a stable rate of low birthweight thereafter. The first year cost of care alone for these low-birthweight babies will add up to more than $6 billion (in 1988 dollars) by the end of the century.

Children left vulnerable to diseases: Millions of American children are failing to receive immunizations that can protect them against diseases that can be prevented, such as polio, measles, and mumps. For example, if the trends in polio immunization rates that prevailed from 1980 to 1985 continue, nearly one in five children will not be fully protected against this crippling disease in the year 2000. More than 2 million preschool children will be inadequately protected against polio.

INFANT MORTALITY THERMOMETER

Deaths of Infants Younger than 1 Year, per 1,000 Births,

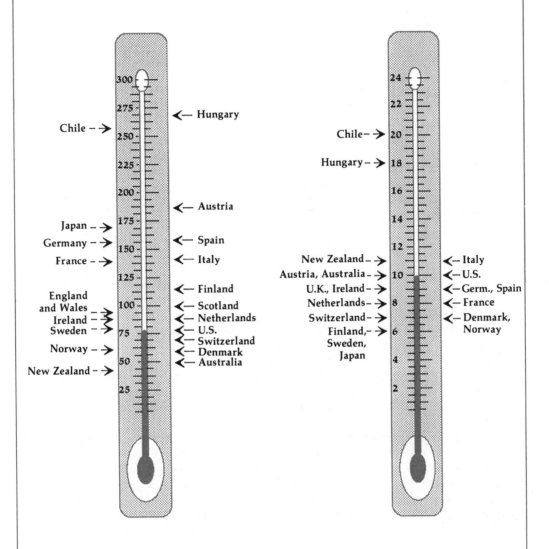

1918

- 300 — ← Hungary
- Chile → 250
- 275
- 225
- 200
- 175 — ← Austria
- Japan → 175
- Germany → 150 — ← Spain
- France → 150 — ← Italy
- 125
- ← Finland
- England and Wales → 100 — ← Scotland
- Ireland → — ← Netherlands
- Sweden → 75 — ← U.S.
- — ← Switzerland
- Norway → — ← Denmark
- 50 — ← Australia
- New Zealand →
- 25

Source: Children's Bureau,
U.S. Department of Labor, 1921

1986

- 24
- 22
- Chile → 20
- Hungary → 18
- 16
- 14
- 12
- New Zealand → — ← Italy
- Austria, Australia → 10 — ← U.S.
- U.K., Ireland → — ← Germ., Spain
- Netherlands → 8 — ← France
- Switzerland → — ← Denmark, Norway
- Finland, → 6
- Sweden,
- Japan
- 4
- 2

Source: UNICEF

• In 1918 the United States ranked sixth in infant mortality rates among selected countries. In 1986, the U.S. rank was thirteenth, behind such countries as Spain, Ireland, Japan, Germany, and France.

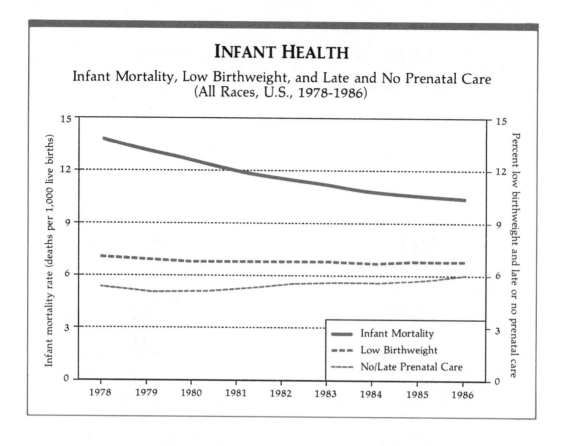

INFANT HEALTH

Infant Mortality, Low Birthweight, and Late and No Prenatal Care
(All Races, U.S., 1978-1986)

There is no vaccine or cure for a deadly disease that threatens a growing number of children: AIDS. Young children get AIDS primarily through transmission during the fetal stage or birth (since the danger of transmission through blood transfusion virtually has been eliminated). As of July 1988, 1,100 children had AIDS. If the number of children with AIDS continues to increase at near-current rates, by the year 2000 the number of infants and children with this fatal disease will reach 13,000. By 1991, the Centers for Disease Control projects that more than 10,000 children younger than 13 will have the virus that can later develop into AIDS.

Millions of children without a way to pay for health care: In 1986 nearly one-fifth of all children younger than 18 and one-third of all poor children had no health insurance, public or private. One crucial reason: the percentage of children younger than 18 who have health coverage through their parents' job fell from 64.6 percent in 1980 to 60.6 percent in 1985. If this drop continues, by 2000 only a minority (48.6 percent) of America's children will be able to get their health care bill paid through a parents' employer-based insurance.

Choosing a Better Future: Health Care Goals for America's Mothers, Infants, and Children

Recently, Congress and many states have taken initial steps toward improving and strengthening publicly financed health programs for low-income children and pregnant women. But America must dramatically step up these efforts if the nation is to achieve the child health goals established by the Surgeon General in 1979. These modest goals were to be met by 1990—an outcome that was possible if the nation's rate of progress in the 1970-1978 period had been maintained or stepped up a little. But instead, the nation moved the other way, with far lower rates of progress on almost all indicators during the 1978-1986 period. At current rates, many of these goals will not be met until well into the next century and beyond. Efforts must be stepped up to meet these life and death objectives.

Infant mortality goal: Cutting the national infant mortality rate to no more than nine deaths per 1,000 live births, with no more than 12 deaths per 1,000 in any county or any racial or ethnic subgroup. Based on the 1978-1986 national rate of progress, CDF projects that the United States will meet the overall goal of nine deaths per 1,000 by 1990. However, it is important to note that based on more recent trends (during 1980 to 1986), the goal would not be met, according to the federal Centers for Disease Control. The 1990 infant mortality goal will not be met for black children until 1996 at the earliest.

Low-birthweight goal: Reducing the percentage of babies born at low birthweight to no more than 5 percent of all births, and no more than 9 percent in any county or any racial or ethnic subgroup. At the 1978-1986 rate of progress, the national goal for all infants will not be met until the year 2031; the goal for black infants will not be met until the year 2055.

Prenatal care goal: Providing prenatal care to at least 90 percent of all pregnant women within the first three months of pregnancy. At the recent rate of progress, the nation will not meet this goal until another century has passed: the year 2094. This goal will not be met for infants born to black women until the year 2153.

Immunization goal: Ninety percent of all two-year-old children should be immunized adequately for measles, mumps, rubella, polio, diphtheria, pertussis, and tetanus. For the youngest children, immunization rates dropped between 1980 and 1985, some to less than 80 percent. After 1985 the Reagan Administration suspended all childhood immunization surveillance activities, making later data unavailable. Based on the 1980-1985 trend, the United States will never meet the Surgeon General's goal for two-year-olds.

Health care access goals: The Surgeon General set three objectives that are essential to help meet the outcome goals:

• Virtually all women and infants should be served at levels appropriate to their need through a regionalized system of primary, secondary, and tertiary care for prenatal, maternal, and perinatal health services.

• All women who give birth should have appropriately attended deliveries.

• All infants should be able to participate in primary health care that includes well-child care, growth and developmental assessment, immunization, screening, diagnosis and treatment of conditions requiring services, and other appropriate counseling.

The nation's health system today is inadequate to meet these Surgeon General's objectives. And the health outcome goals cannot be reached until every American child and mother has access to adequate health care. But today, that achievement is drifting further out of reach.

Among America's Uninsured: 12 Million Children and 9 Million Women of Childbearing Age

Growing numbers of women and children have no way to pay their health care bills and therefore little or no access to care. The reasons are many. First, child poverty has increased during the 1980s. Second, the nation's employer insurance system—the principal source of health care financing for everyone younger than 65—has provided less and less protection to children over the course of this decade. Finally, the nation's publicly funded health programs—though bolstered by increases in recent years—remain woefully inadequate.

NO WAY TO PAY

Insurance Status of American Children in Families in 1986, by Income and Race

	In poor families: Family income at or below the poverty level (approximately $9,100 for a family of three in 1986)	In low-income families: Family income less than twice the poverty level	In low- and moderate-income families: Family income less than four times the poverty level
Percent not insured			
White	33.7%	30.4%	20.5%
Black	30.1%	30.9%	27.6%
Percent insured			
White	66.3%	69.6%	79.5%
Black	69.9%	69.1%	72.4%
Percent with employer coverage			
White	13.4%	37.3%	59.6%
Black	7.9%	23.6%	35.5%
Percent with Medicaid coverage			
White	47.2%	25.2%	12.8%
Black	61.6%	43.8%	33.8%

(Note: Medicaid and employer insurance do not add up to 100 percent of the total insured group because there are other other sources of insurance, such as military, veterans, and family-purchased.)

The working uninsured or partially insured: Most families look to employer health coverage as a source of protection against high-cost medical catastrophes as well as the snowballing costs of routine health care for the whole family. Insurance for both catastrophic and routine care has become increasingly essential to obtain needed health services as medical costs have soared far faster than wages, particularly for younger families.

Since 1980, however, far fewer families can rely on employer coverage to take care of their health needs. The number of uninsured Americans rose by one-fifth, from 30.9 million in 1980 to 37.1 million in 1987. More parents are working at low wage jobs that carry no benefits. Others work for employers that are trying to cut expenses by reducing or eliminating their contribution toward the cost of family coverage. When dependent coverage is no longer available or the cost of paying the premiums for it is switched from employer to employee, spouses and children lose coverage. The loss of dependent coverage was the top factor in the growth in the number of uninsured Americans since 1980, according to the Congressional Research Service, a research branch of Congress.

INSURANCE GAP

White Children in Employed Families
By Insurance Status, 1986

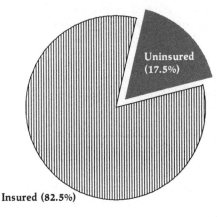

Uninsured
(17.5%)

Insured (82.5%)

Black Children in Employed Families
By Insurance Status, 1986

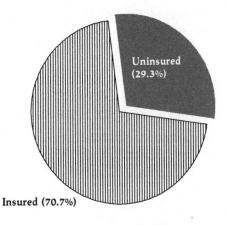

Uninsured
(29.3%)

Insured (70.7%)

- Regardless of family income, black children in employed families are far more likely than their white counterparts to be uninsured.

- By 1986 one out of three children living in families in which at least one family member was employed had no coverage under an employer plan. About half (50.7 percent) of black children in such families were not covered.

- Among children living in moderate-income families (those with incomes between 200 and 400 percent of the federal poverty level), the racial discrepancy is even more glaring. While 80.9 percent of white children in working families with incomes between 200 and 400 percent of the federal poverty level had employer coverage in 1986, only 69.6 percent of comparably situated black children did.

- Among all employer-insured children younger than 18 living in working households in 1986, only 38.2 percent were covered by a plan under which the employer paid the full cost of the premium. Among black children, the proportion was 27.0 percent.

Public Programs: Ill-Equipped To Fill America's Health Insurance Gap

Medicaid's shortcomings: Low-income families often turn to Medicaid to help cover their health costs. But whether or not they get help varies widely depending on the state in which they live.

- Coverage of children ages one to six (rising to age eight in 1991) with family incomes below the poverty line but above the state's AFDC eligibility levels is not mandatory under federal law. Forty-two states have not yet extended Medicaid coverage to all of these children, even though more than one out of four poor children younger than six was uninsured in 1986.

- States do not even have the option to cover children older than eight from families living in poverty but above AFDC levels. The need for such coverage is strong: one out of three poor children ages six to 17 was completely uninsured as of 1986.

- Only 10 states have picked up on their option to extend coverage of all pregnant women and infants with family incomes above 100 percent but below 185 percent of the federal poverty level.

- Even though 30.4 percent of children with family incomes less than 200 percent of the federal poverty level were completely uninsured in 1986, states have no option to cover uninsured near-poor children older than one and with family incomes above the poverty line.

Families and children who are ineligible for Medicaid, or who cannot find a provider who will take Medicaid patients, must rely on a terribly underfunded patchwork of public health programs.

- Our nation's 550 community health centers serve only 5 million patients each year, leaving 20 million eligible people, two-thirds of whom are women of childbearing age and children, without such services.

- A small federal stream of maternal and infant health funding provided to health centers for the first time in 1988 was not even enough to help half of the centers. Further, many of these centers received only half the amount necessary to serve all of the mothers and infants in their communities.

- A health manpower crisis for poor communities looms on the horizon. In 1981, Congress and President Reagan terminated the National Health Service Corps scholarship program, which was mobilizing 6,600 health professionals to work in medically underserved areas of the nation. The pipeline of such essential health manpower is now running dry. Currently, there are approximately 3,600 such professionals in the field. Over the next three years, the number of Service Corps professionals remaining in community placements could fall by more than 1,000, a loss that could directly or indirectly affect some 2 million patients. Recent congressional initiatives to provide additional scholarships and loans will make only a small dent in this problem.

- Funding for the Title V maternal and child health block grant program, targeted on the medically underserved, is so low that fewer than half of all states are able to offer comprehensive prenatal programs on a statewide basis. Only a handful of states pay for hospital delivery services for low-income, uninsured women through Title V. No state is able to offer comprehensive primary pediatric health services on a statewide basis.

- The family planning program is a key player in the effort to help prevent teen pregnancies and halt the spread of AIDS. But its FY 1989 funding of $138.3 million is only a little more than one-half of the amount required to maintain the program's service level in 1981—prior to Reagan era cutbacks and further erosion by inflation.

- The Supplemental Food Program for Women, Infants, and Children (WIC), while operating at funding levels significantly higher than in the beginning of the decade, still reaches less than half of those eligible.

A Promising Start: Recent National Initiatives on Maternal and Child Health

Congress, together with many individual states, has made important strides since 1984 in improving the nation's public system of paying for and delivering basic medical care to low-income pregnant women and children.

- Congress made state Medicaid coverage of all pregnant women and infants with below-poverty family incomes mandatory as of July 1990. This mandate virtually will double the financial eligibility standards for Medicaid that were in effect in 1986. Nearly all of the approximately 700,000 poor infants born each year will be eligible for coverage—extending this crucial help to about 200,000 more pregnant women and 200,000 more babies a year.

- Congress has given states the option to extend Medicaid coverage to all pregnant women and infants with family incomes more than 100 percent but less than 185 percent of the federal poverty level. As of November 1988, 10 states had done so. If it is implemented in every state, this expanded Medicaid program would make an additional 500,000 women and their babies eligible for coverage each year.

- Congress has given states the option to extend Medicaid to all children younger than eight with family incomes less than the federal poverty level. As of November 1988, 22 states had extended coverage to all poor children younger than two, while nine states had extended coverage to all poor children younger than five.

- After several years of vaccine cost inflation far outpacing stagnant federal funding, Congress appropriated sufficient funds to the federal immunization grants program for FY 1989 to purchase the vaccine needed to fully immunize the nation's infants, toddlers, and preschoolers.

- Congress added sufficient funds to the federal community and migrant health centers programs to permit establishment of additional maternity and infant care services at 207 of the nation's 550 such centers.

- As part of the welfare reform bill passed in 1988, Congress created a new part of the Medicaid program that, beginning April 1990, will provide 12 months of Medicaid benefits to thousands of families making the transition from welfare to work. One option states have for providing transitional benefits is to use Medicaid funds to provide assistance in paying premiums to families that are eligible for employer-provided health insurance but cannot afford the employee's share of the monthly cost.

While these are crucial first steps, accelerated efforts are needed to make sure that all American families and children have public or private health insurance and access to care no later than the year 2000.

Health Investments Save Lives and Money

- **Prenatal Care.** Prenatal care saves lives. Children born to women who fail to receive prenatal care are three times more likely to die in infancy than those whose mothers receive comprehensive care. Babies whose mothers receive inadequate care also are at greater risk of being born at low birthweight, a condition that increases the likelihood of such permanent lifelong disabilities as cerebral palsy, retardation, autism, and vision and learning disabilities. Each $1 spent on providing prenatal care to a pregnant mother can save up to $9 over a child's lifetime ($3 in the first year of life alone), taking into account the medical, social, and educational costs and lost earnings that could result from severe impairments that are averted by such timely investments.

  Because they prevent costly health damage, government expenditures on prenatal care both help mothers and babies and pay back the taxpayer, according to a recent study by the congressional Office of Technology Assessment. The report found that prenatal care was so effective in reducing low birthweight and prematurity that the cost of expanding Medicaid to cover all poor women's maternity care would be more than offset by savings to the federal Medicaid program resulting from greater use of such services.

- **Nutrition.** Each $1 spent to provide nutrition help to a pregnant woman under the WIC program saves more than $3 in a child's infancy alone by reducing rates of prematurity and low birthweight.

  WIC is a low-cost way to save lives. A study comparing the cost-effectiveness of various approaches to reducing infant mortality found that WIC could save up to seven lives for every 1,000 women and infants participating in the program. Further, WIC's preventive services cost, at most, $118 for every precious life saved—while neonatal intensive care for underweight babies costs up to $4,778 to save each life.

- **Child immunizations.** Each $1 spent to immunize a child can save more than $10 by reducing childhood illness and death from illness.

  The mass immunization of young American children against preventable disease has saved billions of dollars in averted health costs. A study of the first 20 years in the history of measles vaccine (1963 to 1982) found that this effort yielded an estimated net savings of $5.1 billion in direct and indirect costs averted.

- **Preventive pediatric care.** Children who receive ongoing preventive pediatric care have been found to have fewer health problems. They also have annual health care costs nearly 10 percent lower than children who do not receive such care.

Making a Difference to Children's Health: Successful Initiatives

- **Providing health coverage to uninsured children.** Thousands of Minnesota children who would not otherwise have access to health care are getting their checkups, immunizations, and other vital services thanks to the state's new Child Health Plan. The plan aims to help children from working families that don't have health coverage and are lower income but not Medicaid-eligible. Through an energetic outreach effort, it is working. In the first five months of operation, 4,300 children were enrolled.

- **Reducing the incidence of low birthweight and prematurity.** The Guilford County, North Carolina, health agency's package of extra services to pregnant women has resulted in lowered rates of damaging infant health problems—some 30 percent less than those of infants born to women who receive physician care alone. Working in collaboration with private physicians, the agency provides expectant mothers with such needed supports as health education, strengthened maternity care, and nutritional assistance.

- **Fighting infant mortality.** A remarkable partnership of physicians, local health officials, a charitable foundation, concerned corporations, and others has been fighting to reduce the infant death rate in Lea County, New Mexico. As of 1980, Lea County had one of the highest infant death rates of any county in this nation. The groups worked together to identify women at risk and to lower barriers to getting maternity care. Signs of progress included a dramatic reduction at the local hospital in the number of walk-in maternity patients who had inadequate prenatal care, as well as evidence that the high infant mortality rate is indeed coming down.

A Federal and State Action Agenda

In 1989 the federal government should:

- **Take the next major step in expanding Medicaid.** Congress and the president should require states to provide Medicaid coverage to all pregnant women and all children up to age eight whose family incomes are less than twice the poverty line. The eventual cost of such a crucial step: approximately $1 billion per year. In the first several years, however, the program would cost far less.

Over the next five years the federal government should:

- **Finish the job of Medicaid expansion.** This means extending coverage to all children younger than 21 with family incomes less than twice the poverty level. In combination with the previous agenda item, this reform would reduce by three-fourths the number of children who are uninsured.

- **Increase funding levels for public health programs.** Community and Migrant Health Centers funding should be increased at a real rate of 20 percent per year over the next five years. Funding for the special maternity and infant health program implemented in 1988 should be tripled so that special services can be offered by all existing health centers. The Maternal and Child Health Block Grant and family planning programs must be doubled to reach significantly more underserved women, children, and youths. Even though funding for the purchase of vaccines was sufficient for FY 1989, considerable resources must be invested in outreach and delivery services in the childhood immunization program if the vaccines are to reach infants and preschoolers. And the WIC program must be fully funded so that it can reach all eligible women, infants, and children.

- **Revitalize the National Health Service Corps program.** Sufficient scholarship and loan repayment funds should be provided to permit deployment on a continuing basis of health professionals in all health manpower shortage areas, including the 1,900 areas of the nation that now suffer a shortage of primary health care services for families with children.

In 1989 each state should:

- **Enact the new federal Medicaid options.** States should expand their Medicaid programs to cover all pregnant women and infants with family incomes less than 185 percent of the federal poverty level and all poor children younger than eight.

Over the next five years each state should:

- **Bolster WIC.** States must appropriate substantial funds—as several states do now—to supplement the federal WIC program so that it reaches all women, infants, and children in need of its services.

- **Even out distribution of medical services.** States must provide additional funds for the development of programs for medically underserved areas. These should include maternity and pediatric programs as well as comprehensive family planning services and preventive health counseling.

- **Use financial aid to induce doctors to locate where they are most needed.** States should condition the receipt of state graduate medical education loan and scholarship assistance on young doctors' agreement to serve for a fixed period of time in medically underserved areas.

FAMILY INCOME

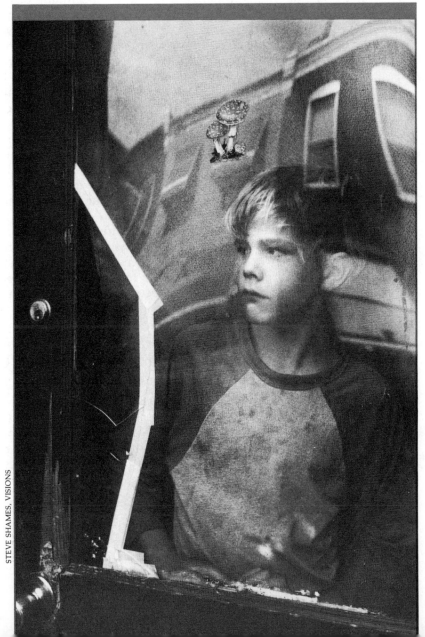

A snapshot of America's children taken in the year 2000 could reveal some alarming changes, unless the nation takes action to reverse the trends of recent years. One out of four children will be poor, a sharp increase from the current shameful rate of one out of five in poverty. Across the United States, on farms and in cities and suburbs, 16 million children will be suffering the hardships of poverty—3 million more than today. This increase is especially remarkable considering that the nation's entire population of children will expand by only 3 million.

America is a nation growing richer while many of its children grow poorer. This pattern has lasted for nearly 20 years, through four recessions and two long spells of sustained economic growth. Child poverty rises during each recession but never falls far enough during the subsequent recovery to restore children's economic status to where it was at the beginning of the cycle. While the rest of the nation enjoys the benefits of the recovery, children are left behind.

Child poverty rose from 16.0 percent in 1979 to 21.8 percent in 1983, after a deep recession, but by 1987 it had retreated only slightly from its 1983 peak, to 20.0 percent, despite the rebounding U.S. economy. At the recent rate of progress, the recovery would have to last until 1995—a sustained rally without historic precedent—to lower the child poverty rate back down to 1979 levels.

Before the end of the century the nation generally will experience economic growth, but also two more recessions, according to the U.S. Department of Labor's official economic projections—on which CDF bases its child poverty prediction for the year 2000. In the event of a severe, unexpected setback to the economy, the child poverty rate could rise even higher than one out of four children.

This nation must take action to make sure that a one in four child poverty rate does not become reality. By the year 2000, every child in America should live in a family that can provide the minimum necessities: shelter that is safe, warm, and well-lit; enough nutritious food to eat; adequate clothing; medical care that will allow the child to become a healthy and productive adult; and enough income so that every day is not a crisis.

In the Midst of Affluence, Child Poverty Casts a Lengthening Shadow

Poor children are those growing up in families with incomes below the amount the federal government says is necessary for bare survival. For a family of three, the official poverty line was $745 a month in 1987. One and a half million more children are poor today than in 1980, swelling the ranks of America's poor children to 13 million. According to the most recent national data:

- Among all children (up to 18 years old) in America, one out of five is poor.

- Among infants and toddlers younger than three, one in four is poor.

- Among children in families headed by young adults (younger than 30), one in three is poor.

- Among black children, nearly one out of two is poor.

All of these poor children live in families with very inadequate incomes, but many are living in extraordinary want, far below the federal government's definition of subsistence. In 1987 more than two out of five poor children lived in households with incomes below half the federal poverty line. For a family of three, this means an annual income of $4,528 or less, according to 1987 figures.

The poorest fifth of America's families now get a tiny sliver—3.8 percent—of America's total income "pie" (in 1986 figures). In contrast, in 1986 the richest fifth of the nation's households increased its share of total family income to almost half—an all-time high. The gap between the rich and the poor is now wider than at any time since the Census Bureau began collecting such data in 1947.

Families, Children, and the Income Crunch

There are four main reasons that so many of America's families are unable to make ends meet.

Hard work is no longer guaranteed to ward off family poverty: Most of the poor in America who can work do work. Roughly two-thirds of the heads of poor households who were not disabled, elderly, or single parents of small children worked either full time or part time at some point during the year studied (1984), according to a report by Sheldon Danziger and Peter Gottschalk of the Institute for Research on Poverty.

But the number of Americans who work yet remain poor has swelled from 6.5 million in 1979 to 8.5 million in 1987. One key reason their effort falls short of conquering poverty is the eroding value of the minimum wage, which has been stagnant at $3.35 an hour since 1981 while the cost of living has climbed 35.4 percent.

Median earnings for Americans have dropped. Median earnings of family heads ages 30 to 64 fell 15 percent from 1973 to 1986. For family heads younger than 30, earnings slumped 30 percent.

Millions of Americans suffer spells of unemployment or under-employment: While unemployment has dropped in recent years, pockets of high unemployment remain in inner cities, in several regions, and among minorities and young workers. And official unemployment rates do not reflect a growing problem: the millions of Americans forced to work part time because they cannot find full-time work.

Women raising children alone face an uphill battle against poverty: In 1987, 34.3 percent of female-headed families were poor, compared with 10.8 percent of all families. Wage inequities that have hampered women's earning power persist: women's hourly wages were only 71 percent of men's hourly wages as of 1987. Child care costs take a bigger proportional bite out of single mothers' smaller paychecks: for example, a typical cost of center-based child care in major cities is $3,000 a year for one child, an amount that is nearly half of the median income of America's single mothers raising one or more children younger than six.

Unlike two-parent families, women raising children alone cannot bring in more money by sending a second adult into the work force. Further, often they cannot rely on any child support help from the absent parent.

Many families getting government help are left desperately poor: Families that are destitute must turn to the government to protect themselves and their children from want. Instead of a single source of help, they find a patchwork of programs, including Aid to Families with Dependent Children (AFDC), Social Security, and Unemployment Insurance—a crazy quilt that budget cuts, inflation, and neglect have torn and tattered. It protects fewer and fewer families.

In 1979 nearly one out of five families with children that otherwise would have been poor was spared the pain of poverty by assistance through these cash benefit programs. By 1986, however, these programs lifted out of poverty only one out of nine families with children that otherwise would have been poor, according to a study by the Center on Budget and Policy Priorities.

The Unmaking of a Decent Family Income

Children rely on their families to protect them from poverty and its harsh impact. But many families cannot provide this protection either through work, child support help, or even assistance from the government. For most American families, the first line of defense against poverty is decent-paying employment. While the unemployment rate has come down in recent years, many families are caught in the cracks in the nation's prosperity.

Pockets of lingering economic hardship: The six-year-old recovery has not reached all regions of the nation. Throughout much of the South, the official jobless rate remains above 7 percent. Employment in scattered states such as West Virginia, Michigan, and Alaska has lagged well behind the rest of the nation. In many rural and inner-city communities, poor job prospects continue to discourage large numbers from even seeking work.

The underemployment problem: The decline in the official jobless rate since 1982 overstates the strength of today's job market. Available jobs are more likely than ever to be part time and usually inadequate to support a family. Newly created service sector jobs in particular are often low-paid, temporary, or part time. The number of Americans forced to work part time because they cannot find full-time jobs has doubled since 1973 to 5 million in 1988.

Lagging earnings: The greatest flaw in the current recovery is reflected in the reduced earnings of American workers. According to a recent study by the Economic Policy Institute, the average weekly earnings of nonsupervisory workers still have not risen above their 1982 recession level and remain nearly 10 percent below their 1979 level.

Average earnings have fallen in part because higher paying jobs in manufacturing industries are disappearing. The Economic Policy Institute found that six of every seven new jobs created between 1979 and 1987 were in the retail trade or service industries—the two sectors with the lowest average wage levels. Industries that have been shrinking since 1979—such as mining and manufacturing—paid 42 percent more annually than those that were expanding during the same period.

More workers also are earning low wages because the minimum wage has not kept pace with the cost of living. In 1979, full-time, year-round work in a job paying the minimum wage lifted a family of three out of poverty. But the minimum wage has not been increased since 1981, and has fallen far below its 1979 level in real terms, and now equals only about 71 percent of poverty for a family of three. In 1986, 26 percent of hourly workers earned less than $4.50 an hour, the wage necessary to keep a family of three above the poverty line. In 1979 only 13 percent of hourly workers earned equal to or less than the equivalent poverty earnings figure ($2.90 an hour). The growth is due substantially to the failure of the federal government to increase the minimum wage.

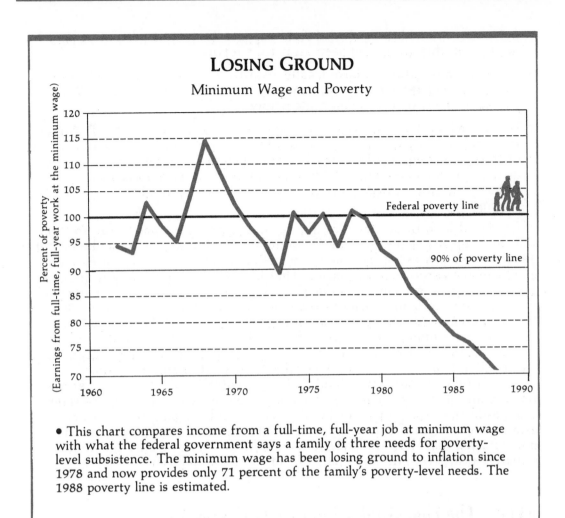

LOSING GROUND

Minimum Wage and Poverty

• This chart compares income from a full-time, full-year job at minimum wage with what the federal government says a family of three needs for poverty-level subsistence. The minimum wage has been losing ground to inflation since 1978 and now provides only 71 percent of the family's poverty-level needs. The 1988 poverty line is estimated.

To minimize losses in total family income in the face of falling earnings, more two-parent families are sending both parents into the work force and working longer hours. These adjustments by parents have kept family income losses smaller, but increased child care costs now take an increasing bite out of that income.

Young families have borne the brunt of these economic changes and are now starting out far behind their predecessors of 15 years ago (see Young Families chapter). For example, the median income of families with children headed by persons younger than 30 fell by 26 percent between 1973 and 1986, compared with 6 percent for families headed by persons ages 30 to 64.

Child Support: An Unfulfilled Promise

Our nation has failed to assure fulfillment of a child's most basic right: to be supported by his or her parents to the fullest extent possible. While the child support provided by an absent parent usually is not enough to provide for a family, or lift a family from poverty, it can be a crucial supplement to other income. For millions of families, however, it is little more than an IOU.

• Of the 8.8 million mothers living with children younger than 21 whose fathers were absent from the home as of the spring of 1986, only 61 percent even had been awarded child support. Only 40.4 percent of poor mothers in this group had been awarded support.

• Of all mothers who had been legally awarded child support in 1985, only about one-half received the full amount due. One-quarter received partial payment; the rest received not one penny.

• Unmarried mothers face the worst odds. In 1986, 22 percent of all women with children younger than 21 whose fathers were absent—and 40 percent of those who were poor—never had been married. Yet less than one-quarter of all women with children born out-of-wedlock have had the father's paternity officially established—the first step in obtaining a child support award.

Faced with these statistics, the federal government has begun to tackle the child support challenge. The Child Support Enforcement Amendments of 1984 began a process of improving the generally dismal performance of state child support enforcement agencies. That law requires states to put in place several effective mechanisms to make sure child support is awarded and paid.

Because of inadequacies in the policies and enforcement of the 1984 law, Congress made changes through the Family Support Act of 1988 to improve upon some of the earlier reforms. The new law will prod states to implement the 1984 requirements more quickly and effectively by: beginning withholding from a noncustodial parent's wages automatically, rather than waiting until payments fall behind; following equitable guidelines in setting the amount of awards; updating the amount of awards periodically to reflect changes in the cost of living or family income; and stepping up paternity establishment efforts. But many state child support agencies are so severely understaffed that they are likely to have difficulty making sure this new initiative translates into more dollars and cents for children.

AFDC: The Floor Under Families Is Caving In

Every year millions of American families turn to public assistance to help them weather bad times. What they find is far from a safe haven. While the amount of help they receive varies widely depending on the state in which they live, virtually all AFDC families in America get so little public help that they still have to scrounge for food, shelter, clothing, and health care.

One AFDC mother of two learning-disabled children, herself handicapped, asks: "Why must my daughter endure the pain of a chipped tooth because Medicaid will not pay for a cap? Why must I visit our local food pantry and have to be selective about what I accept from them because of the kids' special diet? Why must I roll pennies and collect cans and bottles to buy gas to take them to the pediatrician for their check-ups? Why must we be at risk of being homeless every year when our rent goes up and our check doesn't?"

The numbers bear out this mother's story. Each state sets its own AFDC eligibility and benefit levels. The AFDC "standard of need," used to determine eligibility, is supposed to represent what a family needs to maintain a minimum standard of living—in theory. The reality is quite different. As of July 1988, the AFDC need standard for a family of three was less than the 1987 federal poverty line in all but four states, and considerably less in many.

As low as these needs standards are, the benefits states actually pay to poor families are often far worse, since states need not pay benefits equal to their standard of need. According to 1987 federal poverty guidelines, a family of three needs $754 per month for subsistence. Yet the maximum AFDC benefit for a family of three in July 1988 was less than one-half of this poverty level in

INADEQUATE HELP

AFDC Benefits for a Family of Three, Compared with SSI Benefits for
One Individual
(1977, 1988, and the Year 2000, Assuming the Same Trends)

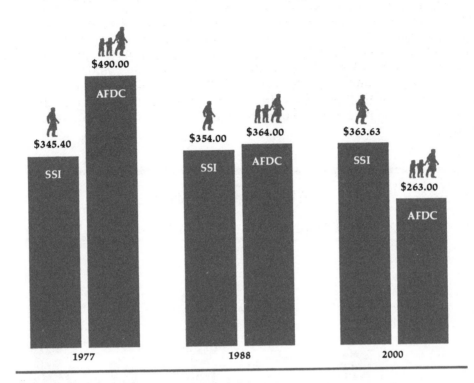

• This chart compares in 1988 dollars the differences between the median state maximum AFDC grant for a family of three and the maximum federal SSI benefit for a single individual.

AFDC benefits are set by each state. Federal law does not require that they be updated to reflect increases in the cost of living. Benefits under the Supplemental Security Income (SSI) program for poor aged, blind, and disabled individuals are set by the federal government and must be updated annually. Neither program meets poverty-level need. In 1987 the maximum SSI benefit provided 70 percent of the poverty guideline for one individual, while the median state maximum AFDC grant for three provided 47 percent of the federal poverty guideline for three.

Note: All figures are in 1988 dollars. Figures for 1977 and 1988 are based on actual state and national data. Projections for SSI benefits in the year 2000 are based on the rate of SSI benefit increases between 1977 and 1988. Projections for AFDC benefits are based on the rate of increase during the same period for the state that had the median benefit for a family of three in 1977 and had the median proportional increase in benefits from 1977 to 1988.

31 states. The real value (adjusted for inflation) of the median state AFDC monthly benefit for a family of four fell by 30 percent between July 1970 and July 1988.

The availability of food stamps does not make up for the inadequacy of cash benefits. As of July 1988, the maximum AFDC grant plus the maximum value of food stamps left a family of three below the 1987 federal poverty line everywhere but Alaska, California, and parts of New York.

Here in America we spend far more on our cars than we do on our poor children. According to the National Automobile Dealers Association, the average monthly installment payment for a new car purchased in 1987 was $298—more than twice as much as a child's share of the median state AFDC grant, which is the highest a state will pay for a family of three (as of July 1988).

Many poor families cannot get any help from AFDC at all. In 1973 AFDC benefits were provided to 83.6 children per every 100 poor children in this nation. By 1987 that ratio had dipped to 59.8 children for every 100 poor children.

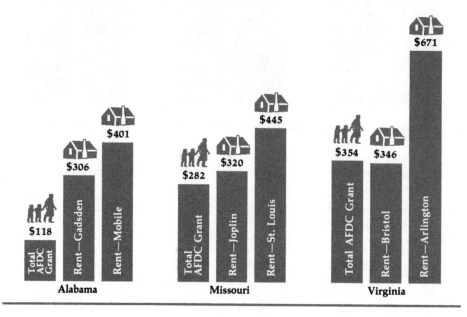

AFDC AND RENT

AFDC Grants Compared with Rental Costs, in Sample States

Alabama
- $118 — Total AFDC Grant
- $306 — Rent—Gadsden
- $401 — Rent—Mobile

Missouri
- $282 — Total AFDC Grant
- $320 — Rent—Joplin
- $445 — Rent—St. Louis

Virginia
- $354 — Total AFDC Grant
- $346 — Rent—Bristol
- $671 — Rent—Arlington

• This chart compares for three states the total AFDC grant for a family of three[1] with the costs of modest rental housing in the least expensive and most expensive area in each state.[2]

[1]July 1988 data, Congressional Research Service, "Aid to Families with Dependent Children (AFDC): Need Standards, Payment Standards, and Maximum Benefits," (September 1988).

[2]Fair market rental values based on United States Department of Housing and Urban Development levels for existing housing under Section 8 Housing Assistance Program, effective October 1, 1988. Fair market rent represents amount determined by HUD as necessary to rent a two-bedroom, privately owned "decent, safe, and sanitary rental housing of a modest (nonluxury) nature."

AFDC Families Can't Pay the Rent

More and more AFDC families are joining the ranks of the homeless. These families are forced out of their housing because they don't have enough money to pay the rent and still buy food, heat, clothing, and medical care not covered by Medicaid insurance.

- Eighty-three percent of the women with children in homeless shelters in the Twin Cities of Minnesota in 1988 received AFDC. Thirty percent had left their last housing because they had been evicted, 21 percent had experienced a change in their ability to pay the rent, and 10 percent had received a rent increase.

- Sixty-four percent of women with children in homeless shelters in Atlanta were receiving AFDC, according to a 1987 survey, but the grants were not enough to meet the families' needs. The maximum monthly AFDC grant for a Georgia family of three was $263 in 1987; the fair market rental cost for a modest two-bedroom apartment in Atlanta was $504. Fifty-nine percent of those in night shelters said they had been evicted from their housing.

AFDC benefits today are so low and housing costs so high that these families are forced to spend far more than the 30 percent of their income experts agree is the maximum they should be spending on rent.

- In all but four states, the amount the federal government estimates is necessary to rent a modest two-bedroom apartment in the least expensive metropolitan area in the state is more than 75 percent of the entire state AFDC grant for a family of three.

- In 35 states the cost of a two-bedroom apartment is more than the entire AFDC grant for a family of three.

For AFDC families that live in the most expensive metropolitan areas, the picture is darker still. For example:

- A two-bedroom apartment in Toledo, Ohio, a high-cost area, is $448 a month; the AFDC grant for an Ohio family of three is $309.

- A two-bedroom apartment in Nashville, Tennesee, costs $454; the maximum grant for a three-person family is only $173.

Federal housing subsidies don't begin to make up the difference between rents and AFDC benefits. According to a study by the Urban Institute, only 22 percent of all AFDC families get housing assistance.

One reason fewer families are helped is because of the decline in eligibility levels in the 1970s and 1980s. Families must be much poorer now to qualify for assistance. Other families get snarled in arbitrary eligibility rules:

- During the 1980s, Congress slapped new restrictions on AFDC eligibility for first-time pregnant women and for children ages 18 to 20 who are still students.

- No matter how poor they are, two-parent families cannot get help if the breadwinner works more than 99 hours a month. And even if he or she is totally unemployed, the family can be disqualified unless a complex past earnings history requirement is met. These rules mean that only a tiny fraction of poor two-parent families qualify: in North Carolina, for example, only 120 two-parent families received AFDC as of September 1988.

- The federal government never has required states to give AFDC to destitute unemployed two-parent families at all, and about half have not. While the Family Support Act of 1988 requires that all states provide assistance to these families (beginning in 1990), unfortunately states newly entering this program can restrict their assistance to six out of 12 months, even if a family is still destitute at the end of six months. The 1988 Act also allows states to impose on these two-parent families "make-work" requirements that make them work for no pay but do not necessarily provide skills or experience that will lead to paid employment.

While it will do only a little to help more families gain AFDC assistance, and nothing to make AFDC benefit levels more humane, the Family Support Act does provide important help to families who work their way off AFDC. These families will be able to continue their Medicaid health coverage and child care assistance for one year—crucial benefits that most low-wage jobs will not cover. This transitional assistance removes one major barrier to families' efforts to become independent of AFDC.

To help prepare more AFDC parents to compete in the job market, the Family Support Act creates a Job Opportunities and Basic Skills (JOBS) Training Program that allocates new federal funding for education, training, employment, and supportive services, including child care. Whether or not the JOBS initiative really helps AFDC recipients will be up to the states: the program gives states extraordinary flexibility to create their own programs.

If they are to foster long-term self-sufficiency, state programs must offer support services such as quality child care and transportation, as well as intensive educational and training services that are carefully tailored to the needs of the individual recipient and available over an extended period. Three-fifths of adults on AFDC have not completed high school, and data from the National Longitudinal Survey of Young Americans indicate that the average 17- to 21-year-old AFDC mother has reading skills below the sixth-grade level. Clearly, punitive or "quick-fix" programs will provide few long-term prospects for economic self-sufficiency. Putting the Family Support Act to work for children and families will be one of the major challenges advocates and states face in the coming months and years.

A Federal and State Action Agenda

The nation's long-term priority must be to ensure that every child and family has enough income to live with health and dignity. This means enabling families to provide for themselves through work, wages, child support, and (as a last resort) public assistance that is free of the humiliation and stigma of the

Innovative Programs Strengthen Families' Independence

A creative solution to the child support dilemma. Young fathers in Marion County, Indiana, who cannot pay child support are developing the job skills they will need to support their children in the future. Under a county pilot program, fathers 21 years old and younger acknowledge paternity and with the mother's consent enter into a novel support agreement: If they cannot pay support in cash, they can partially satisfy their obligation by participating in alternative education or a high school equivalency program, by working with an agency that provides employment and training, or by attending a parenting skills class. Forty-nine young fathers completed the program during its first six months, and 89 percent of the participants were making at least minimal child support payments by the time they completed the program.

Maine gives welfare parents a chance to become self-sufficient. A pilot program that offers education, training, employment, and other support services to recipients of Aid to Families with Dependent Children (AFDC) helped 4,500 participants find employment in its first four years of operation. The program, in effect since 1982, provides jobs subsidized through diversion of welfare grants into paid employment, cooperative pretraining programs with Displaced Homemakers, links with adult and vocational education providers, as well as transportation and child care services. Under the expanded statewide program that started in January 1989, each participant will be assigned a case manager who will be available after the participant leaves the welfare rolls to make sure necessary support services such as transportation, health, and child care benefits continue for one year.

Helping AFDC families stay in their homes. Two states, recognizing that AFDC payments are too low to meet skyrocketing housing costs, are using modest AFDC special needs grants that supplement the basic AFDC grant to help families pay the rent. Massachusetts provides a $40 a month rent supplement to AFDC families that live in private, nonsubsidized housing. Connecticut has authorized a $50 a month special needs grant, effective April 1989, for AFDC families that pay more than half their incomes in rent.

current welfare system. Adequate income that realistically meets a child's needs must be available regardless of family composition, or where in the country a family lives. The federal government should take the first steps in this direction in 1989 by increasing the minimum wage, making child care available so families can work more hours at the increased wages, and starting to build a system of adequate support to families with inadequate wages:

- **Shoring up the eroding value of wages.** The minimum wage must be increased to at least $4.55 per hour over the next three years, with the first step coming in 1989. Over the longer term, the minimum wage must be pegged to a percentage of the nation's hourly wage and adjusted annually to keep up with increases in the cost of living.

- **Passing the Act for Better Child Care.** This nation must make sure that there is decent, safe, accessible, and affordable care available to children so their parents can work and provide for their families' basic needs.

- **Improving refundable tax credits for lower income families.** President Bush has proposed a new refundable tax credit of up to $1,000 for working families with children younger than four, if family income is less than $10,000 per year. Creation of something resembling this type of tax credit to provide income support to poor families, along with possibly improving the existing Earned Income Tax Credit to reflect the needs of larger families, would be an important first step toward adequate income assistance to lower income families.

Over the next five years the federal government should:

- **Improve and expand the system of family support tax credits.** All families with children should be eligible for tax credits on a sliding scale, according to need, whether or not the parents are working and regardless of the children's ages. Such credits would be an important first step toward an adequate children's allowance—an approach that has proven effective in protecting children from poverty in many western democracies. It is an essential complement (but not a replacement) for targeted public help in such areas as health insurance, housing assistance, and child care.

- **Improve the AFDC program.** Federal leadership is essential to increase benefits and wipe out narrow categorical restrictions and time limitations on assistance for two-parent families. Until the needs of all children can be more fully met through a children's allowance, these incremental AFDC improvements are essential.

In 1989 each state should:

- **Take steps to implement the new federal JOBS programs in ways that benefit families and are not punitive.** This means long-term investments in education and training, placement in jobs that pay a living wage, and the provision of quality child care to families on AFDC as a lever to help them become independent. The new federal law says that states must implement most JOBS provisions no later than October 1, 1990, and may do so as early as July 1, 1989. States also must implement transitional child care and medical benefit provisions in ways that maximize coverage for families that leave the welfare rolls for work.

Over the next five years each state should:

- **Raise AFDC need standards and benefits to realistic levels.** First, the standards should be adjusted to reflect the actual needs of poor families. Then, benefit levels should be raised so that by 1994 food stamps and welfare benefits provide families with income equal to at least 100 percent of poverty-level need.

- **Bolster child support enforcement.** The first step is to implement the federal amendments in the Family Support Act and devote adequate resources and staff to the job. Implementation efforts must focus on improving paternity establishment, putting in place fair child support guidelines (an effective mechanism for periodic review and adjustment of awards), and broad application of the immediate wage withholding provision. States also should make sure that gains to state treasuries from child support collections are recycled to meet the desperate needs of poor children for better income supports and services.

HOUSING AND HOMELESSNESS

By the year 2000, if current trends continue, millions of American children will have spent at least a part of their childhoods without a place to call home. Throughout their lives, these youngsters will bear the physical, educational, and emotional scars that result from a childhood punctuated by cold, hunger, sporadic schooling, and frequent moves among temporary shelters and "welfare hotels" riddled with violence and drugs.

Throughout the country, families are the fastest growing segment of the homeless population. Because counting the homeless is difficult—and has become highly politicized—there is no single, accepted count of homeless families. There is virtual unanimity, however, that the 1980s have produced a homeless population—and a rate of homelessness among families—far larger than at any time since the Great Depression of the 1930s. Estimates of the total number of homeless persons range from 350,000 to 3 million; it is generally thought that members of homeless families with children make up about one-third of this population.

Every night, according to 1988 estimates by the National Academy of Sciences, 100,000 American children go to sleep homeless. Families are homeless today primarily because there is a shortage of affordable housing, and the number of homeless families will continue to grow unless the country addresses the pressures that are forcing more and more families out of their homes.

Current trends indicate that these pressures will continue to grow. For example, in 1974 the median rent paid by the poorest families consumed 35 percent of their income—about the maximum level considered affordable; by 1983 it consumed 46 percent of their incomes. If this rate of increase were to continue, by the year 2000 median rents would consume 60 percent of poor families' incomes—placing these families at high risk of homelessness.

At the same time, the supply of housing available for poor families has continued to shrink. Nationwide, the U.S. General Accounting Office predicts, as many as 900,000 units now dedicated to low-income housing under federal agreements with landlords and developers may disappear from the low-income housing market and return to the open market by 1995. And as many as 1.7 million low-cost units could be lost by 2005—an amount equal to 40 percent of all federally assisted housing units in 1986.

Today's "Housing Poor" are Tomorrow's Homeless Families

Families caught in a housing cost squeeze: Family incomes generally have stagnated over the past 15 years. But the median income for some families, especially those headed by parents younger than 30 and by single parents, actually has declined. The number of poor families has grown, and the poor are poorer. During this same period, housing costs for poor families have risen sharply—far faster than inflation. Poor families, therefore, have a much harder time finding housing within their means.

Skyrocketing rents have forced poor families with housing to spend an ever-greater percentage of their incomes on rent and proportionately less on heat, food, medical care, clothing, and other necessities. The National Low

The Homeless: Families At High Risk Today

AFDC families: Rents have risen dramatically in most urban centers in the past decade, and AFDC grants have fallen far behind the increased cost of living. As a result, more and more AFDC families are finding themselves priced completely out of the housing market. In 36 states in 1988, the entire AFDC grant for a family of three was less than the amount HUD estimated as the fair market rent for a modest and low-cost two-bedroom apartment. In 1987 in Atlanta, where the maximum AFDC grant was $263 for a family of three and the fair market rent for a modest two-bedroom apartment was $504 a month, 64 percent of the families in shelter were receiving AFDC.

Single-parent families: These families, generally headed by women, are far more likely than two-parent families to be poor and to spend most of their income in rent. According to H. James Brown and John Yinger (of the Joint Center for Housing Studies of MIT and Harvard University), in 1983, 34 percent of single mothers with children younger than six were spending more than 75 percent of their incomes on rent. The younger the parent the worse the housing cost squeeze. William Apgar (of the Joint Center for Housing Studies) estimates that single parents between ages 25 and 34 pay an average of 58 percent of their incomes for rent, but single parents younger than 25 pay an even more alarming average of 81 percent. It is not surprising, therefore, that single-parent families (one-fourth of all American families) make up about two-thirds of all homeless families, according to the U.S. Conference of Mayors.

Minority families: The wrenching combination of decreasing income among poor families and rising rents have taken a high toll in homelessness among minorities. In Philadelphia, for example, where rents in general went up by 8 percent (in real dollars) between 1975 and 1986, and real median wages decreased by the same percentage, this gap widened even more dramatically among blacks, according to a study prepared by Cushing Dolbeare for the Public Interest Law Center of Philadelphia. Median rent paid by blacks (again, in real dollars) increased by 15 percent, while their median income dropped by 20 percent. Predictably, a disproportionate number of blacks are showing up in the homeless population. A 1988 report by the Coalition on Homelessness in Pennsylvania—a state with a 9 percent black population—found that 64 percent of the homeless population was black.

Income Housing Coalition estimates that one out of four households with incomes of less than $15,000 now pays more than 60 percent of its income for rent. Families that routinely live on the edge of economic crisis are at high risk of homelessness when faced with a period of unemployment, an unexpected rent increase, or any other unexpected expense.

The housing dispossessed: Low-income Americans literally are losing their homes as the nation's low-cost housing stock gradually shrinks. Many older units are being abandoned because they are too expensive to rehabilitate; others are being gobbled up by condominium conversion and gentrification. And the federally supported units disappearing from the low-income stock are not being replaced.

Instead of allowing more families and children to become homeless, the nation must embrace a basic goal: by the year 2000 every American family will live in safe, decent, and affordable housing. Children should never have to live in a car or eat from a dumpster because their parents cannot afford a place to live. And no low-income family should have to forgo food and heat and live at constant risk of becoming homeless because it pays most of its income for rent.

Reaching this goal will require a new level of national commitment to and investment in affordable housing for low-income families. In addition to reducing poverty sharply and addressing these long-term housing needs, the nation must bolster community supports that can intervene to help stave off homelessness among families that are at immediate risk and assist already homeless families in reestablishing stable lives.

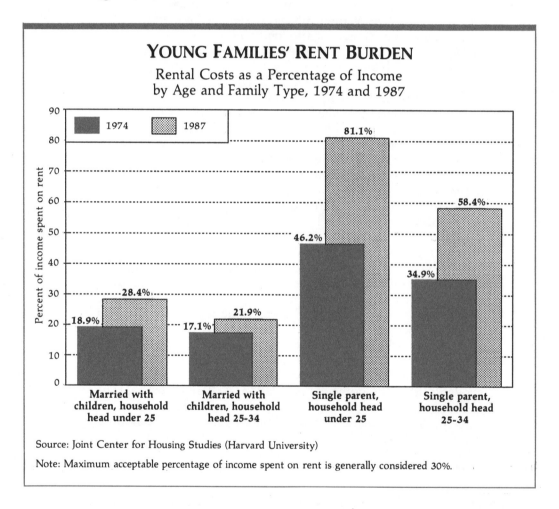

YOUNG FAMILIES' RENT BURDEN
Rental Costs as a Percentage of Income
by Age and Family Type, 1974 and 1987

Source: Joint Center for Housing Studies (Harvard University)

Note: Maximum acceptable percentage of income spent on rent is generally considered 30%.

America's Shame: The Plight of Homeless Children

Most homeless families rely, at least for a time, on some kind of emergency shelter. Despite the best efforts of the staff and volunteers who run such shelters, they are always harsh environments for children. Many are squalid welfare hotels shared by drug dealers and prostitutes; others only take in mothers and children or only take in young children. As a result, two-thirds of the cities surveyed by the U.S. Conference of Mayors in 1987 reported that families had to separate in order to find shelter for all members.

The human stories heard every day illustrate how homelessness affects children:

- In a Los Angeles shelter, two homeless youngsters always looked for a couch or a large chair to play on instead of playing on the floor with the other children. The two had lived with their family in the back seat of a car for so long that they needed the familiar configuration of such a seat in order to feel at home.

- In Washington, D.C., three-year-old Denise spends her nights with her mother, Barbara, and five-year-old brother James in a cubicle in a school gym that is now a homeless shelter. They used to live in an apartment. Barbara lost her job when her boss lost his patience with her unreliable child care arrangements, and she lost her home soon after that. Now little Denise is awakened every morning at 5:30 when a staff member pounds on the side of their cubicle. At 7:00 a.m. a bus takes her family across town to the welfare hotel where they wait for breakfast. After breakfast, the family boards another bus, this time to take James to Head Start, and they return to the hotel for lunch. Most days, Denise is worn out because there is no place for her to take the afternoon nap she needs. But her exhausting daily routine is not over yet. Later, there is another bus ride, to pick James up, dinner at the welfare hotel, and a final bus ride back to the gym. Without some help caring for her children, Barbara doesn't know how she will find the time to look for a new job or a new home.

How Homelessness Devastates Families

Homeless families resemble poor families with stable homes in many respects: similar income, educational achievement, work history, family structure, drug use, and psychiatric history. Recent research suggests that they differ, however, in their support networks. By the time a family becomes homeless, it has few people who can help. Without a friend's couch to sleep on, or a relative to borrow money from, a poor family is more likely to end up without shelter when a crisis strikes.

While the lack of supports can lead to homelessness, it also can be an outcome. Homeless families may be sheltered in unfamiliar settings far from their neighborhoods and lose touch with friends, families, churches, and other community supports. In a recent study comparing homeless families to housed poor families, Ellen Bassuk of Harvard Medical School and Lynn Rosenberg of Boston University School of Medicine reported that 31 percent of the homeless mothers named a minor child as their primary emotional support. Only 26 percent named three adult supports. In contrast, just 4 percent of the housed poor mothers named a child as a primary support, while 74 percent named three adult friends or relatives.

Once homelessness occurs, children and their parents face dire consequences. The life of a homeless child is far worse than that of other children who still have a roof overhead.

Health deficits: Homelessness hurts children's health even before they are born and continues to damage it as they grow. According to a 1987 study by Wendy Chavkin of the New York City Department of Health, more than 39 percent of the homeless pregnant women she studied in that city had received no prenatal care. This rate is three times higher than that of women in low-income housing projects and four times higher than that of all city residents. It is not surprising, therefore, that the rates of infant mortality and low birthweight among homeless infants were also very high—25 deaths per 1,000 live births, compared with 17 among housed poor women.

James Wright, reporting on the Johnson-Pew Health Care for the Homeless Program, found that homeless children were twice as likely as their housed counterparts to suffer from such chronic health problems as cardiac disease, anemia, and upper respiratory infections. Homeless preschool children are only one-third as likely as other poor children to be fully immunized, and they are more than twice as likely to have elevated levels of lead in their blood, a condition associated with educational and psychological problems (according to a 1988 study by Garth Alperstein at St. Luke's Hospital).

Children's mental health also suffers when they are homeless. More than half of the homeless children interviewed in Boston family shelters by Ellen Bassuk in 1986 showed signs of serious developmental lags as well as clinical depression and anxiety.

Disrupted schooling: Homeless children suffer myriad educational difficulties. Because many homeless families move frequently, their children's education lacks coherence and continuity. But whether or not they change schools often, homeless children may fall behind academically because their chaotic living arrangements mean they often come to school tired, hungry, anxious, or unprepared. Public shelters are uniquely bad places for children to do homework or get a good night's sleep.

Sometimes homeless children are not even allowed to go to school. Although school districts increasingly are making efforts to accommodate homeless children, some still require proof of residence, birth certificates, and other documents that homeless families often cannot provide.

Family stress and disintegration: Being homeless puts poor families under severe stress. Such stress, often experienced by parents as well as children, can lead to or increase domestic violence against women and children. Sometimes homelessness causes at least temporary dissolution of the family, and homeless children may be placed in foster care. A 1985 New Jersey study showed that homelessness was the primary reason for 19 percent of the foster care placements studied and a contributing reason for 40 percent.

Government Housing Help: A Crumbling Refuge Against Homelessness

The increase in homelessness has been inevitable, given the federal government's cutbacks in housing assistance during a period in which rents have soared and poor families have gotten poorer (see Family Income chapter). The National Low Income Housing Coalition estimates that between 1970 and 1983, median rents rose twice as fast as median incomes.

Instead of providing more help as lower income families needed more assistance, the federal government cut funding for low-income housing by a staggering 81 percent (in real dollars) between 1980 and 1988. This reduction in the federal low-income housing investment (including Public Housing, Section 8, and other programs) was far greater than the cuts in any other area of federal spending during this period.

None of the existing federal programs intended to provide housing assistance to low-income families even comes close to meeting the need: only one-fourth of all households living in poverty currently receive any form of federal housing assistance.

Dwindling public housing: Throughout the country, the Public Housing program currently houses approximately 500,000 families with children. Many public housing authorities have waiting lists larger than their total number of units, and families on these lists can expect to wait as long as 12 years for a unit to become available.

The public housing crunch is worsened by the estimated 70,000 uninhabitable units that need major repairs before they can be filled. Additional units are lost every year. Because funds for both construction and repairs are so limited, many of these units cannot be repaired, and new ones are not built fast enough to replace them.

Cuts in Section 8 housing: Under programs such as Section 8 and Section 236, the federal government has provided low-cost mortgages and loans to landlords and developers on the condition that they reserve some or all of the resulting housing units for low-income tenants for a stated time period.

The number of units available under Section 8 is—and has always been—inadequate to meet the need, and the shortage will worsen in the future. Many of the agreements under which these units are reserved as low-cost housing

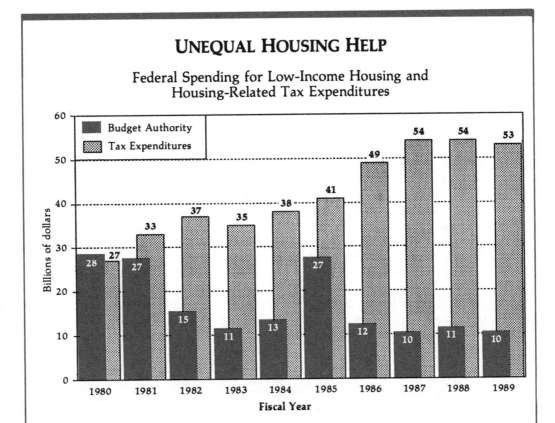

UNEQUAL HOUSING HELP

Federal Spending for Low-Income Housing and Housing-Related Tax Expenditures

Legend: ■ Budget Authority ▨ Tax Expenditures

Fiscal Year	Budget Authority	Tax Expenditures
1980	28	27
1981	27	33
1982	15	37
1983	11	35
1984	13	38
1985	27	41
1986	12	49
1987	10	54
1988	11	54
1989	10	53

(Billions of dollars)

• Budget authority: The level of funding that Congress and the president agree to provide for certain programs. Actual spending may be less (but not more) than this amount.

• Tax expenditures: This category includes revenues not collected by the federal government because of deductions allowed (primarily to homeowners) for mortgage interest, property taxes, capital gains, and investor deductions. Approximately 52 percent of all federal housing expenditures (including spending and revenue losses) go to the 17 percent of all American households earning more than $50,000 a year.

Source: National Low Income Housing Coalition

were made during the 1960s and 1970s, and they are beginning to expire. For example, in Minnesota, 49 percent of Section 236 agreements and 67 percent of Section 8 agreements will end during the next five years, according to the Minnesota Housing Project. These expirations could eliminate 900,000 low-income housing units nationwide by 1995 and as many as 1.7 million low-cost units by 2005.

An inadequate voucher program: While cutting the Public Housing and Section 8 housing programs, the Reagan Administration focused its low-income housing efforts almost exclusively on a voucher program. Serving about 32,000 households in 1986, the program provides an eligible family with a certificate worth the difference between 30 percent of its income and the fair market rent

---

Homelessness Prevention Is Better Than Emergency Shelter

Around the nation, innovative programs are using cost-effective methods to prevent homelessness and resettle homeless families.

Housing assistance saves money: A private Washington, D.C., program called ConServe helps homeless families find permanent housing using subsidies from the District government and offers them a range of services to get them back on their feet. The cost is $765 per family per month, including rent. In contrast, the Washington, D.C., government shelters and feeds other homeless families in squalid "welfare hotels." The cost is at least $3,000 per family per month, and the program provides no permanent solution to a family's homelessness.

Eviction prevention: A Trenton, New Jersey, program works to prevent homelessness among families that are withholding rent from landlords because of physical problems with their units. The city inspects the unit to verify that the complaint is legitimate; combined city and federal funds provide half of the rent and the tenant pays the other half to the court. Eviction is stopped until the court rules on the case. If any of the rent is abated by the court, it is returned to the city for use in other cases. This program serves two purposes: it helps maintain the housing stock by pushing landlords to make needed repairs rather than evict the tenants who ask for them, and it is cost effective. The costs are estimated at $2.50 per day per person, compared with $15 per day per person in emergency shelter.

Neighborhood-based efforts: The Grace Hill Settlement House in St. Louis, Missouri, is staffed and operated by people from the neighborhood and provides a continuum of services for low-income families. Grace Hill works to help prevent homelessness by providing emergency services (including small cash grants), job training, and referrals to other services that can help avert family crises. Grace Hill's community-based staff also helps homeless families find new homes by linking them with interested landlords and providing cash assistance with security deposits and other help as needed. Of 200 homeless families helped to find homes since 1986, all but 20 are still stably housed—a much better record than most programs demonstrate.

(FMR) in its geographical area, as determined by the U.S. Department of Housing and Urban Development (HUD).

Each family shops for rental housing on the open market. If the family finds housing that is more expensive than the FMR determined by HUD, the family must make up the difference. Fully 54 percent of the families receiving vouchers paid more than the acceptable 30 percent of their income for rent, according to HUD. And 25 percent had to spend more than 40 percent.

The low-income housing cuts are more than just numbers in a budget: they add up to millions of families struggling to hold on to the very basic security of a safe and stable home and countless children who wake up not knowing where they will get their next night's sleep.

Every child deserves a place to call home. This nation must recommit itself to the long-standing public policy goal of providing decent and affordable housing for every American family, regardless of income. And quick action is necessary to minimize the damage already being done to homeless children and their families.

A Federal and State Action Agenda

In 1989 the federal government should:

- **Begin to restore housing assistance.** To ensure that every American family has a decent home by the end of this century, the federal government must begin now to restore funding for low-income housing assistance. This means a commitment to fund enough additional units of subsidized housing in 1989 and each year thereafter to end homelessness and the low-income housing shortage by the year 2000.

Over the next five years the federal government should:

- **Provide decent income supports so families can afford housing.** The federal government must strengthen the system of income and related supports (including the minimum wage, the Earned Income Tax Credit, AFDC, and unemployment benefits) for low-income families, both working and nonworking, so they are better able to pay for decent housing, with supplemental assistance when necessary.

- **Ensure families' access to housing without discrimination.** The federal government must enforce aggressively the Fair Housing Amendments Act of 1988, which in general strengthens enforcement tools against housing discrimination and for the first time makes housing discrimination against families with children illegal.

- **Assist state and local (public and private) efforts to address homelessness.** The federal government should make targeted funds available to help maintain effective programs that prevent low-income families in crisis from losing their housing and help already homeless families find permanent housing.

In 1989 each state should:

- **Increase the number of available low-income housing units.** States should work toward increasing the low-income housing supply by at least 2 percent in 1989 and each year thereafter until the supply is adequate. To do this, states must capture all available federal low-income housing funds, including tenant subsidies, rehabilitation, and construction funds, and use state and local money to supplement federal funds.

Over the next five years each state should:

- **Bolster state income supports.** Each state should work to improve the adequacy of state income supports for poor families, including AFDC benefit levels, unemployment benefits, and low-income tax credits.

- **Improve services for homeless families.** Each state should assess community-based support programs as well as current educational and health care policies as they apply to homeless families and make those changes that are necessary to better meet these families' needs.

- **Increase funding for community support programs.** Community-based programs that help prevent homelessness and provide shelter and other services for homeless families should be expanded to reach all families at risk or in need.

FOOD ASSISTANCE

JIM HUBBARD

In the year 2000, this nation is likely to be paying a high human cost for the increase in hunger in America during the 1980s. Among the new generation of young Americans approaching adulthood in 2000 will be many whose potential has been limited in some fashion by lack of adequate nutrition during their fetal period, infancy, or childhood.

The connection between inadequate nutrition and health damage is well established. A woman who is malnourished during pregnancy is more likely to give birth to a low-birthweight infant—a baby weighing less than 5.5 pounds. Low birthweight is a leading cause of infant death, and the small babies who survive face an increased risk of being impaired for life by autism, retardation, cerebral palsy, epilepsy, learning disabilities, and vision or hearing loss. Nutrition deprivation can hurt an infant's development, delay or stunt growth, and weaken resistance to infections.

Widespread hunger in America, documented in dozens of local, state, and national reports, shows little sign of abating. Hunger also increases a child's vulnerability to environmental poisons such as lead. Because of growing concern about hunger in America, Congress recently made partial restorations in some food assistance programs that were cut deeply during the early Reagan years. But the total amount of food stamp benefits—the nation's first line of defense against hunger and malnutrition for Americans who cannot feed themselves—remains below the levels provided in 1981, before the cuts were made. In addition, the economic recovery has been uneven, leaving wages for lower paid workers depressed and large pockets of persistent want scattered across America. And finally, for growing numbers of poor Americans, rapidly rising rent burdens are consuming an ever-increasing share of their small incomes, leaving less and less money in these families' budgets for purchasing food and other necessities.

Our nation cannot wait passively for hunger and malnutrition to go away. The consequences of inaction are far too severe. Congress began to recognize this truth in 1988 by passing major anti-hunger legislation. Such efforts must continue in the years ahead. Substantially eliminating hunger by the end of the century is an achievable—and essential—national goal.

The Spread of Hunger and Malnutrition Among America's Children and Families

Studies conducted during the past few years in all regions of this nation have reached the same troubling conclusion: the country has a widespread, persistent hunger problem.

- Many millions of Americans experience hunger at some point each month, and malnutrition affects almost 500,000 American children, the Physician Task Force on Hunger in America found in 1985. The task force, coordinated through the Harvard University School of Public Health, traveled the nation to examine the hunger problem. In a 1987 update of this initial report, the task force found that hunger not only had failed to abate, but that working

Hunger in Middle America

It startles the visitor to drive into Waterloo, [Iowa] surrounded by fields of corn, to find a van with the words "Food Bank" painted on its side. But feeding the hungry has become serious business here.

"Last summer we offered a feeding program for town children," explained a local school official. "We expected 300 children, but more than 2,000 came the first day. We thought we knew our community but we were in for a big surprise."

In Cedar Falls, requests for an evening meal at the Community Meals Program zoomed from 1,102 families in 1986 to 1,527 this year. The Salvation Army was forced to open a lunch program due to rampant hunger among farm families. Ruth Toney, who operates the local food bank, says that she served over 10,000 families in seven months, up from 7,800 all last year. The county population is 86,000 people.

Families try to cope but not always successfully. The People's Clinic reports seeing more cases of childhood malnutrition in the first three months of 1987 than in the last three years.

From *Hunger Reaches Blue
Collar America: An Unbalanced Recovery in a Service Economy,*
Physician Task Force on Hunger in America, October 1987

Americans in depressed regions of the nation have been forced increasingly to turn to bread lines and soup kitchens to feed themselves and their children.

- Requests for emergency food assistance increased in 1987 by an average of 18 percent in 24 of the 26 major U.S. cities surveyed by the U.S. Conference of Mayors. The mayors' study, published in December 1987, also found that 25 of the 26 cities reported a substantial rise (averaging 18 percent) in the number of families with children requesting assistance. This group accounts for the majority of those requesting emergency food assistance in the cities surveyed, according to the conference.

- Four out of five low-income families with children in the city of Seattle and in Yakima and Pend Oreille counties in Washington State who were interviewed by the Governor's Task Force on Hunger had experienced at least one food shortage problem due to lack of resources, according to a report published in October 1988. Of these families, 21 to 42 percent experienced severe monthly food shortages directly affecting children. "We have people lining up at 7 a.m. to get food bags at 1 p.m., and we are out of food by 2:30," says a staff member of Seattle's El Centro de la Raza Food Bank.

Some of the millions of families and children who cannot get enough to eat will suffer damage to their health and often permanent harm.

- The Massachusetts Department of Public Health, in a study issued in 1983, found that 10,000 to 17,500 poor children in that state suffered stunted growth, largely due to chronic malnutrition. Nearly one in five low-income children studied in the survey was stunted, anemic, or abnormally underweight.

- A survey of families with children in a low-income neighborhood of New Haven, Connecticut, in the summer of 1986 found that one-quarter of the families sampled either were experiencing chronic food shortages or were at risk of this problem. Children in families chronically short of food had suffered from twice as many instances of health problems as children from families not experiencing chronic food shortages during the preceding six months.

Root Causes of Hunger in America

Poverty worsened among families and children during the 1980s: One of every five children in America (or a total of approximately 13 million children) is poor today. Despite five years of economic recovery, the child poverty rate was higher in 1987 than in any year of the 1970s, even the period of the 1974-1975 recession.

Also, the poor have been getting poorer. The Census Bureau's definition of poverty in 1987 for a family consisting of a man or woman and two children was an income of less than $9,056 a year. But increasing numbers of poor children live in households in which incomes are so low they are less than *half* the poverty line. The number of children in these very poor households grew from 3.398 million in 1979 to 5.434 million in 1987.

There are several reasons for the high poverty rate afflicting children and families. Many families have lost ground economically in the past decade, especially young families just starting out in life (see Young Families chapter). The median income of families with children headed by persons younger than 30 fell by 26 percent between 1973 and 1986, after adjusting for inflation. This dramatic drop is comparable to the per-capita income loss Americans in general suffered between 1929 and 1933, at the bottom of the Great Depression.

Also, needy households lost government help due to the Reagan-era cutbacks. In 1979 nearly one of every five families with children that would have been in poverty without government help was lifted out of poverty by programs such as AFDC, unemployment insurance, and Social Security. As of 1987, a far smaller proportion of families was being rescued from poverty by government assistance: only about one out of 10 families, according to the Center on Budget and Policy Priorities.

Adequate food and nutrition help is not available to millions who need it: America's food assistance programs never have received enough funding to provide adequately for all of the families and children who do not have enough to eat. These efforts collectively have lost more ground during the past eight years, due in large part to the budget cuts of the Reagan era.

- **Food stamps:** The largest federal food program for the poor currently fails to serve millions of low-income Americans—between one-third and one-half of those who are eligible, according to a recent Congressional Budget Office study. Although poverty has grown, food stamp participation has fallen. As a result, the ratio of people receiving food stamps for every 100 poor persons fell from 68 in 1980 to 58 in 1987, according to the Center on Budget and Policy Priorities. While the poverty population and the food stamp-eligible population are not identical, the comparison indicates a widening gap between the need for food help and the nation's readiness to meet it.

- **The Special Supplemental Food Program for Women, Infants, and Children (WIC):** Although this program has grown during the Reagan era because of congressional initiatives, it serves only about half of the low-income infants, young children, and mothers who are eligible to receive its help. WIC's prescription food supplements and nutrition counseling—proven effective in reducing low-birthweight births as well as health problems among children—reach 3.7 million people, or about one-half of the 7.45 million estimated to be eligible. In many counties, significant numbers of eligible mothers and children cannot be served because there are not sufficient resources to provide for them.

- **Child nutrition:** Several of the government programs that provide nutritious meals to low-income children who might otherwise have empty stomachs—the school lunch, school breakfast, and summer food programs—are serving fewer children than they were in 1981, before the federal budget cuts took effect. For example, the number of low-income children receiving free school lunches each day was reduced by 600,000 from 1981 to 1987.

Nutrition Programs: Documented Successes

Government-sponsored studies have shown that anti-hunger programs do an effective job.

- **WIC saves babies' lives and averts costly medical care.** Major research funded by the U.S. Department of Agriculture (USDA) and issued in January 1986 found direct links between WIC and a reduction in late fetal deaths. WIC also was credited with decreasing the incidence of premature and low-birthweight births. Other research has indicated that $1 invested in the prenatal component of WIC has saved as much as $3 in short-term hospital costs.

- **Food stamps help close the nutrition gap.** According to USDA survey information, the nutritional gap between low-income Americans and those more well-off narrowed significantly between 1965 and 1977-1978. This is precisely the period in which the food stamp program and other food aid programs were created or expanded.

- **The school lunch program improves the nutritional status of children.** A major USDA evaluation of this program found in 1982 that school lunches enhance the nutritional status of school children, especially low-income children who need this help the most.

Recognizing the reality of growing hunger and shrinking help, Congress acted in 1988 to begin to shore up the national effort to fight hunger and malnutrition in America. The Hunger Prevention Act of 1988 made important steps in the right direction. The law made an increase in the basic food stamp allotment, which will increase the help that eligible families receive—by $7 to $8 a month in 1991 for a family of three, for example. This increase in food stamp benefits, however, only partially offsets the loss of surplus food distribution to the needy, which has diminished sharply as government surplus food stocks have dwindled. The law also modestly increases funding for child nutrition programs. This important new federal direction may signal a willingness to address a problem that is now almost universally acknowledged. We must build on this beginning.

A Federal and State Action Agenda

In 1989 the federal government should:

• **Increase WIC funding by at least $100 million to $150 million over current service levels.** This would make benefits available to approximately 200,000 to 300,000 additional pregnant women, infants, and children.

Over the next five years the federal government should:

• **Expand the WIC program.** By 1994 it should reach all eligible pregnant women, infants, and children who apply. To ensure this program's steady growth in a way that allows states to plan expansion, a specified amount of federal funds should be guaranteed to it each year, increasing gradually until the program reaches the entire eligible population. One mechanism to help do this is to make WIC a "capped entitlement." This approach will enable states to plan for steady expansion to meet more of the unserved, will avoid fluctuations in funding levels (and lack of certainty of funding levels until several months into a fiscal year), and will assure that WIC is not affected by across-the-board reductions in appropriations bills. Every other federal program of this size that provides monthly help to children has entitlement status. The approach will protect WIC from some of the ups and downs of the federal budget process.

• **Improve food stamp benefits.** Food stamp benefits are still too low for poor families to purchase an adequate diet. As long as AFDC benefits remain abysmally low, the federal government should consider further general increases in food stamp benefit levels, building on the 1988 increases. Second, the benefit computation must be revamped so that it takes into account the high housing costs of all poor households—not just households headed by elderly or disabled Americans. Food stamps are supposed to ensure that households have enough resources to purchase a minimally adequate diet after meeting the costs of certain other necessities such as rent. The current structure does not do that for families with children. With rental costs rising for poor families, this policy must be changed. Finally, the program must stop penalizing poor single mothers for receiving child support and must encourage child support enforcement: the current policy of counting all child support payments so that food stamp benefit levels are reduced should be changed so the first $50 of income is not counted, as in the AFDC program.

• **Let charitable organizations help feed poor children in the summer.** The federal government should permit charitable, nonprofit organizations to operate summer food programs for poor children who otherwise would go without this help when no public agency or school is willing or able to operate the program in the area. This step should be accompanied by strong safeguards and antifraud provisions to protect program integrity.

In 1989 each state should:

• **Launch food stamp outreach efforts and cut red tape.** Legislation enacted in 1988 makes federal money available to states, for the first time since 1981, to educate potentially eligible households about the food stamp program. To reach the approximately one-half of eligible households that do not currently participate in the program—including many working poor families—and make them aware that they can get food stamps, states should enlist the help of a range of social service agencies, community groups, and churches. Many poor families simply don't know they can get food stamps or think only welfare recipients are eligible. States also should remove unnecessary administrative barriers to participation, such as monthly reporting requirements, which can hinder participation.

Over the next five years each state should:

- **Enact a state supplement for WIC.** Every state should—as 13 states do now—appropriate its own funds to reach more mothers, infants, and children in need.

- **Cut WIC costs so more can be served.** Every state should institute cost containment methods to make WIC benefits available to more women and children. States should implement competitive bidding for infant formula contracts unless another approach would produce equal or greater savings. For example, competitive bidding introduced in Texas in 1988 saves $1 a can on the price the state pays for infant formula; the savings will enable the state to serve 80,000 additional needy residents annually. A number of other states using competitive bidding are receiving even larger savings. The savings then should be converted into substantially expanded participation in the program. In conjunction with cost containment, states should undertake intensified outreach efforts to add as many new WIC participants as the savings will allow.

- **Start school breakfast programs in poor areas.** Each state should follow the lead of the states that now require schools with large numbers of low-income children to institute breakfast programs. Recent federal funding increases for these programs will ease this process.

VULNERABLE CHILDREN AND FAMILIES

A s the nation approaches the year 2000, the social and economic pressures on many of America's families and children are mounting.

Child poverty: CDF projects that between 1988 and the year 2000, unless recent trends are reversed, the number of poor children in this country will increase by 3 million. By the year 2030, at least one in three children will be poor. As their families struggle to survive, these children are likely to lack adequate health care, child care, and educational programs, and may often lack food and shelter.

Single-parent households: These poverty-related deprivations are often most prevalent among children who live in female-headed single-parent families, which are expected to increase by 2.8 million by the year 2000. Female-headed families are generally poorer than two-parent families because they lack a second wage earner, because women's wages are generally lower than men's, and because women who become single parents at a very young age frequently lack education and job skills. Families with one parent also are more vulnerable to unpredictable or adverse events such as the loss of a job, parental sickness, or the difficulty of meeting the multiple needs of a severely disabled or otherwise troubled child.

AIDS, drugs, and alcohol: AIDS will take a drastic toll on families and children in the next decades. The Centers for Disease Control estimate that 10,000 to 20,000 children—disproportionately poor and minority children—will be infected with the AIDS virus by 1991. Many of these children will need help from the child welfare system because their parents are ill, drug-addicted, or otherwise unable to care for them. Almost all will need public help in other forms.

Alcohol and drug abuse will continue to threaten young people as long as poverty, the lack of community supports, ineffective schools, and hopelessness are the realities that a large portion of American children face every day. Drug abuse among adults also has serious implications for their children.

All these problems place phenomenal strains on families and may erode their ability to provide for their children. Consequently, unless this nation can start reversing these trends, more and more young people will flood local child-serving agencies. Too many of these children will end up in costly state care of one type or another because of abuse, neglect, or unmet physical or emotional needs, or because their families are no longer able to cope with poverty-related stresses. Looking only at the child welfare system, CDF estimates that the number of children and adolescents in care will grow to half a million by the year 2000, assuming increases comparable to those of the past several years.

The agencies that care for troubled children are already overwhelmed by the demands placed on them. Unless this nation takes drastic action, the child-serving systems, now stretched too thin, will be unable to serve the growing numbers of children and families that need help, thus placing them at even greater risk. However, if support is provided early enough, it can both reduce the number of children who enter substitute care and better serve those whose special needs require such care.

This nation cannot afford to write off the needs of several million of its most vulnerable young people. Doing so will cost dearly in lost human potential and in greatly increased future burdens on the criminal justice, health care, and welfare systems—three institutions that must deal with the consequences of earlier neglect of families' and children's needs.

This society's goal for the year 2000 must be to give every vulnerable child and family access to a unified system of family support services designed to help them overcome the problems they face. For children whose needs cannot be met in the family, the states, with federal assistance, must provide a continuum of services and care that will appropriately address children's needs and allow them to develop their potential and move toward self-sufficiency.

In Harm's Way: The Growing Vulnerabilities of Children

Being abused and neglected: Reports of child abuse and neglect have increased steadily since 1976. Between 1981 and 1986, reports increased by more than 90 percent. In 1986, 2.2 million children and adolescents were reported abused, neglected, or both, according to the American Association for Protecting Children.

While it is true that not all reports are reliable, verified reports have increased. And not all actual cases of abuse or neglect are reported. A recent incidence study commissioned by the National Center on Child Abuse and Neglect in the U.S. Department of Health and Human Services showed a 66 percent increase nationally between 1980 and 1986 in the number of cases in which children were endangered by maltreatment. About half of these cases were not known to local child protective services agencies as substantiated reports, which suggests either that many cases are not being reported at all or that the child protection agencies are screening out valid cases due to insufficient resources and support.

The increasing reports and incidence of abuse reflect in part a broader incidence of family violence. About 40 percent of children whose parents suffer spousal abuse also are abused themselves.

Neglect—parents' failure to care adequately for a child's physical, emotional, or educational needs—represents a far more common form of maltreatment than physical, sexual, or emotional abuse. A disproportionate number of children described as neglected come from poor families, which are more likely to come within the purview of public agencies. These families often could function well except for severe economic stresses.

Maltreated children can suffer damage to their social, emotional, and cognitive development as well as physical harm. Many respond by running away from home, using drugs or alcohol, or getting in trouble with the law. They also are more likely to grow up to be abusive parents. An estimated 30 percent of children who are physically or sexually abused or extremely neglected become abusive parents.

Lacking permanent families: More than 250,000 children in this country are living apart from their families in foster families, group homes, residential treatment centers, and child care institutions. A disproportionate number are minority children. More and more very young children, most often younger than two, are entering public care in many states. Often these are babies born to drug abusing parents, and they are at high risk for medical and developmental problems. Some states also are reporting growing numbers of teens in care. Compared with such children in the past, young people in care have more severe physical and emotional problems and a greater need for specialized services.

Children enter state care for various reasons. Most have been abused or neglected; an increasing number come from families in which substance abuse is a serious problem. Some children have parents who are unable or unwilling to cope with their children's disabilities or behavior problems. Other children come from families that have become homeless or are struggling to raise children on grossly inadequate incomes. In Iowa, for example, more than half of the state's foster care children come from AFDC families, yet families receiving AFDC account for less than 8 percent of all Iowa families.

Many children continue to face risks while in care. Frequently they are placed in overly restrictive group care settings or with foster families that do not have the resources and supports necessary to meet the children's special needs. Teens especially may be shuffled from home to home and institution to institution, developing no sense of security or permanence. Nor are teens sufficiently helped to make a successful transition to independent living when they leave care.

Having emotional problems: Between 7.5 million and 9.5 million children and adolescents in this country suffer from emotional problems that require mental health services. Some of these problems result from parental abuse and neglect or from mistreatment during out-of-home care. Other emotional problems stem from the numerous pressures facing youths today.

No more than 30 percent of the children in need of mental health services are getting the attention they need. Even among the 3 million children who are severely emotionally disturbed, two-thirds do not receive appropriate treatment.

Running away: About 1.5 million children and adolescents run away from home each year. Many others run away from foster care placements or other residential care settings that fail to meet their needs. Although most of these youngsters return to their families within a short time, as many as one-third do not. Because many children who return home go back to the same problems that drove them away, they frequently run away again. Too many runaways eventually end up on the streets, where their poverty, fear, anger, depression, and hopelessness make them especially vulnerable to crime, drug abuse, prostitution, and now AIDS.

Getting in trouble with the law: As of February 2, 1987, there were 53,503 young people in public juvenile detention facilities. More young people entered care in 1986 than in any year since 1977, despite the fact that the arrest rate declined significantly during that decade.

Between 1985 and 1987, the rate at which juveniles were in custody increased 12 percent. The number of black and Hispanic youths held in public juvenile facilities increased 15 percent and 20 percent respectively, while the number of nonminority youths in custody decreased slightly. The increases were not due to increases in violence; the number of youths held for serious violent crimes or property offenses fell between 1985 and 1987, but the number held for alcohol and drug offenses increased by 56 percent.

Youths who end up in the juvenile justice system typically have been failed earlier in their lives by other public agencies. A significant number are former state wards who have lived in various foster care settings. With a few notable exceptions, these young people also are failed by the juvenile justice system, with its bias toward institutional care and restrictive settings. Minority children in particular are likely to be served inappropriately. They are confined in numbers disproportionate to their share of responsibility for criminal activity, and they are often more likely to be housed in the most secure facilities.

Severe overcrowding in many training schools and detention centers limits opportunities for education and treatment and seriously compromises the quality of care. Reports of juveniles being mistreated in institutions are on the rise. Holding juveniles in adult jails is another way in which states continue to expose children to risk of harm.

Too Little Help Too Late: Child-Serving Systems Under Siege

For children and families in trouble, support from extended families, neighbors, churches, and community resources is often scarce. As a result, many vulnerable children and families are flooding public child-serving systems. But the help they receive from child welfare, mental health, and juvenile justice agencies is generally too late and too fragmented.

Preventive services are hard to come by: Prevention is generally cheaper and more effective than crisis intervention and remediation. Nonetheless, our society generally has committed few resources to preventive services for vulnerable families. They often are denied basic health care, nutrition, and shelter when they need it. Service agencies lack the staff and resources that would enable them to identify and use young children's behavior and learning problems as valuable warnings of more severe problems ahead. Instead of intervening early, child-serving systems generally offer little help to families until children are seriously harmed or strike out at others. Even when prevention programs are available in a community, they generally serve only small numbers of families each year.

Many families with severe problems have considerable strength and can weather life's crises intact if they receive timely outside help. But supports must be early, comprehensive, intensive, and flexibly designed to meet a wide range of needs, including basic shelter and other survival needs. The handful of states that have implemented intensive, family-based service programs report that they have been able to maintain families and improve family functioning as well as assure the safety and well-being of the children involved. At the same time they have avoided the long-term expense of costly out-of-home care for the children.

In many states, however, child welfare agencies almost completely neglect preventive services because increasing reports of child abuse are forcing a shift of resources from prevention to investigation and disposition of abuse and neglect reports. Moreover, federal resources to help states provide preventive services have fallen further and further behind the demand. The appropriation for the Title XX Social Services Block Grant, which funds child abuse investigation, prevention, and treatment, among other services, was reduced more than 50 percent in real dollars between FY 1977 and FY 1988. Funding for activities under the Juvenile Justice and Delinquency Prevention Act was reduced 30 percent in 1981, and the program has been held at $70 million since then, squeezing the tiny preventive programs states had operated with a portion of the funds.

Perhaps the most chilling evidence of the overload on state child welfare systems is the number of children's deaths caused by maltreatment. In both 1986 and 1987 more than 1,100 children died from abuse or neglect, resulting in an average of three child abuse related deaths every day. Compounding the tragedy is the estimate that as many as half of these child victims were known to local child protection agencies before they died, which suggests that at least some might have been saved with the right kind of intervention.

Pigeonholing interferes with treatment: Arbitrary labels conceal children's needs and deny them appropriate care. In most states children in trouble are routed into one of three separate agencies and their cases pigeonholed accordingly.

Children identified as abused, neglected, or dependent—those "in need of protection"—are shuttled into the child welfare system. Youths who are considered runaways, status offenders, or adjudicated delinquents—those "in need of rehabilitation"—generally are placed under the jurisdiction of the juvenile justice system. Seriously emotionally disturbed or mentally ill children—those "in need of treatment"—enter the mental health system.

Programs to Keep Families Together Work and Are Cost-Effective

State programs that provide short-term, intensive, family-based services to families that have children at risk of placement in out-of-home care are having good results and are cost-effective as well. They are a critical component of an effective system of family supports for vulnerable children and families.

- Homebuilders in Tacoma, Washington, the prototype for many other family preservation efforts, has been in operation since 1974. With caseloads of two to four families each, specially trained staff members provide intensive home-based services for no more than 12 weeks and connect families with other longer term supports. A 1986-1987 study showed that one year after Homebuilders' services ended, 87 percent of the assisted families had remained intact. Program costs range from $2,600 to $4,000 per family, a significant savings compared with the averted costs of out-of-home placements, which range from $7,186 to $22,373 and more.

- Familystrength in New Hampshire serves families of abused and neglected children as well as youths adjudicated delinquent or in need of supervision. In 1986-1987 the average length of treatment for the 180 families served was 4.4 months, at an average cost of $4,800 per family of five. Seventy-six percent of the client families were still intact at the end of treatment, despite the fact that earlier they had been at imminent risk of placement. The per-family cost represented less than half of the average cost of foster care placement for even one child for one year.

- Maryland's Intensive Family Services Program (IFS) delivers comprehensive services to families through public agency teams made up of a social worker and a paraprofessional parent aide. Each team serves approximately six families at a time for a period of 90 days. At the end of that time, approximately two-thirds of the cases are closed with no further service needed; other families are linked to auxiliary supports. A detailed evaluation of 100 IFS families revealed that at the end of a one-year follow-up these families were less than one-fourth as likely to be placed in out-of-home care as families receiving traditional child protective services. The IFS families also had a much lower recidivism rate after two years. Based on these findings, the state estimates that serving approximately 600 families each year in the IFS program can save approximately $2.5 million a year in averted out-of-home care costs.

These systems are separately funded, bureaucratically distinct, and often are restricted rigidly in what kinds of help they can provide.

Although such divisions are tidy, families' lives and children's problems are not. Most at-risk children have similar backgrounds and overlapping, multiple problems. Very little distinguishes the children in one kind of care from those in another besides the fact that they enter through different doors. For example, more than one-third of the 1.5 million children who run away from home each year are running away from physical or sexual abuse, and 40 percent are running from such family problems as alcoholism and marital conflict. Judges polled in a national survey by the National Council of Juvenile and Family Court Judges said child abuse figured in the backgrounds of at least 70 percent of the boys and girls who come before them, including those charged with juvenile offenses.

An increasing number of children in the child welfare and juvenile justice systems have serious emotional and behavioral problems as well as severe education and health deficits. A 1987 Ohio study showed that two-fifths of the children in state care had problems that overlapped departmental boundaries.

It is counterproductive to children to label them arbitrarily and to divide services for them into rigid administrative compartments. Children end up being bounced from system to system and frequently get no help at all. Vulnerable children and adolescents need integrated services, based on individualized assessments that treat the whole child.

An overburdened staff: In every state the demands for strengthened child and family services fall on beleaguered staffs. Poor salaries, insufficient training, and inadequate support make it difficult to recruit and retain staff for public child-serving agencies. Annual staff turnover rates approach 100 percent in some communities, and unfilled vacancies contribute to extremely large caseloads. It is not unusual for caseworkers—who are charged with nothing less than protecting children's lives—to carry caseloads of 60 to 80 families. Yet competent, caring staff members with realistic caseloads are the key to the successful implementation of effective programs and policies for at-risk children and families.

Out-of-home care creates its own problems: All three child-serving systems report increasing numbers of children with more severe problems seeking help, a lack of sufficient community-based programs designed to address children's needs appropriately, and the failure to prepare children appropriately for the return home or for independent living when they leave care.

Although many states report increases in requests for foster home placement, most face a serious shortage of foster parents. In the Washington, D.C., metropolitan area, increases in drug abuse, births to teens, and economic hardship have contributed in part to a 71 percent jump in foster care requests since 1985. However, the number of available foster homes lags far behind the need.

The explanation is partly economic. Foster care reimbursement rates fall far below the estimated costs of raising a child even in modest circumstances. But foster parents need more than adequate funds; they also need training and special support services to help them cope with the increasingly severe problems of many foster children. Such services are generally unavailable. And although new models exist for therapeutic foster homes and other specialized settings, few states have undertaken such initiatives.

In the mental health and juvenile justice systems, overreliance on the most restrictive institutional placements continues to be the norm in many

Alternatives to Detention Save Money and Maintain Public Safety

By using a comprehensive approach with juvenile offenders, Utah significantly reduced the number of youths confined in secure facilities and maintained public safety. Under Utah's system, every youth referred for detention receives a thorough individual assessment and, where possible, is placed in one of a range of in-home or community-based programs. As a result, Utah now spends far less to operate secure facilities. It is estimated that the state can save as much as $10,000 annually per participant by providing alternatives to secure detention. The state maintains only 70 secure beds for violent and chronic juvenile offenders, compared with 350 before the new system started. Moreover, the National Council on Crime and Delinquency reported that 75 percent of the seriously delinquent youths in Utah who were diverted from secure confinement to community-based programs were crime-free for at least one year after leaving state custody, a far higher percentage than for youths placed in secure facilities. The council also documented a decline in the severity of offenses among recidivist youths.

states. The National Association of Private Psychiatric Hospitals reported an estimated 450 percent increase in children admitted to private psychiatric hospitals between 1980 and 1984. This increase was driven in part by the availability of private health insurance funding for such hospitalization and the lack of alternative community-based resources or funding for them. Public funding, too, favors institutional care over less restrictive settings.

Despite evidence of the effectiveness of community-based programs for youths in the juvenile justice system, only a small number of states have shifted substantial proportions of their juvenile correction dollars away from large institutions into smaller community programs.

Many youths in out-of-home care are failing to get the help they need to return successfully to their families. Rather, communities report increases in the numbers of children reentering care. A New Jersey study reported that one-third of the children leaving foster care over an 18-month period had returned to care within a year. In Baltimore, Maryland, almost one-fourth of the children entering care had earlier been in state care.

Teenagers need special help in making a transition from state care to self-sufficiency if they are to avoid continuing as state wards in the adult mental health or criminal justice systems or ending up in homeless shelters or on the streets. A 1985 federal independent living initiative has encouraged state child welfare agencies to provide transitional help for teens in the child welfare system. Programs have been developed to help 16-year-old and older youths in care acquire daily living skills and take full advantage of education and employment opportunities. The estimated 20,000 young people being served represent only a small portion of youths who need such assistance. Help for teens in the juvenile justice and mental health systems is lagging in particular.

The inadequacy of children's services reflects America's failure to make a national commitment to vulnerable youths and their families. Too frequently both the public and policy makers write off troubled children and families, believing they have caused their own difficulties and are undeserving of assistance. It is more comfortable, for example, to assume that all child abusers are unworthy of help than to sort out the most effective forms of help for those who are likely to respond. The same is true for delinquent youths and their families. Yet to walk away from these problems and the potentials of the young people involved is costly in the long run and diminishes the economic health and social fabric of society.

A Federal and State Action Agenda

As a nation we must begin to build in every state a unified continuum of services for vulnerable children and families. Family supports must begin with preventive services to build resilience and strengthen family functioning, continue through intensive crisis intervention that treats the family's needs as an interdependent whole and seeks to preserve the family unit, and include a variety of options for caring for children in appropriate out-of-home care when that is essential. At every stage, families' and children's needs—not arbitrary labels and administrative categories—must determine the help they receive.

In 1989 the federal government should:

- **Modify selected statutes to encourage preventive services.** The government can do this by eliminating the serious imbalance between federal funds for out-of-home care and federal funds for services that can reduce the need for unnecessary placements. Funding should shift toward preventive services designed to help families function adequately and remain intact. Current provisions that favor out-of-home placements should be examined. This means modifying the federal foster care program, the Child Welfare Services program, Medicaid, the Juvenile Justice and Delinquency Prevention Act, and the Alcohol, Drug Abuse and Mental Health Block Grant to give states incentives to develop appropriate alternatives to out-of-home placements.

During the next five years the federal government should:

- **Continue to increase resources for family support services and community-based placements.** The federal government must redirect existing dollars and provide new funds for state expansion of in-home services and community-based alternatives to institutional placements. In addition, the federal government should allow states that reduce the number of children entering out-of-home care to retain the equivalent of the saved federal foster care dollars for use in developing alternative services.

- **Encourage unified children's services.** Through amendments to existing child welfare, juvenile justice, and mental health programs, the federal government should provide fiscal incentives to state child-serving agencies to jointly fund and staff services for youths at risk of placement and for those already in care. Money for developing and implementing family preservation services, therapeutic foster homes, and independent living services to help older youths make a successful transition to adulthood should be provided to states that document interagency collaborations in these areas. In addition, the federal protections currently guaranteed by the Adoption Assistance and Child Welfare Act to children supervised by state child welfare agencies should be extended to all children under the jurisdiction of state mental health and juvenile justice agencies.

- **Rebuild basic supports for poor families and youths.** Increased federal investments in more adequate income supports, health care, food, shelter, and employment assistance will enable families to meet their children's needs better and avoid the economic stress that so often leads to abuse, neglect, or other problems. Improvements in education, particularly in the areas of remedial education and dropout prevention, will help many youths develop the basic skills and enhanced self-esteem they need to avoid getting into trouble.

    In 1989 each state should:

- **Devote more resources to in-home services.** Each state should increase its allocation of funds for in-home family support services and establish intensive short-term family preservation programs, at least in those areas of the state serving the greatest proportion of vulnerable children and families. Each state also should plan to develop these services statewide as part of its overall system of care.

    During the next five years each state should:

- **Develop an individualized assessment package.** Each child and family seeking help, whether from the child welfare, juvenile justice, or mental health system, should receive the same comprehensive developmental assessment. The assessment should identify the child's strengths and needs and the needs of other family members, and should designate specific services to meet those needs. Aggregate data from these assessments should form the basis for interagency program development.

- **Establish a comprehensive system of services.** Each state's vulnerable children and families need a full range of nonresidential and residential service programs. The continuum must include, at a minimum, early intervention and a variety of in-home services, respite care, therapeutic foster family homes and group homes, and residential treatment centers. A limited number of secure treatment beds also should be available for the small number of young people who need them. A case advocate or case manager should be responsible for making sure each child and family receive the care most appropriate to their needs in the least restrictive setting possible. Access to programs should be based on need for the service, not on arbitrary labels attached to the child.

- **Strengthen staff quality.** States should evaluate the job requirements, salaries, training, and supports provided for staff assigned to work directly with children in the child welfare, mental health, and juvenile justice systems and improve them wherever necessary to ensure quality care.

CHILD CARE

A child care crisis confronts this nation. It grows more severe every day and will intensify further as America approaches the new century.

Demand for child care is climbing rapidly: As recently as 1970, only three out of 10 preschool-aged children in America had mothers in the work force. Today, five out of 10 do; the proportion will climb still further, to seven out of 10 by the year 2000, if current trends continue. At the turn of the century, four out of five women in America ages 25 to 54 will be working.

For more and more families, child care spells work and self-sufficiency: Two-parent families increasingly need two incomes to provide for their children. Between 1973 and 1986, median annual earnings of men ages 20 to 30 plummeted by 28 percent. Many young families can only cushion the impact of this drop if mothers bring home a second paycheck.

At the same time, more and more families are headed by single parents who need child care to work at all. Families without two wage-earners face a high risk of sinking into poverty: almost half of those headed by a single mother ages 25 to 44 are poor today. For growing numbers of American working families struggling to make ends meet—whether on one income or two—child care has become a necessity of economic survival.

The quality of child care will help shape the work force of the next century: The millions of American children who will spend a significant part of their childhood in child care are vital to the nation's future economic health and competitiveness. To prepare the next generation to be productive workers, the nation must ensure that every child gets a strong early foundation for learning. For most children who need child care, this means access to care that is safe, affordable, and high quality. For disadvantaged youngsters, who need extra help to compensate for poverty's deprivations, it means offering a chance to experience the extra boost provided by comprehensive early childhood programs such as Head Start.

America's patchwork child care system—already swamped by existing demands—is ill-equipped to cope with stepped-up pressures. Unless the nation acts now, the future will only bring longer day care waiting lists and more children left in substandard day care or waiting home alone because no affordable care is available.

Twenty-Six Million American Children In Search of a Child Care Solution

Every day, millions of children—infants, preschoolers, and schoolagers—are affected directly by the nation's child care dilemma. This is because the sole parent living with them, or both parents, are in the work force.

Five million infants and toddlers: The past few years have witnessed a surge in demand for child care for an especially vulnerable group: babies and one- and two-year-old youngsters.

Because this nation's employment policies have not kept pace with changing realities, many parents who would like to stay home with their infants cannot do so. They cannot afford the economic risk. Unlike all other western industrialized nations except South Africa, the United States does not have a parental leave policy that guarantees new parents a leave of absence and job security when they return to work. In the absence of such protections, and with more and more mothers of infants having to work, more working families must seek infant care.

Fifty percent of mothers of babies one year old or younger are working. They find the costs of infant care especially high and the choices few. In Arizona, for example, less than 3 percent of licensed child care centers offer slots for infants. Nearly half of the women who went back to work four to seven months after childbirth faced significant problems finding child care, according to *Mothers in the Workplace*, a 1987 study conducted by the National Council of Jewish Women's Center for the Child.

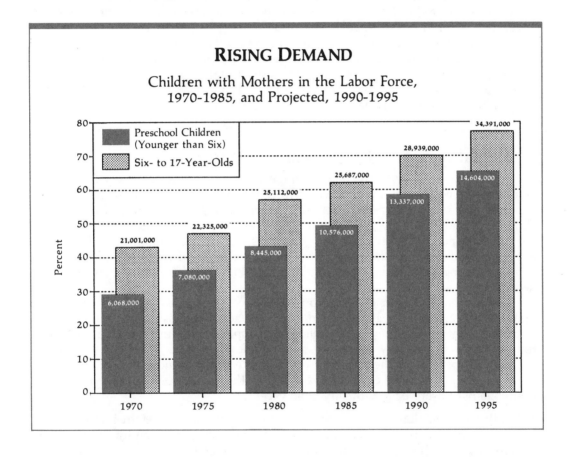

RISING DEMAND

Children with Mothers in the Labor Force,
1970-1985, and Projected, 1990-1995

Around the country, parents are competing just to get their infants and toddlers on child care waiting lists. At the Children's Edition, a child care center in Louisville, Kentucky, for example, 96 youngsters younger than two are among the 130 children on the waiting list for the center's 86 child care slots. The average wait is nine months to a year.

Five million three- to five-year-olds: Although more programs are available for preschoolers than for infants, many for three- and four-year-olds are run on a part-day basis. Most parents, however, do not work part time. As a result, bewildered youngsters must shuttle among as many as three care-giving situations in a single day, increasing their anxiety and disrupting their normal learning and play patterns. Only the luckiest children are placed in a single stable arrangement. In Vermont, for example, only one out of four preschool children with working parents is cared for in a regulated full-time day care slot.

Sixteen million six- to 13-year-old youngsters: The dearth of after-school care for school-age youngsters leaves them to loiter in streets or playgrounds, or go home alone or with other children to an empty house.

- A survey in Los Angeles, California, found nearly one-quarter of seven- to nine-year-olds in self-care after school.

- In Columbus, Ohio, one-fourth of the 500 households surveyed relied on self-care for school-age children age 12 and younger. Not surprisingly, half of these families said they were uncomfortable with their child care arrangements.

- In a 1987 study conducted by Louis Harris and Associates for the Metropolitan Life Insurance Company, a majority of more than 1,000 teachers interviewed cited isolation and lack of supervision after school as the major reasons children have difficulty in school.

In 1984, when children were invited by the language arts magazine *Sprint* to write about a situation they find scary, the editors were stunned by the response. Nearly 70 percent of the 7,000 letters that poured in from fourth-, fifth-, and sixth-graders from across the United States described fears of being home alone, mostly while parents were working.

The Quality of Child Care Makes a Difference

Parents, teachers, and child development experts agree that good child care makes a positive and permanent difference to a child's development. Child care that works for children is that which keeps group sizes small and has fewer children per adult caregiver. Children in such settings receive more attention and get more chances to improve their cognitive, social, and language skills. In addition, good child care is staffed by caregivers with solid training and has low caregiver turnover, qualities that can best be achieved by paying employees decent wages.

Parents want their children to have a good child care experience. They know that the current system does not provide adequate assurance of that outcome. That is why they overwhelmingly support minimum national standards for child care. In a survey conducted by NBC News and *The Wall Street Journal*, for example, 69 percent of the surveyed public backed such standards.

Today, millions of children live in states that do not adequately protect them against unsafe or low-quality child care:

- South Carolina allows one caregiver to care for as many as eight infants. In Georgia and North Carolina, one caregiver may care for seven infants. Ten states allow staff-to-infant ratios of one to six or worse.

- Twenty-eight states have such low expectations of family day care providers that they require neither training in child development nor any prior experience. Twenty-eight states require no training before teachers come to work at day care centers.

- Twenty-eight states do not protect parents' right to drop in unannounced to check on their children.

- In Colorado, each case worker on the state's licensing staff monitors an average of 211 child care facilities. While the day care licensing caseload has nearly tripled since 1971, the licensing staff has declined from 8.5 positions to 6.5.

When Parents Cannot Afford Quality Child Care, Children Pay the Price

Recently, in a community near Chicago, 47 youngsters—half of them younger than two—were discovered being cared for in a basement by only one adult. At $25 a week, the program was one-third of the cost of most child care in the community. When the state closed this "center," many of the parents objected. No concerned parent would happily put a child in such a child care situation. But the parents could afford no better. When parents cannot afford decent child care, children suffer and often are placed in care that is dangerous.

It costs an average of $3,000 a year to send one child to full-time child care—money that is getting harder to find in many families' budgets. The median income of America's families with children fell 6 percent between 1973 and 1986 and would have fallen more except for increased numbers of working mothers. For younger families with children the child care burden is greater still, because they have suffered a 26 percent income drop since 1973.

While purchasing child care is a struggle for many working families, poor and near-poor families cannot afford decent child care at all unless they stop eating, buying shoes, or paying the rent. For example, America's single mothers who are raising one or more children younger than six have a median income of $6,595 (as of 1986). The annual cost of child care for one child would eat up nearly half their entire income.

INCOME DRAIN

Percentage of Income that Low-Income
Parents Would Have to Pay for Child Care

Families	One Child in Child Care (Average Cost: $3,000/yr.)	Two Children in Child Care (Average Cost: $6,000/yr.)
One parent working full time at minimum wage ($6,700 annual income)	45 Percent	90 Percent
One parent working full time, earning poverty-level wages for a family of three ($9,700 annual income)	31 Percent	62 Percent
Two parents working full time at minimum wage ($13,400 annual income)	22 Percent	45 Percent
A single mother with at least one child under six, earning the median wage for that group ($6,600 annual income)	45 Percent	91 Percent
A couple aged 18 to 24 with the median earnings for their age group ($19,900 annual income)	15 Percent	31 Percent

The Gaps in America's Child Care System

Meeting the nation's child care crisis calls for a working partnership among the federal government, the states, the private sector, and America's families to assure an adequate supply of quality child care and to provide help to lower income families so they can keep working. But the federal government has walked away from any significant role in improving quality or expanding supply, and has provided scant help to lower income families that are working hard to provide good child care for their children.

The federal government has been the missing partner: Despite the demographic and economic convulsions that make child care a pressing national concern, the nation still has no broad federal policy or program that addresses the availability, affordability, and quality of child care.

Federal child care help through the Title XX Social Services Block Grant has dwindled. On average, states use about 18 percent of their allotment of Title XX funds—funds that must meet a broad range of human service needs—to help lower income families pay for child care. But Title XX funding never has come close to meeting the need. In FY 1977 the program served only 12 percent of the 3.3 million poor children younger than six. Today the money is stretched even more thinly. The overall Title XX appropriation for FY 1989 is less than half of what it was in FY 1977 (after adjusting for inflation), while the number of preschool children in poverty has soared to almost 5 million.

Federal tax breaks do not build a good child care system. The dependent care tax credit is the only federal source of child care help that has increased significantly in recent years. The credit allows families to offset some of their federal tax bill by claiming a portion of their child care expenses. More than 8.4 million families received $3.127 billion of credits in 1985. But the credit does little for the lower income families that most desperately need child care assistance, because these families have little or no federal income tax liability to offset, and because the credit covers only a fraction of the cost of care. Nor does the tax credit have any impact on the two other key child care problems: availability and quality of care.

Under the Family Support Act of 1988, AFDC families will receive federal child care help. The welfare reform bill is expected to provide $1 billion over five years to defray child care costs for AFDC parents who participate in education and work preparation programs, work, or are in a one-year transitional period after their earnings make them ineligible for AFDC. But millions of poor and near-poor working families who do receive AFDC benefits are still without child care help.

States cannot handle the child care crisis alone: Some states are struggling to address the child care crisis by boosting state contributions to Title XX-funded child care or by launching new child care programs. But more states are sliding backward. In 1988, 26 states spent less in real dollars for child care funded through the Title XX Social Services Block Grant than they did in FY 1981. Only 20 states are serving more children than they did in 1981, while 23 states are serving fewer. Even California, which annually invests more than $300 million in child care, serves only 7 percent of the children eligible for child care assistance.

These numbers mean that children are at risk. Lashwana, a two-year-old toddler who lives in Broward County, Florida, is one of close to 30,000 on the state's waiting lists for child care help. Lashwana is often left in the care of her seven-year-old sister, who stays home from school to babysit so their mother can go to work.

Private sector efforts are growing, but still very scarce: While employers are increasing their involvement in child care, only approximately 4,000 employers out of 6 million across the United States provide any child care help to their employees. Very few of even these 4,000 employers provide the most needed help: assistance to families in paying their child care bills.

Tackling the Child Care Challenge: Programs That Work

- **Helping parents find child care:** Using local dollars to supplement state and federal money, the Office for Children in Fairfax County, Virginia, has become a partner in parents' quest for good, affordable child care. The agency provides a subsidy to help low- and middle-income families pay for child care, offers a resource and referral service, operates before- and after-school programs in elementary schools throughout the county, and provides training to child care providers. In addition, the county has a special program to encourage employers to invest in child care.

- **Multiple strategies that increase and improve child care:** Maine has a multipronged campaign for child care. To help parents find care, the state funds 10 resource and referral centers that also recruit new family day care providers. To help parents pay for child care, Maine has increased direct family subsidies and expanded the state dependent care tax credit. To improve quality, the state has increased salaries for child care workers in government-funded programs, expanded training opportunities for child care workers, and initiated loan forgiveness programs for child care workers who earn two- or four-year degrees. To increase supply, Maine gives tax credits and other assistance to employers that start child care programs and offers loans and grants for ongoing providers. In addition, since 1985 Maine has invested almost $7 million to increase the number of children enrolled in Head Start.

- **Public/private partnership strengthens child care:** In California, 33 corporations, foundations, and government entities (including federal, state, and local agencies) are working together to increase the supply of licensed child care. The statewide California Child Care Initiative has contributed more than $3.2 million to help community-based resource and referral agencies recruit and train new family day care providers. Since its inception in 1985, the program has generated more than 1,000 new licensed family day care homes, creating about 6,500 new places for California children.

Head Start: An Early Childhood Program That Helps Our Neediest Children

All children need a strong early childhood experience as a foundation for later learning. But disadvantaged three- and four-year-olds, struggling under the hardships of poverty, need something extra before they go to school: the comprehensive services provided by the federal Head Start program.

Head Start, however, only has the funds to serve one out of six eligible children. As a result, poor children are far less likely than more affluent children to have the opportunity to enroll in an early childhood development program. In 1986 fewer than four out of every 10 four-year-olds with family incomes below $10,000 a year were enrolled in a preschool program. In contrast, two out of three four-year-olds whose families had incomes of $35,000 a year or more attended such programs.

Early Investments Yield Big Dividends

Every $1 invested in high-quality preschool programs such as Head Start saves $6 in lowered costs for special education, grade retention, public assistance, and crime later on. Children formerly enrolled in these programs are more likely than other poor children to be literate, employed, and enrolled in postsecondary education. They are less likely to be school dropouts, teen parents, dependent on welfare, or arrested for criminal or delinquent activity.

The shortage of help to poor preschoolers is extremely short-sighted. The business-led Committee for Economic Development (CED) in its 1987 report, *Children in Need: Investment Strategies for the Educationally Disadvantaged*, stated that such programs represent a "superior educational investment for society." CED recommends that the nation expand the Head Start program until every eligible child has an opportunity to participate.

Research shows that the benefits of early education programs last through school and into adulthood (see Early Investments Yield Big Dividends box).

The hallmark of Head Start's effectiveness is its multifaceted approach to helping children learn, develop, and grow. Head Start succeeds by:

• **Providing a broad range of needed services:** "Head Start is much more than just preschool education," Sharon Glynne, a Fairfax County Head Start coordinator, told Lisbeth Schorr, author of *Within Our Reach: Breaking the Cycle of Disadvantage.* "Our new child-initiated learning curriculum is exciting, it works, but it wouldn't work without the health and nutrition and social services we also provide.... Our teachers understand that a child whose family got evicted that day can't pay a lot of attention to classroom routines." Head Start addresses a broad range of children's needs. In 1988, for example, almost 100 percent of all Head Start children received vaccinations, medical screening, dental checkups, and needed treatment.

• **Involving and energizing families:** Four out of five Head Start parents volunteer in the program, helping youngsters and learning new skills and new self-respect. More than one-third of all Head Start employees are parents of current or former Head Start children.

Although 2.5 million disadvantaged youngsters are potentially eligible for Head Start, only 18 percent of those children are lucky enough to be admitted. Many of the others are waiting for an open slot:

• In Bath, New York, where the Head Start program has an enrollment of 119, 90 remain on waiting lists.

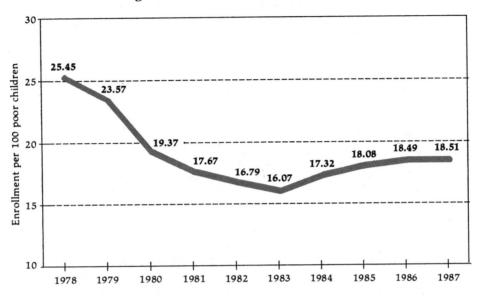

FALLING BEHIND

Head Start Enrollment Per 100 Poor Children
Ages 3 to 5 Years Old, 1978-1987

Enrollment per 100 poor children

25.45
23.57
19.37
17.67
16.79
16.07
17.32
18.08
18.49
18.51

1978 1979 1980 1981 1982 1983 1984 1985 1986 1987

• The portion of poor children served by Head Start has decreased significantly.

Note: This chart compares the total number of Head Start enrollees with the total number of poor children. Not every Head Start enrollee is poor.

• In Phipsburg, Pennsylvania, 313 children receive services, while 188 children wait for a slot to open up.

These children have to wait because federal funding for Head Start has not kept pace with spreading child poverty during the 1980s. But inadequate funding also has meant that program quality has been harder to maintain. All around the country, Head Start programs are struggling to attract and retain qualified staff, to maintain or renovate their facilities, and to provide pre-schoolers with transportation to the programs. While a few states have boosted their investment in early childhood programs for youngsters, their total spending on such programs was less than $250 million in 1988.

A Federal and State Action Agenda

In 1989 the federal government must enact a broad range of measures to help children and families. No single program is going to solve America's child care crisis. Different groups of children and families need different levels and types of help. Together, three initiatives would move the country a long way toward a system that helps all American children—regardless of their age, income status, or whether both their parents are at work:

• **Pass the Act for Better Child Care.** ABC is comprehensive legislation that will lay the foundation for a national system of safe and affordable child care. It will bring the federal government into an active child care partnership with state and local governments as well as the private sector. ABC authorizes $2.5 billion annually to address the essential child care problems:

Affordability: ABC will provide child care assistance to low- and moderate-income families, targeting the most help to the poorest families. The assistance will enable parents who currently cannot afford care or can afford only substandard care to choose among good child care programs on the basis of their children's needs. Programs operated by nonprofit or for-profit organizations, employers, schools, churches, community-based organizations, group homes, neighborhood family day care providers, and relatives all will be available choices.

Safety and quality: After a phase-in period, programs receiving ABC funds will be expected to meet realistic and practical minimum protections for quality and child safety. These standards are derived from the experiences of states as well as the knowledge of child development experts, the private sector, and parents. ABC will help providers meet these standards.

Supply: ABC will increase child care options by supporting the recruitment and training of new family day care providers and offering low-interest loans and grants to establish and expand child care programs.

- **Enact low-income tax credits.** Assistance through the tax system is necessary to help low-income families defray the high costs of raising a family today. President Bush has proposed a children's tax credit—a payment through the tax system of up to $1,000 per child younger than four to families earning less than $10,000 a year. The credit would be available regardless of whether one or both parents work. This type of measure (like proposals to expand the Earned Income Tax Credit to give added help to larger families)—while not substantially removing the cost of child care for most low-income families— will ease the financial strain.

  Congress also should make the current Dependent Care Tax Credit refundable so that lower income families can benefit from it. While refundability by itself will not provide enough help to the poorest families that do not have enough income to pay out-of-pocket for quality child care, it would provide some assistance to lower income families that will not be able to obtain ABC services.

- **Expand Head Start.** The final piece of the puzzle is the beginning of a substantial expansion of Head Start. Congress must appropriate sufficient additional funds in 1989 and each year thereafter so that by 1994 all eligible three- and four-year-olds who want Head Start can participate. This means boosting authorizations and appropriations levels by $400 million a year for each of the next five years. There also must be federal administrative efforts to maintain the program's effectiveness, to enable programs to offer full-day, year-round services—a crucial need for working families—and to address the problem of low salaries paid to Head Start workers.

In 1989 each state should:

- **Act to implement the child care provisions of the Family Support Act of 1988.** Necessary state steps include providing adequate state matching funds, assuring that the child care offered under the program is of high quality, and designing the program to foster AFDC parents' continued self-sufficiency.

Over the next five years each state should:

- **Make its own substantial commitment to help low- and moderate-income families within its borders to pay their child care bills.** No federal program will be able to help all who need assistance. States must provide matching funds under ABC.

- **Work to assure safe, quality child care for every child.** States must make sure their licensing systems are strong enough to protect children from harm and to help them learn and develop; ensure that an adequate number of trained staff members are available to monitor programs and help them meet state standards; expand parents' roles in the monitoring of their children's child care settings; and invest in the training and compensation of child care employees.

- **Allocate state funds to give more children a strong start.** This means expanding the number of children receiving comprehensive early education experiences such as Head Start and strengthening program quality by increasing the salaries and benefits providers receive and lowering staff turnover.

EDUCATION

T he children attending America's schools today will need to be able to read, write, compute, and think clearly to become productive members of the work force in the year 2000. They will need stronger academic skills than any preceding generation of Americans.

The U.S. job market is growing fastest in occupations that require more education (see Tomorrow's Jobs chart). According to the U.S. Department of Labor, more than half of the new jobs created between 1984 and 2000 will require some education beyond high school, with almost one-third requiring four or more years of college. Another major crop of new jobs—in such fields as service and sales—will demand far more solid basic skills than did past jobs that did not require college. An increasingly educated work force will be essential to the nation's long-term economic health and ability to be internationally competitive.

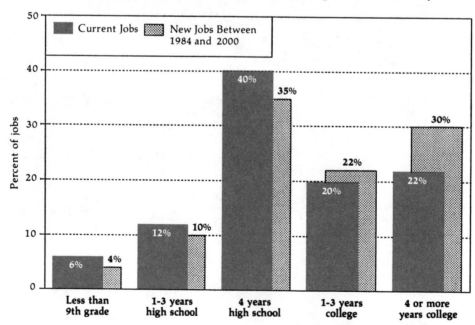

TOMORROW'S JOBS

Future Jobs Will Require More Years of Schooling Than Current Jobs

Source: Adapted from Hudson Institute, Inc., *Workforce 2000: Work and Workers for the 21st Century,* 1987.

Note: Totals exceed 100% due to rounding.

Unless the educational success of poor and minority youths improves dramatically, however, a considerable proportion of young workers in the year 2000 will lack the skills they will need to fill the available jobs. By the year 2000 the proportion of young workers who are minority will increase to more than 30 percent. Yet far too many of today's disadvantaged students—who are disproportionately from minority groups—are leaving school ill-prepared for today's and tomorrow's work place. Growing up in poverty dramatically reduces a young person's chances of keeping on grade level, acquiring strong basic academic skills, graduating from high school, or having the opportunity to attend college.

The business-led Committee for Economic Development warned in 1987 that, unless corrective action is taken, "our industries will be unable to grow and compete because an expanding educational underclass will be unable to meet the demands" of new jobs in a changing economy.

America must heed this warning. To ensure the economic health of the nation, every effort must be made to ensure that by the year 2000 every young American has the minimum requirements for becoming a productive member of our economy: strong basic academic skills, a high school diploma or its equivalent, and an excellent opportunity to obtain postsecondary education or training.

Poverty: A Key Roadblock to Educational Progress

Overall, America's young people—including some of the most disadvantaged students—have made remarkable educational gains over the past three decades. In 1960 only six out of 10 young adults had graduated from high school. By 1986 more than eight out of 10 had done so.

Further, thanks in significant part to the help of federal educational programs put in place during the 1960s, minority students have been able to narrow the long-standing gaps in educational attainment. As recently as 1967, only a little more than one-half of black 18- to 24-year-olds had high school diplomas—a graduation rate more than 20 percentage points behind that of their white peers. By 1985, three-quarters of black youths had high school degrees, and the black/white gap had narrowed to 8 percentage points. If current trends continue, black and white youths could be graduating from high school at equal rates in the year 2000.

Although these achievements are impressive, too many disadvantaged youths—including a disproportionate share of minority young people—are not yet reaping the full benefits of our educational system. While their families' often enormous commitment to education may be pushing more of them to complete high school, the ill effects of poverty continue to block their progress to full educational equality.

Poor teens fall behind their peers: Among 16-year-olds who have lived at least half of their lives in poverty, four out of 10 have repeated at least one grade—twice the repetition rate for 16-year-olds whose families have never lived in poverty (see Lagging Behind chart). Because they are more likely to suffer early disadvantages, black youths 15- to 17-years-old are more than twice as likely as white youths to have repeated a grade. Hispanic youths, often hampered by both poverty and language barriers, are almost three times as likely to have repeated a grade.

Poverty often spells poor skills: Poor teenagers are four times more likely than nonpoor teens to have below-average basic academic skills. According to data from the National Longitudinal Survey of Young Americans, more than half of the 15- to 18-year-olds from families with incomes below poverty had reading and math skills that placed them in the bottom 20 percent of all teens. The data on minority teens, who bear a disproportionate burden of

LAGGING BEHIND

Percent of 16-Year-Olds Who Have Fallen Behind in School by Years in Poverty

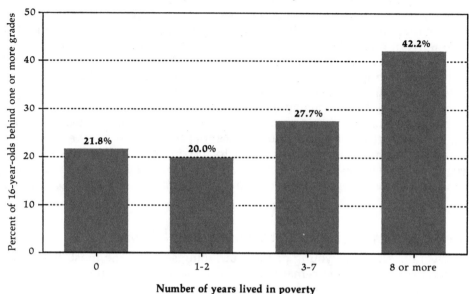

- 16-year-olds who have lived half of their lives in poverty are twice as likely as those who have never been poor to be behind in school.

Source: U.S. Dept. of Education, Office of Educational Research and Improvement, 1986.

poverty, reflect these disadvantages. Although black and Hispanic students have made gains in reading achievement, the average reading level of minority 17-year-olds is only slightly better than the average reading level of white 13-year-olds.

Poor teens are more likely to drop out: Despite overall improvement in the dropout rate, a distressingly large proportion of disadvantaged young people still leave school before graduation. Regardless of race, poor youths are almost three times more likely than their more well-off peers to drop out. In 1986 more than one in four poor 18- to 21-year-olds had dropped out of high school, compared with only one in 10 of their nonpoor peers. In large part because young black students face high poverty rates, a troubling gap in educational attainment between blacks and whites remains—though it has closed substantially over the past two decades and may narrow further as we approach the year 2000.

Poor students are more likely to miss out on college: Although poor young people are more likely to have a high school diploma today than in the mid-1970s, these disadvantaged teens—especially black teens—are now much less likely than their peers to attend college. In 1975 poor high school graduates of all races were only slightly less likely than other high school graduates to attend college—about one-third of all 18- to 21-year-old high school graduates, poor and nonpoor, had completed a year or more of college. By 1986, however, the gap had widened significantly. The proportion of poor young people attending college had dropped by about 4 percentage points while the proportion of

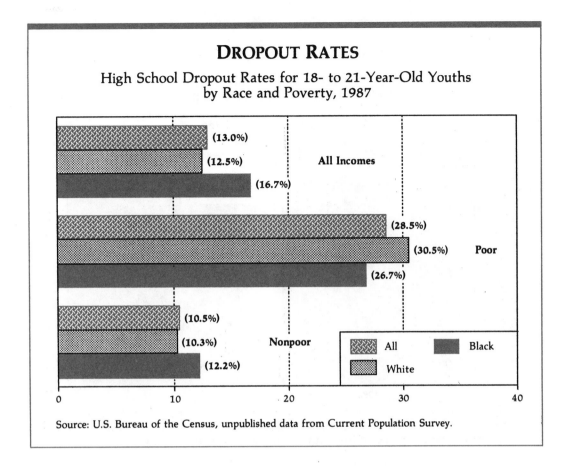

DROPOUT RATES

High School Dropout Rates for 18- to 21-Year-Old Youths
by Race and Poverty, 1987

(13.0%)
(12.5%)   All Incomes
(16.7%)

(28.5%)
(30.5%)   Poor
(26.7%)

(10.5%)
(10.3%)   Nonpoor
(12.2%)

All   Black
White

0   10   20   30   40

Source: U.S. Bureau of the Census, unpublished data from Current Population Survey.

nonpoor high school graduates who managed to gain at least one year of a college education increased 5 percentage points. Poor black high school graduates suffered the most severe setbacks. Their college attainment rates fell from 33 percent in 1975 to 20 percent in 1986, while poor white high school graduates saw only a two-point decline. Further, the dimming college hopes of poor black young people contrast with the gradually improving fortunes of black youths as a whole. The proportion of all black high school graduates getting some college education has increased slightly since the mid-1970s (rising from 29 to 33 percent).

The consequences to young adults and their families of truncated educations and low basic skills are far graver than in earlier decades. From 1973 to 1986 the median annual earnings of young family heads (younger than 30) who were high school dropouts fell 53 percent, after adjusting for inflation. Even young family heads who were high school graduates (but did not attend college) saw their earnings drop 31 percent. In contrast, the earnings of those young family heads who were college graduates fell only marginally (3 percent).

Why Child Poverty Raises the Odds of School Failure

Poor children often get a weak start in life: In 1987, 23 percent of all children younger than six lived in poverty. Youngsters who grow up in poverty are already at a disadvantage when they first enter school.

Poor parents are less likely to be able to afford prenatal care, which increases their babies' risk of being born at low birthweight, a condition that can lead to learning disabilities. As they grow up, poor children are less likely to

COLLEGE INEQUITY

Percentage of High School Graduates Age 18-21 With at Least 1 Year of College

By Poverty, 1975 and 1986

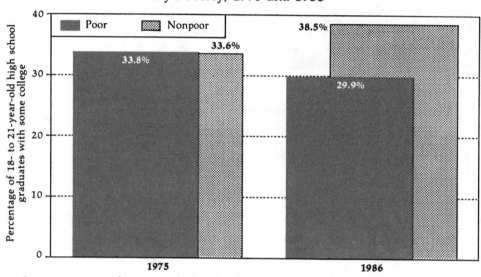

• In 1975 poor and nonpoor high school graduates were equally likely to have obtained at least one year of a college education. By 1986, however, there was a 9 point gap between the college attainment rates of poor and nonpoor youths.

By Poverty and Race, 1975 and 1986

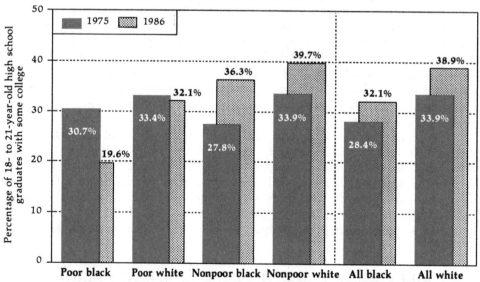

• While the percentage of 18- to 21-year-old high school graduates who completed at least one year of college increased for both blacks and whites between 1975 and 1986, the percentage of poor high school graduates—in particular, poor black high school graduates—who were able to attain some college education dropped.

Source: U.S. Bureau of the Census, *Current Population Reports.* Calculations by Children's Defense Fund.

receive key building blocks of early development—adequate nutrition, decent medical care, and a safe and secure environment. Children who are under-nourished and ill are less alert, less curious, and interact less effectively with their environment than healthy children, making them generally less prepared to start school than more affluent youngsters.

Also, a substantial number of poor children live with parents who have less than a high school education. These parents, however motivated to help their children learn, often lack the personal and economic resources to do so. The option of supplementing learning in the home with early childhood develop-ment programs—a crucial opportunity for poor children—is more often available to affluent children. In 1986, for example, two out of three four-year-olds in families with annual incomes of $35,000 or more were enrolled in some type of preschool program, compared with only four out of 10 four-year-olds in families with annual incomes less than $10,000.

Poor children are more likely to attend schools with poor resources: Students from disadvantaged backgrounds often need an enriched educational experience to overcome early learning deficits and the special problems of poverty. Poor youths, consequently, have the most to gain from their school experience. They need the highest quality teachers, the most advanced classroom equipment, a low student/teacher ratio, and educational programs that supple-ment classroom learning.

They are often disappointed. Schools with large poor and minority populations usually have the least money to serve children well. The state of New Jersey, for example, has attempted to make up for fiscal inequities among school districts, yet per-pupil expenditures in 1986-1987 were $3,540 in one poor district and $7,642 in one wealthy district.

Extra federal help for needy students has declined: Inadequate funding has curtailed the effectiveness of the major federal programs that are designed to provide extra assistance to disadvantaged students:

- **Chapter 1.** This program offers remedial education aimed at helping poor youngsters who are at risk of falling behind in school. While the number of poor children has gone up in the 1980s, the proportion of needy children served by Chapter 1 has gone down. In 1980 the program served 75 children for every 100 poor school-aged children. By 1985 Chapter 1 served only 54 students for every 100 poor children.

Chapter 1: A Preventive Investment in Learning

Chapter 1 is a proven, cost-effective way to promote literacy and adequate basic skills through preventive investment. Designed to give poor children the extra help they need to avoid falling behind in school, Chapter 1 resulted in reading gains by element-ary students of four to five percentile ranks in 1983-1984. In math, elementary students gained five to seven percentile ranks. By helping students keep up with their classmates, Chapter 1 saves the high costs of grade repetition, which are four times as much as one year of preventive services through Chapter 1.

- **The Education for All Handicapped Children Act (Public Law 94-142).** Under this legislation every handicapped child between the ages of three and 21 is supposed to receive a free and appropriate public education in the least restrictive environment. But the current federal contribution to this program —approximately 10 percent of the national per-pupil expenditure for such students—is only about one-fourth of the commitment made in the original legislation.

- **Bilingual education.** This program is intended to build a language bridge to help young students for whom English is a second language. According to U.S. Department of Education estimates, only a small minority of the millions of students with limited English proficiency currently are getting this help.

Young people in poor communities get few opportunities to grow outside the classroom: School, home, and community—working together at their best— create a positive climate for learning. The lessons learned in school are reinforced and applied at home and in the community. Too often, however, the weak learning experience many disadvantaged youths have at school is mirrored in their homes and communities. Their parents often lack the credentials and skills they are hoping their children will acquire. Poor youths are more likely to have parents who have not completed high school than their nonpoor peers. This is a significant disadvantage: parents' education level is one of the strongest predictors of their children's success in school. Research suggests that, if other factors are the same, each additional year of education attained by a mother translates into half a year of educational attainment for her child.

Most poor young people live in communities where opportunities to apply academic skills and build new ones are either not available or not accessible. The lack of community resources is especially destructive during the summer months, the time when children doing least well in school (a group that is disproportionately poor) slide backward the farthest. Recent research shows that most of the learning gap between poor and nonpoor children is due to this summer learning loss. But this is not a new phenomenon. Summer learning loss, the National Advisory Commission on Civil Disorders (Kerner Report) warned 20 years ago, is "both a substantial factor in producing disorders and a tragic waste of time and facilities. Financing should be provided . . . for large-scale year-round programs in the disadvantaged areas of our cities. . . . What is needed is not 12 months of the same routine, but innovative programs tailored to total educational needs, and providing a wide range of educational activities (verbal skills, culture and arts), recreation, job training, work experience and camps."

A dearth of educational alternatives: As a nation, we have not invested resources in developing effective education and training programs for the millions of young Americans who do not function well in mainstream classrooms, who are not college-bound, or who are too old to reenter the public school system. This costs the nation both the productivity of many young citizens and millions of dollars on useless grade repetitions for those youths who gain little from sitting in the same course or same grade for a second time. Every one of these youths has the capacity to learn—but few schools and communities have sufficient capacity to teach them appropriately, provide a range of settings for learning, and offer useful skills and information.

The opportunities for poor young people to go to college are shrinking. A college education is still one of the smartest economic choices a young person can make: college graduates earn twice as much over the course of their lifetimes as do high school graduates, and the gap is growing. Yet disadvantaged students increasingly cannot make that choice.

For decades federal support for college education has improved poor young people's options, allowing many to attend college. But in the 1980s, funding for the combination of grants and subsidized loans that opened college doors to more youths has not kept pace with the skyrocketing costs of tuition. Between 1980 and 1988, the cost of attending a four-year public college increased 28 percent (after adjusting for inflation); the cost of attending a private university increased 52 percent. Yet the number of students receiving Pell grants (the major federal grants for low-income students) increased by only 6 percent; the average grant given increased by only 11 percent. Sadly, college enrollments among poor students have declined.

Education Plus: Innovative Programs Get High Marks

- **An alternative school offers a rich learning experience.** Central Park East Secondary School (CPESS) in New York City provides 225 students in grades seven through nine a school experience based on the growing body of knowledge about what works for young people in middle-grade education. To reduce anonymity, students are grouped into "houses" of 75 students, each with a separate faculty, and classes are kept small (18 students maximum). To foster participation, every student has a faculty adviser and belongs to a small advisory group that meets every day for study and discussion. The results are clear: students' attendance rates and achievement test scores are high compared with those of similar students in traditional schools.

- **An early boost helps preschoolers.** Washington State is spending several million dollars a year on a preschool program for low-income children who meet Head Start eligibility guidelines. Head Start programs and child care providers in cooperation with school districts may participate. Because the state requires all providers to follow the federal Head Start guidelines, the preschools offer the same comprehensive services as Head Start and can expect the same record of demonstrable success.

- **Preventive attention encourages students to look ahead.** Career Beginnings, a comprehensive college/business initiative operating at 25 sites nationwide, targets youths who have demonstrated ability and ambition but are at risk of dropping out for financial or other reasons. Career Beginnings assigns each participant a personal mentor and provides summer employment and summer enrichment workshops. Preliminary evaluations show low program attrition rates, improved high school graduation rates, and nearly doubled rates of education or training after high school.

A Federal and State Action Agenda

In addition to strengthening its commitment to early childhood education through expansion of the Head Start program (see Child Care chapter), the federal government must reaffirm and bolster its commitment to the education of disadvantaged students at the primary, secondary, and postsecondary levels.

In 1989 the federal government should:

- **Increase funding for Chapter 1 by at least $750 million.** When this compensatory education program was reauthorized in 1988, a legislative commitment was made to increase funding by at least $500 million each year for the next five years in order to reach the goal of serving all eligible children. To speed progress toward this goal and strengthen services to middle-school students, appropriations should be set at $5.3 billion in 1989, reflecting the additional $500 million commitment, plus $257 million not committed last year.

Over the next five years the federal government should:

- **Continue to build Chapter 1.** This means continuing annual increases of at least $500 million until the commitment to full funding is fulfilled, as well as expanding existing requirements for increased parental and community involvement. It also means spelling out and carefully monitoring the new requirements set by the 1988 reauthorization that demand performance goals for local programs as well as better coordination between Chapter 1 and regular school programs.

- **Reaffirm its commitment to handicapped and non-English speaking students.** The federal government must step up the amount of its educational investment in both groups, whose participation in regular classrooms hinges on receiving targeted help through the Education for All Handicapped Children Act (PL 94-142) and the Bilingual Education Act.

- **Ease financial barriers to postsecondary education and training.** There are several ways federal help can put opportunities within reach of low- and moderate-income students. First, the government should ease the college cost burden for disadvantaged students by reversing the trend of providing loans rather than grants. By 1993, 75 percent of all aid should be in the form of grants, up from 47 percent of federal aid in 1987-1988.

    In addition, the government should offset the negative impact of skyrocketing tuition costs by indexing maximum grant and loan amounts to average public four-year college tuition costs. And the government should explore ways of relieving the burden of student debt on disadvantaged young people by canceling part or all of student loans in return for public service, by extending deferment periods, and by linking repayment to postcollege income.

    Finally, the government should boost funding to increase outreach, career counseling, and support services to help low-income youths prepare for postsecondary programs. Upward Bound, Talent Search, and Educational Opportunity Centers are three services that should receive more funding.

The states should continue their increasingly aggressive role in improving education.

In 1989 each state should:

- **Expand its investment in early childhood education.** To supplement the federal commitment to Head Start, states should increase appropriations for comprehensive early education programs, which have proven so effective in helping lay a learning foundation for four- and five-year-olds.

Over the next five years each state should:

- **Build a comprehensive system of early childhood programs.** Working collaboratively with school administrators, early childhood educators, and Head Start providers, states should build a system with slots in quality early childhood and preschool programs for all disadvantaged three- to five-year-olds.

- **Work to eliminate funding inequities and increase funding accountability.** Where such inequities persist within states and within districts, states must make sure that districts with greater needs get greater funding. Such districts should be required to develop plans and goals and should be held accountable for making reasonable improvements as a condition of assistance. At both the state and local levels, administrators should streamline administrative budgets and move education money out of the offices and into the classrooms and school buildings.

- **Ensure that education reform serves disadvantaged students.** The recommendations for increased accountability for the education of disadvantaged students made by the Council of Chief State School Officers provide a good framework. States should take steps to set in place: guidelines for identifying as early as possible students who are at risk of dropping out; incentives for systemwide and schoolwide adoption of promising approaches to educating all students; mechanisms for developing, monitoring, and enforcing schoolwide improvement plans for schools that are not adequately meeting their students' educational needs; and within-school procedures for developing individual teaching and learning plans for students who are at risk of school failure.

YOUTH
EMPLOYMENT

America's pool of young workers will look very different in the year 2000. The number of young adults in our nation will dwindle rapidly during the next decade. At the turn of the century, there will be 4.1 million fewer Americans between the ages of 18 and 24 than there were in the mid-1980s, reducing the potential young work force by 14 percent. The shrinking pool of young workers means our nation will need every young person to take his or her place in our offices, farms, and factories.

Only one out of every seven new entrants to the work force between 1988 and 2000 will be a white male born in the United States, from the group that employers traditionally have looked to most often to fill available jobs. The vast majority of new workers will be women or members of minority groups. Nearly a third of the nation's 18- to 24-year-olds will be minorities in 2000, compared with less than one-quarter in 1985.

Unless we act quickly, many of these young adults will be ill-prepared for the work place of the year 2000. About 14 percent of young Americans now reach their early twenties without obtaining the basic key to the working world—a high school diploma or its equivalent. There was a time when our nation's economy could function without the contributions of these young men and women. But no more: our shrinking work force means that every young worker will be needed to keep our nation strong and competitive into the twenty-first century.

To protect our future, our nation's employment goal for the year 2000 must be to build academic and job training programs that will prepare every young adult to become a productive worker and to make sure that a decent job opportunity is always there.

Slipping Down the Job Ladder: The Growing Struggle of Young Workers

A growing proportion of young, noncollege-educated workers cannot find jobs that will support themselves and their families. Those who drop out of high school face the greatest difficulties, but many of our high-school educated youths are floundering as well.

Youths with limited reading and math abilities are at a serious disadvantage in the job market. Those who by age 18 have the weakest basic skills (in the lowest fifth of their age group) are between four and seven times more likely to drop out of school and be jobless in subsequent years than those with above-average skills.

Young people who do not go on to college, even if they have high school diplomas, are finding it difficult to compete in a labor market that places a growing premium on cognitive abilities. More than one-quarter of all high school graduates younger than 20 and not enrolled in college did not have jobs in October 1988. Employment rates among high school dropouts were even lower: fewer than half had jobs. And full-time jobs are particularly scarce for young workers. Less than half of the total pool of high school dropouts and graduates not going on to college held full-time jobs in October 1988.

YOUTH EMPLOYMENT

Employment Rates for Noncollege-Bound Youths Ages 16 to 19[1]
October 1988

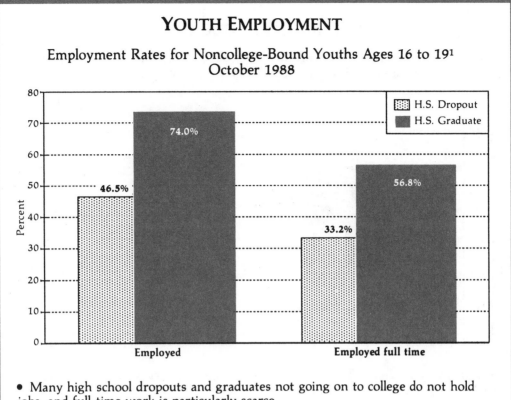

• Many high school dropouts and graduates not going on to college do not hold jobs, and full-time work is particularly scarce.

[1]Subjects' major activity was not schooling at time of interview.

Even when young Americans do find jobs, they are having a harder time supporting themselves and their families. There are many differences between today's young adults and those who entered the work force during the 1970s.

More young workers make low wages: The proportion of all hourly workers between the ages of 20 and 24 who earned less than $4.50 per hour (in 1986 dollars) nearly tripled from 1979 to 1986. There are two major causes of this trend. The federal minimum wage has not been increased since 1981. And roughly 85 percent of all new jobs created in the United States since 1979 have been in the lowest-paying industries: retail trade and personal, business, and health services.

More young men cannot support even a small family: As a result of falling wages and employment rates, young men's annual earnings have plunged. Between 1973 and 1986, the median earnings of men in their early twenties plummeted 26 percent. The median earnings of young male high school dropouts declined even more sharply—by 42 percent.

Falling earnings make it harder for young men to support a family. In 1973, nearly two out of every three men ages 20 to 24 who had not finished high school earned enough to lift a family of three out of poverty. By 1986, only one out of three did. Young men with high school diplomas also lost economic ground during that period: the share with earnings at or above the three-person poverty level dropped from 76 percent to 57 percent.

As wages fall, marriage rates sink and the proportion of births that are out-of-wedlock rise: Young men who earn enough to lift at least a small family out of poverty are three to four times more likely to be married than those who

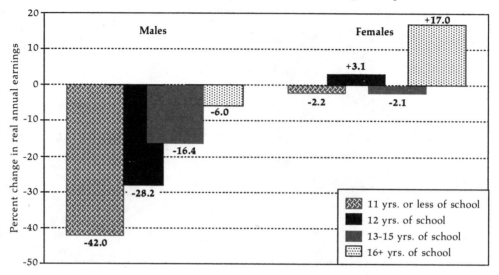

EARNINGS BY EDUCATION

Percent Change From 1973 to 1986 in Annual Earnings of 20- to 24-Year-Olds
(Adjusted for Inflation) by Years of Schooling Completed[1]

Legend:
- 11 yrs. or less of school
- 12 yrs. of school
- 13-15 yrs. of school
- 16+ yrs. of school

Males: -42.0, -28.2, -16.4, -6.0

Females: -2.2, +3.1, -2.1, +17.0

• Young men's earnings have fallen sharply. Women's wages were lower to begin with, but young women without college education have barely held that ground.

[1]Subjects' major activity was not schooling at time of interview.

do not. As fewer young men have been able to bring home adequate earnings, their marriage rates have fallen by one-half. Not surprisingly, the proportion of births to women ages 20 to 24 that were out-of-wedlock has nearly tripled, jumping from 11 percent in 1973 to 29 percent in 1986.

Young women can rarely support a family alone: Women have always been paid dramatically less than their male counterparts and have had far less access to better-paying jobs. These historical realities persist. The average hourly wage for female workers in 1987 was equal to only 71 percent of that for male workers. All single-parent families, regardless of the gender of the head of household, face a much greater risk of living in poverty than married-couple families that have two possible incomes. This problem is compounded for female-headed families because women's wages are so low. Nearly three-fourths of all families headed by women younger than 25 were poor in 1986—a poverty rate that has risen substantially since 1973.

The Changed—and Harsher—Economic Landscape

Sweeping changes in the American economy since 1973 have caused the decline in the earnings of young workers. Those who lack strong basic academic skills are virtually shut out of any success in the job market.

The U.S. job market is changing: Today's industries and jobs are dramatically different from those that dominated the American economy just a few decades ago. Every day more young people don the various uniforms associated with jobs in the mushrooming service industries, but many of them

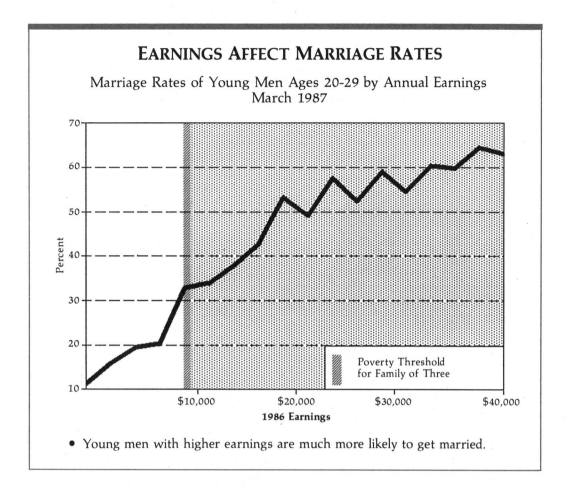

EARNINGS AFFECT MARRIAGE RATES

Marriage Rates of Young Men Ages 20-29 by Annual Earnings
March 1987

Poverty Threshold
for Family of Three

1986 Earnings

• Young men with higher earnings are much more likely to get married.

take home a minimum wage paycheck, lack the security of benefits such as health insurance, and can get only temporary or part-time work. Part-time employment is three times more prevalent in the growing service sector than in the declining goods-producing industries. Since 1979, changes in the job market have helped push up by one-half the proportion of workers younger than 25 who work part time because they cannot find full-time work.

As the manufacturing sector of our economy shrinks, so do young workers' hopes of earning a middle-class income by holding jobs that often require less skills and formal education but provide decent pay for physical strength, manual dexterity, or tolerance of unpleasant working conditions. Some of America's most prominent manufacturing industries have been hardest hit by the forces of economic change. The result has been the "silent firing" of a generation of young workers, according to Gordon Berlin and Andrew Sum in *Toward a More Perfect Union*, a 1988 report for the Ford Foundation. For example, only 1.26 million workers were employed in the automobile and basic steel industries in 1986, compared with 1.82 million in 1973. While more than one-third of all employed men ages 20 to 24 who had not gone on to college held manufacturing jobs in 1973, fewer than one-fourth did so in 1986.

As the manufacturing sector shrinks, job opportunities for less-educated young people are vanishing, particularly in our major cities. A study by John Kasarda of the University of North Carolina at Chapel Hill found that between 1970 and 1984 the number of jobs available to young people without a high school diploma declined by 34 percent in New York City, 39 percent in Baltimore, 43 percent in Philadelphia, and 45 percent in St. Louis.

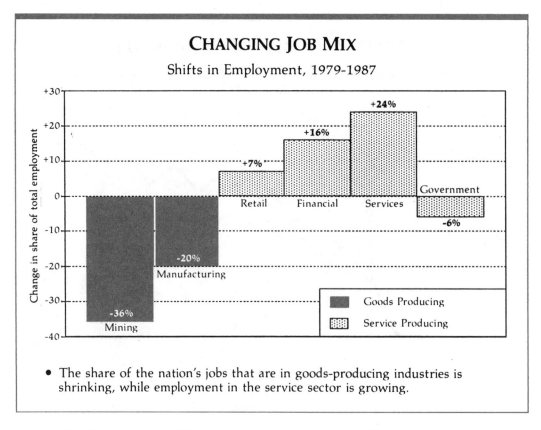

CHANGING JOB MIX

Shifts in Employment, 1979-1987

Change in share of total employment

+24% Services
+16% Financial
+7% Retail
Government
-6%
-20% Manufacturing
-36% Mining

Goods Producing
Service Producing

- The share of the nation's jobs that are in goods-producing industries is shrinking, while employment in the service sector is growing.

The disruption to the youngest and most vulnerable part of the nation's work force caused by these shifts has been exacerbated by government inaction.

The minimum wage is no longer a living wage: Almost 8 million young Americans, more than half of all hourly workers ages 16 to 24, are employed at or near the minimum wage. Young people are dependent on a fair minimum wage to support a family in decency. Yet despite eight years of inflation, the minimum wage has not been increased since 1981, the longest period without an adjustment since it was first established in 1938.

The government's failure to make sure the minimum wage has kept up with the cost of living has meant that workers earning the minimum wage have

The Job Corps Pays Off

Participants in the federally funded Jobs Corps come from very poor households, enter the training program with an average sixth-grade reading level, and often have prior arrest records. Yet the Job Corps record is impressive: every $1 the Job Corps spends returns $1.45 to society in increased employment, earnings, school completion rates, and reduced crime and welfare costs. The Job Corps success formula combines basic education, vocational training, and counseling with a residential program offering housing, food, and medical attention.

Most Job Corps centers are successful public/private partnerships, operated by major private employers to ensure that the vocational training is closely tied to job opportunities in the private sector.

seen nearly 30 percent of their purchasing power erode during the past eight years. A full-time, year-round, minimum wage worker now earns only 71 percent of what is necessary to support a family of three at the poverty line.

Job training misses the mark for many youths: The federal government's major employment and training program for disadvantaged youths and adults, the Job Training Partnership Act (JTPA), fails to help those who need it most. The act prohibits using federal funds to create paid work opportunities for young people, even when unsubsidized jobs are not otherwise available. And JTPA's heavy emphasis on immediate results makes it extremely difficult for local agencies to help young people who need long-term or intensive remedial education and vocational training. The average JTPA program for youths lasts only 18 weeks, at a cost of $1,800 to $2,000 per participant, an investment too short and too meager to make a lasting difference for most low-skilled or poor youths.

Programs Prepare Young People for the World of Work

Harlem program meets two needs at once. Youths who need jobs are being put to work building desperately needed low-income housing, thanks to East Harlem's Youth Action Program. For nearly a decade, poor and minority youths have worked in carefully supervised teams, learning the construction trade while improving their academic skills. Funded by New York City from local tax revenues, the program builds participants' self-esteem and leadership skills by giving them responsibility for structuring and operating the program.

Education and job training in a downtown department store. Rich's Academy in an Atlanta, Georgia, department store is an alternative school for high school dropouts and potential dropouts. Special coordinators work with students on an individualized basis to connect them with appropriate city and county services and jobs. Students also get instruction in English, math, and social studies, along with counseling. Rich's contributes space, utilities, and telephone services for the academy as well as employment opportunities in the store.

Texas helps community agencies bolster basic skills. Local agencies serving Texas youths can turn to Texas BASICS for assistance in meeting their educational needs. Established by the state as a nonprofit corporation, the Texas Basic Skills Investment Corporation works with more than 40 learning centers to implement the Comprehensive Competencies Program (CCP). The CCP program is a model that tailors learning to individual needs and pacing. Texas BASICS also seeks to stimulate the creation of new CCP learning centers by building linkages with the federally funded summer employment program and the Texas Department of Education.

A Federal and State Action Agenda

In 1989 the federal government should:

- **Target federal job training funds more effectively.** A portion of the funds now available under JTPA should be invested in more intensive remedial education and long-term vocational training for young people for whom the services of the current program are not enough. The federal government should earmark a portion of JTPA funds to support preapprenticeships and other structured training programs that move noncollege-bound young people into clearly defined career paths with opportunities for advancement. At the same time, it should provide the flexibility such programs need so they can pay for child care, stipends, and other support services to keep youths in training. To reinforce this effort, the Job Corps program should be expanded to enable it to open new centers and serve more young people.

Over the next five years the federal government should:

- **Help expand a network of locally based community learning centers.** To supplement the efforts of our public schools, we need to create a widespread network of community centers—in youth-serving agencies, alternative schools, churches, public housing projects, recreational centers, libraries, and other community facilities—that can strengthen the basic academic skills of young people in out-of-school settings. The centers should be available both to reinforce public school education during after-school hours and summer months (the latter in conjunction with the federal summer youth employment program for teenagers) and to provide alternative education options for school dropouts. Building on but substantially expanding the efforts of existing youth-serving agencies, funds would be available to a wide range of locally based groups to help them provide effective, personalized instruction so youths acquire the skills demanded by today's work place.

- **Guarantee help for noncollege-bound youths seeking training.** Low-income youths who enroll in college now receive at least some financial help through federal and state student aid programs. In contrast, our society does nothing to help many of those young people who seek to move directly from high school into the labor market—the group called the "forgotten half" of American youth in a recent report by the William T. Grant Foundation Commission on Work, Family and Citizenship. Yet these noncollege-bound young Americans are the ones who need the most help to cope with a changing economy.

  As a first step, the federal government should support large-scale demonstration projects such as the Fair Chance proposal developed by the Grant Commission. These demonstrations would test the feasibility of community-based efforts guaranteeing remedial education, vocational training, and work experience to all noncollege-bound youths needing assistance. These experiments also should test varying ways for young people to earn opportunities for advanced training or job placements, thereby providing clear incentives and rewards for individual effort and achievement.

- **Restore the value of the minimum wage.** To make sure that young workers can earn enough to support themselves and their families, the minimum wage must be adjusted to compensate for the inroads of inflation since 1981. Modest steps consistent with past increases would raise the minimum wage to at least $4.55 per hour over the next three years. Over the longer term, the minimum wage must be pegged to an established percentage of the nation's average hourly wage and adjusted annually to prevent dramatic erosion of its real value.

In 1989 each state should:

- **Build alliances between schools and employers.** Programs that provide counseling, peer support, and job placement assistance to high school juniors and seniors cost little and accomplish much to help noncollege-bound youths make the transition directly from school to work. Jobs for America's Graduates provides one promising approach. These steps to ease the transition into the work force are particularly important for poor and minority teenagers, who seldom have access to the informal family and community networks through which many middle-class youths find jobs with a future.

Over the next five years each state should:

- **Expand youth conservation and service corps programs.** Thirteen states already operate such programs on a year-round basis, putting unemployed youths to work in valuable projects within state parks or their own communities. Corps members typically work in closely supervised teams, learning new job skills while also participating in remedial education programs to improve their basic academic skills. All states should launch similar efforts, providing paid work experience for youths and tackling projects that address state and community needs.

- **Strengthen opportunities for out-of-school learning.** States can play an important role in helping community agencies develop effective education programs, both by training staff in the best approaches to individualized instruction and by making it possible to obtain necessary equipment and materials. States can also work to avoid the fragmentation or duplication of services that occurs when such activities are funded under diverse federal or state programs.

- **Allow school districts to pass along state funds to alternative educational programs.** Most states stop making their per-pupil expenditures for education when a student drops out of the regular public school. By doing so, they halt their investment in the very young people who most desperately need educational assistance. As an alternative, all states should follow the example of such states as California, Oregon, and Colorado, which allow schools to transfer a dropout's per-pupil allotment to community agencies when he or she enrolls in an alternative education program that meets certain standards.

ADOLESCENT PREGNANCY PREVENTION

In the year 2000, the 1,804,000 girls who are nine years old in 1989 will celebrate their twentieth birthday. If current trends continue, more than two out of five will have been pregnant at least once, and one in every five already will have become a parent. And hundreds of thousands of their male contemporaries will have fathered a child.

These young mothers' life prospects will be bleak. At current rates:

- Only six in 10 will have a high school diploma, compared with nine in 10 of their peers who delayed parenthood.

- More than one in three will have such low-level reading and math skills that they will be able to get only low-paying jobs, if they can get jobs at all.

- Almost one in five of these mothers will have not one, but two or more children.

- More than than four out of five of these 20-year-old parents will be unmarried if recent trends toward greater rates of out-of-wedlock childbearing continue. The vast majority of these unmarried mothers will be poor, which means their children will be at increased risk of later becoming teen parents themselves, placing yet another generation at risk.

Early childbearing has serious implications for the future of young parents and their children. But it is not merely a personal issue. By depriving the country of educated, productive workers, too-early parenthood also has serious implications for the nation's economic future.

To avoid losing productive workers, the nation must make sure by the year 2000 that every teenager—male and female—has both the means and the reasons to delay parenthood. Teens who do become parents also need help establishing strong, self-sufficient families so that their lives and those of their children will improve.

The High Price of Teen Pregnancy and Parenthood

In 1986 there were roughly 1 million pregnancies and almost half a million births among women younger than 20. Most of the pregnancies were unintended. While 18- and 19-year-old girls accounted for nearly two-thirds of the births, 179,000 births were to girls age 17 and younger, and 10,000 were to girls 14 and younger.

Teenage parenthood is not a new phenomenon; it is age-old, and the phenomenon has in fact declined in the United States in recent decades. The teen birth rate (the number of births per 1,000 teenage girls) decreased sharply in the 1970s and has remained fairly stable in the 1980s. In 1970, for example, there were 68.3 births per 1,000 young women ages 15 to 19. By 1986 this rate had fallen to 50.6 births per 1,000 young women.

What has changed for the worse, however, are the rates at which two-parent families are forming and the severity of the economic consequences of too-early parenting:

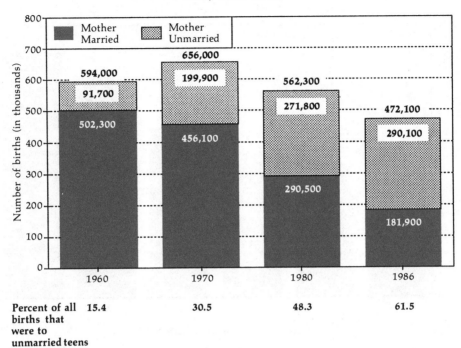

BIRTHS AND MARRIAGES

Births to Mothers Younger Than 20 by Marital Status, U.S., 1960-1986

	1960	1970	1980	1986
Total	594,000	656,000	562,300	472,100
Mother Unmarried	91,700	199,900	271,800	290,100
Mother Married	502,300	456,100	290,500	181,900
Percent of all births that were to unmarried teens	15.4	30.5	48.3	61.5

- After peaking in 1970, the number of births to teens has declined steadily. But the proportion of teen births that are to unmarried teens has been growing fast.
- In 1960, 15.4 percent of all teen births were to unmarried teens. By 1970, the proportion had doubled. By 1986 it doubled again.

Source: National Center for Health Statistics. Calculations by Children's Defense Fund.

- Many teen parents cannot compete for permanent jobs that pay decent wages. In this country's technologically sophisticated economy, the lack of at least a high school diploma is an increasingly serious barrier to economic self-sufficiency. Since the 1960s, the earning power of high school dropouts has fallen 22 percent in relation to the earning power of graduates. Yet half of all young women who give birth before age 18 do not obtain a high school diploma by their mid-twenties, and a disproportionate number of young fathers drop out of school as well.

- Many teen mothers raise their children alone. Marriage rates among all teens, including pregnant teens and teenage mothers, have fallen in recent decades. For example, the proportion of teen girls 15 to 19 years old who had ever been married fell by three-fifths between 1960 and 1984, from 16 percent to about 7 percent.

   This decline in teen marriages is in turn related to the increase in out-of-wedlock births. In 1960 only 15 percent of all teen births were to unmarried

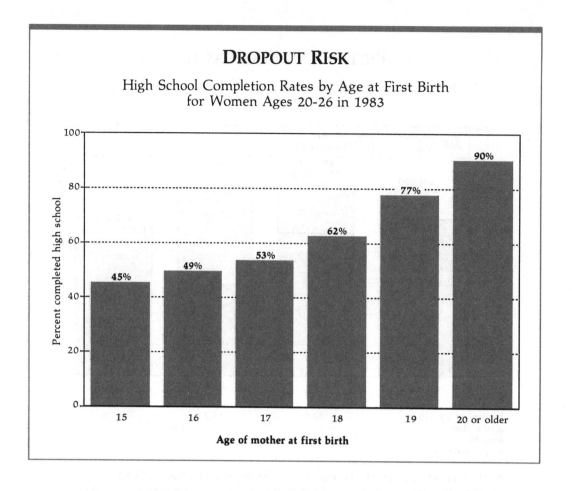

DROPOUT RISK

High School Completion Rates by Age at First Birth
for Women Ages 20-26 in 1983

Percent completed high school

45% — 15
49% — 16
53% — 17
62% — 18
77% — 19
90% — 20 or older

Age of mother at first birth

mothers. By 1970 this proportion had doubled to about 30 percent, and by 1986 it had doubled again to more than 60 percent.

The decline in marriages has been due in part to the diminished earnings prospects of young men. Young men with low earnings are far less likely to be married than are their peers with higher earnings, perhaps because they are bad marriage prospects. The median earnings of young men have fallen substantially since the early 1970s.

- Early childbearing often spells poverty. Becoming a parent too soon is not simply a temporary disruption in a teen's life. It often means a long-term—and often losing—struggle against poverty. Because the wages of young workers have dropped significantly since 1973, two incomes are increasingly necessary to maintain a young family above the poverty line. From 1973 to 1986 the median earnings of family heads younger than 25 with children fell from $15,049 to $6,000 (in 1986 dollars).

Furthermore, the inadequate education and low wages of young parents, combined with the fact that they are more likely to be unmarried than earlier generations of young parents, restricts young families' future economic prospects far more severely than in the past. In 1987, two-thirds of all children younger than three who lived in families headed by a parent younger than 22 were poor.

Profile of Teens At Risk of Early Parenthood

Teen pregnancy and parenthood are problems that afflict all groups in our society—rich and poor; black, white, and Hispanic; urban and rural populations. In fact, two-thirds of teen births occur to nonpoor teens, two-thirds occur to white teens, and two-thirds occur to teens who do not live in big cities.

Nonetheless, even though they do not account for the majority of teen births, disadvantaged teens are disproportionately likely to fall into the trap of early parenthood. Their academic and nonacademic failure and their severely limited prospects for a successful work life mean they perceive very little hope of

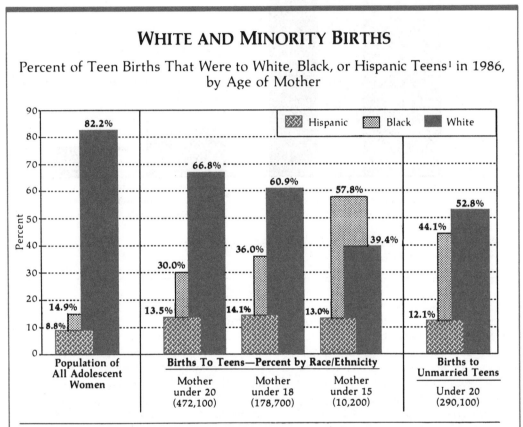

WHITE AND MINORITY BIRTHS

Percent of Teen Births That Were to White, Black, or Hispanic Teens[1] in 1986, by Age of Mother

[1]Note that percentages will add to more than 100 percent because Hispanics can be of either racial group.

Source: National Center for Health Statistics. Calculations by Children's Defense Fund.

becoming full participants in society. Without a vision or hope of a future, they are likely to lack the reasons or the desire to delay parenthood.

There is an established relationship between poverty, limited schooling and life options, and early parenthood. In fact, poverty and low basic academic skills appear to be the key factors that account for the higher rates of early childbearing among minority teens. White, black, or Hispanic, about one of every five teenagers (ages 16 to 19) with below-average basic academic skills and from families with incomes below the poverty level is a parent. In contrast, only about one of every 20 teens in the same age group who have average or better skills and family incomes above the poverty level is a parent, regardless of race or ethnicity. Nonetheless, because they face a much higher risk of being poor and

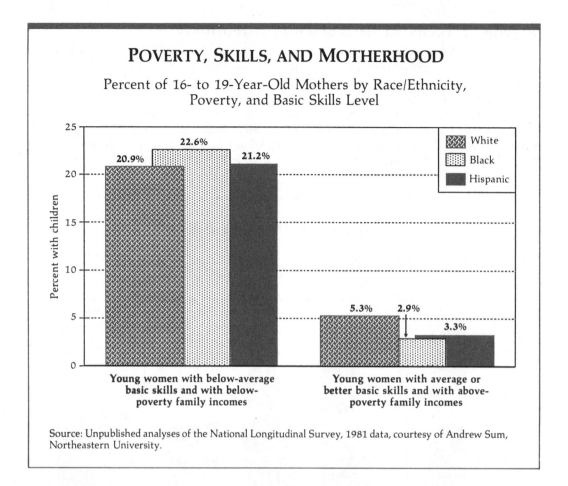

POVERTY, SKILLS, AND MOTHERHOOD

Percent of 16- to 19-Year-Old Mothers by Race/Ethnicity,
Poverty, and Basic Skills Level

Source: Unpublished analyses of the National Longitudinal Survey, 1981 data, courtesy of Andrew Sum, Northeastern University.

having lower academic skills, minority teens face a higher than average risk of pregnancy and parenthood.

The nation pays a high price, which is steadily mounting, for leaving millions of young people vulnerable to the risk of early parenthood. As the work force ages, society becomes increasingly dependent on each young worker. By the year 2000, the number of 18- to 24-year-olds will have decreased almost 20 percent from its peak in 1980, and the proportion of young workers that are minorities—and are at greatest risk of early parenthood—will have increased to almost one in three.

To maintain a healthy economy, the United States needs every person in this shrinking pool of young workers to be a fully productive member of society. It is imperative to break the wasteful cycle of poverty, inadequate skills, early parenthood, and new families in poverty that is so typical among children who grow up without dreams of a successful future.

Roadblocks to Preventing Teen Pregnancy

Too little help: This society fails to give teenagers the information and services they need to avoid too-early sexual activity, pregnancy, and parenthood. All teens—male and female—need easy and timely access to information, counseling, and health services to help them either delay sexual activity or be responsible sexual partners if they are sexually active. Data show that this need cannot be ignored:

- Sexual activity among U.S. teenagers increased by 43 percent between 1971 and 1982, although it appears to be leveling off. Consequently, more teens are now at risk of early parenthood than in earlier generations.

- Although a majority of big-city school systems studied in 1982 offered some form of sex education, only one-fifth devoted as much as one class period before the ninth grade to such topics as sexual decision making. Only one-tenth allowed that much time to be spent on the topic of contraception.

- Only one-half of sexually active teen girls use contraception.

- Despite generally similar rates of sexual activity among teenagers in the United States, England, France, and Canada, pregnancy rates for U.S. teens are twice as high as those for teens in the other countries.

- Adolescent boys are often left out of pregnancy prevention strategies, despite their higher rates of sexual activity and lower levels of knowledge about pregnancy risk and contraceptive use. The double standard regarding acceptable sexual behavior is one of the most serious roadblocks to encouraging teens to delay sexual activity and pregnancy.

There is no national policy that attempts to cope with these realities, nor is there a national attitude that would foster the development of such a policy. On the contrary, recent federal efforts to delay early parenthood, including the Adolescent Family Life Act, have been limited to policies that encourage sexual abstinence for avoiding pregnancy and adoption for dealing with unplanned babies. These desirable approaches cannot by themselves prevent widespread teen pregnancy and parenthood.

An essential prevention strategy for those teens who are already sexually active—access to contraceptive services and counseling—has suffered in the 1980s. Federal funds for the Title X Family Planning Program, which is the major source of money for family planning services and serves many teens, has been reduced significantly. The Reagan Administration also sought to limit teenagers' access to contraceptive services by challenging confidentiality requirements, the eligibility of service providers, and the kinds of services providers may offer. While some states have moved to fill these gaps in contraceptive services—as well as to expand access to family life education—the extent and quality of state-level efforts vary widely.

Too little hope: The United States fails to give millions of teens the essential ingredient they need to delay parenthood: hope for a better future. In order to believe they have a reasonable chance for a successful and self-sufficient adulthood, teens must receive a range of services and experiences:

- Education that builds basic academic skills, and remedial instruction that takes over when schools have failed.

- Employment-related experience and skills, including access to job training programs and specific help in finding entry-level positions.

- Access to comprehensive health care services that include preventive care and mental health services.

Programs in these areas are currently too few in number, too narrow in scope, and too fragmented to give poor teenagers a sense of having good options for the future.

But even at their best, these services would not be enough. Too many teens lack adult supervision, positive role models, and productive activities. They have too few chances to experience success, either inside or outside of school. Disadvantaged teens, in particular, need after-school and summer programs

State, Local, and Private Initiatives Give Teens Hope

- **Providing teens with a range of preventive services.** In New Jersey's schools, help is available to 13- to 19-year-old students who are at risk of dropping out, becoming pregnant, using drugs, developing mental illness, or other problems. The state's School-Based Youth Services Program offers young people all the health, education, and social support services they may need. Implemented in 1988, the program now operates in 29 school districts at sites located in or near schools and is managed by a variety of community-based agencies.

- **Helping teen parents beat the odds.** Pregnant and parenting teens get continuous case management and support services through California's Teenage Pregnancy and Parenting (TAPP) project. Begun in 1981 in San Francisco and Lawndale, California, TAPP coordinates the participation of more than 48 different agencies to make sure young mothers and fathers have access to all the health, education, and social services for which they are eligible. In San Francisco, 60 percent of the teens enrolled in TAPP were still in school six months after the birth of their children, compared with 20 percent for California's teen parents in general. The program is being replicated through the State Department of Health in 29 locations.

- **Giving teens an academic boost.** Fourteen- and 15-year-olds who are failing in school have an opportunity to improve their chances in life through the Summer Training and Education Program (STEP), sponsored by Public/Private Ventures, a nonprofit Philadelphia-based research and evaluation corporation. Demonstration sites were set up in Boston, Massachusetts; Fresno and San Diego, California; Seattle, Washington; and Portland, Oregon. Day-to-day management and operation of STEP is the joint responsibility of schools, businesses, and community organizations. Participants work at summer jobs in addition to receiving remedial education and instruction in life skills, including issues of sexuality and parenthood. For three consecutive years, STEP students have improved their math and reading scores. STEP programs at 66 sites are planned for the 1989-1990 school year.

that provide varied opportunities for learning and success. They also need to interact with adult mentors and role models. As yet, the nation has developed no strategy for meeting the enormous nonacademic, nonjob-related needs of poor teenagers. And while some local programs do address these needs, their scope is still severely limited.

Too little support for teen parents: When teen parents are neglected, the nation invites long-term poverty among young families. Pregnancy and birth immediately increase teen parents' need for economic and social supports: health care, child care, transportation assistance, special school arrangements, remedial education, and job training. Without such services, many young parents will find it difficult, if not impossible, to become self-sufficient and support their children.

Some states and localities have programs that provide teen parents with comprehensive services or coordinate service delivery. However, these programs typically have little funding stability and serve only a small proportion of the teen parents who need help.

Federal and state concern about teenage parents too often has focused solely on young mothers who receive welfare assistance. A far wider range of teen parents needs help. And even the programs for families on welfare must address the wide range of young parents' individual needs and be realistic; strategies to improve young parents' long-term earning capacity must be comprehensive and include education and remediation, child care, personal supports, and other support services, as well as job training and employment.

A Federal and State Action Agenda

In 1989 the federal government should:

- **Invest in programs that build the academic and work place skills of disadvantaged youths.** Because early parenthood is only one of a number of risks faced by young people who have no dreams for their future, efforts are best focused on prevention services that help disadvantaged teens avoid the many pitfalls of adolescence. The federal government should provide funds to support a network of locally based community learning centers to strengthen young people's basic academic skills after school, on weekends, and during the summer. The centers also would serve dropouts and young high school graduates not going on to college who need to build their skills.

  At the same time, to give disadvantaged teens the full range of supports they need, the federal government should support a set of demonstration projects that provide comprehensive services to youths. These projects should either provide or coordinate a broad array of preventive services that includes at least a core of key elements: life skills education, arts and recreation, tutoring and academic enrichment, comprehensive health services, volunteer and community service, group counseling, and job readiness and job training. Projects should provide assessments, referrals, and follow-up on services that are not provided on site. Priority should be given to projects that offer preventive services after school and during the summer.

  Over the next five years the federal government should:

- **Fund model programs that provide supervised service opportunities to young adolescents.** During the crucial early adolescent years, many students who are not doing well in school begin to drift away from school and into trouble. Opportunities for service to others can be the grounding experiences that keep these young students in school, bolstering their self-esteem and helping them understand the importance of learning. The federal government should support structured, school-linked opportunities for volunteer service to young adolescents in junior high school and even in the late elementary grades. Poor and minority youths and students of all incomes and backgrounds who are not doing well in school should be priority candidates for these programs, not as recipients of services, but as volunteers.

- **Increase access to family planning services.** To assist sexually active teens to delay pregnancy, the federal government must immediately reauthorize the Title X Family Planning Program, which served more than 5 million low-income women in 1987. The government should reverse nearly a decade of cuts and inflation erosion by increasing Title X funding during this five-year period so that its 1994 funding and services are equal to its 1981 funding and service levels.

- **Expand services to teen parents.** Congress should enact legislation—similar to that introduced in the 100th Congress—to create a new set of service projects for teen parents. This legislation should reflect what demonstration projects have identified as the necessary range of comprehensive services teen parents need to be self-sufficient and to ensure a good start in life for their children. New legislation should encourage parental participation in the programs and strong evaluation components to test the efficacy of varying approaches.

In 1989 each state should:

- **Improve the quality and availability of family life and life skills education.** State departments of education should develop and assure implementation of guidelines for program content, teacher selection and training, and program evaluation. Courses should offer instruction and counseling in interpersonal relations, human sexuality and development, and decision making. Family life education should be available in every school district in the state.

Over the next five years each state should:

- **Coordinate services to teen parents and teens at risk of early parenthood.** Each state should establish a mechanism to coordinate the funding and delivery of services to prevent teen pregnancy and of services to teen parents and their children. Representatives from all public agencies serving teens, as well as representatives from county and city governments should participate to ensure joint planning, funding, and staffing of programs. Such entities should oversee joint data collection and documentation of the effectiveness of various approaches in serving teen parents and teens vulnerable to early parenthood.

- **Fund local efforts to improve services for youths.** States should provide incentive grants to communities to develop preventive support services such as after-school and summer programs, counseling, preventive case management, recreation programs, and opportunities for community service.

- **Provide educational opportunities for young parents.** Each state should make alternative education, adult education, and vocational education more responsive to young parents' educational needs. These programs should be expanded to accommodate all young parents who do not have a high school diploma or a GED. In addition, states should develop special outreach and tuition support programs to enable teen parents with high school diplomas to enroll in higher education. All education programs should include child care and the other supportive services young parents need in order to participate.

YOUNG FAMILIES

As the nation approaches the year 2000, a growing number of America's young families—those headed by a person younger than 30—face very bleak prospects. Between 1973 and 1986 the median income of young families with children fell by 26 percent. If current trends continue, with young families lagging further behind the rest of society even during periods of economic growth, very large numbers of young families will have a harder time getting established economically than earlier generations. Fewer young families will be able to look forward to achieving the standard of living that the average American family once took for granted.

The consequences for children are enormous. Since a majority of America's children are born into and spend crucial early developmental years in young families, their well-being is threatened directly by falling incomes and rising poverty rates.

Demographic trends suggest that even tougher times lie ahead for young families. If the proportion of young families headed by single parents continues to rise at the pace of the past two decades, only three out of five young families will be headed by a married couple in the year 2000. Only slightly more than half of all children in young families would be living with two parents. Even if economic prospects for young workers do not worsen, this demographic shift by itself would raise the poverty rate for young families by one-fourth, to 27 percent in the year 2000.

Vital, productive young families are essential to this nation's future. As providers and caregivers for the majority of the youngest and most vulnerable children, young families are the cradle of the next generation of Americans. The strengths and weaknesses of young families will determine in large part whether this new generation grows into good citizens, workers, and parents.

To build a strong future, this nation must reinvigorate efforts to see that every young family has the opportunity and the means to secure an adequate income and provide for its children.

Economic Disaster Has Struck America's Young Families

In the past, most young families have struggled when starting out. But the struggle for many of today's young parents has become more desperate. The 26 percent drop in median family income that young families with children experienced between 1973 and 1986 was virtually identical to the 27 percent drop in per capita personal income that occurred for the country as a whole from 1929, the last year before the Depression, to 1933, the worst year. Nearly three-fourths of the income decline for young families took place during the 1980s.

While older, more established families have been holding their ground, income losses have hit almost all types of young families. The major exception has been young families without children. The median income of such childless families rose slightly during the 1973-1986 period. Other groups of young families have seen their incomes (and their hopes) diminish.

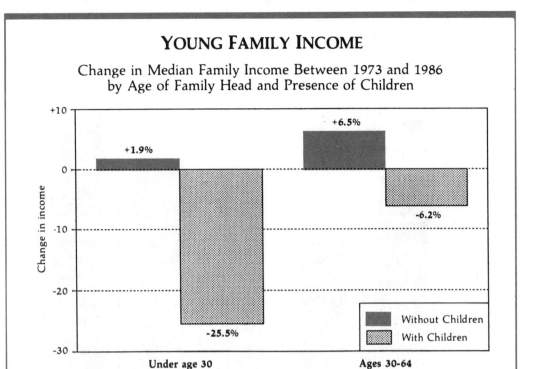

YOUNG FAMILY INCOME

Change in Median Family Income Between 1973 and 1986
by Age of Family Head and Presence of Children

- Young families without children enjoyed a slight increase in median family income between 1973 and 1986, while the income of young families with children plunged by more than one-fourth.

Young married-couple families: The median income of young married-couple families with children fell by 8 percent between 1973 and 1986, even though many women went to work during this period in order to make up for the drop in their husbands' earnings. While sending a second earner into the work force or increasing that earner's hours of employment was a partially successful strategy for married couples for staunching income losses, the increased child care costs they incurred meant their effective income loss was considerably greater than 8 percent. As their incomes have declined, these young couples have found it increasingly difficult to shoulder rising housing and child care costs.

Single-parent families: The median income of young female-headed families plunged by 26 percent between 1973 and 1986. Young single mothers are virtually shut out of the job market: their median annual earnings from employment were only $1,560 in 1986. Reductions in public assistance payments also were a major factor in these income losses.

Young black and Hispanic families: Since 1973 the median income of young minority families has plummeted—by more than one-fourth for young black families and by one-sixth for young Hispanic families. As a result, the income gap between young white and young minority families has widened.

Young families whose heads have the least education: This group's income drops have been the steepest. The median income of young families headed by high school dropouts fell by more than one-third between 1973 and 1986. A high school diploma, however, is no longer an adequate defense against declining income. Families headed by high school graduates not going on to college lost one-sixth of their median income. In contrast, the median income of young families headed by college graduates rose slightly during this period.

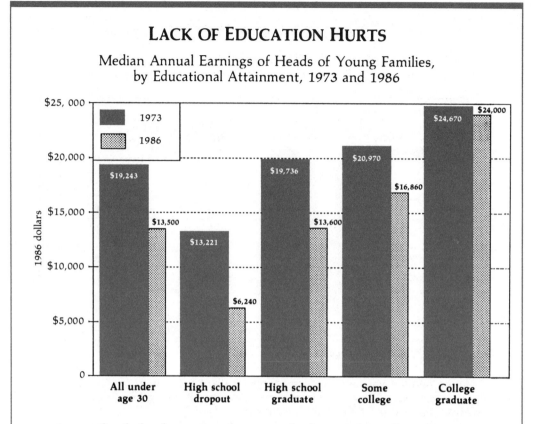

LACK OF EDUCATION HURTS

Median Annual Earnings of Heads of Young Families, by Educational Attainment, 1973 and 1986

Legend:
- 1973
- 1986

1986 dollars

	All under age 30	High school dropout	High school graduate	Some college	College graduate
1973	$19,243	$13,221	$19,736	$20,970	$24,670
1986	$13,500	$6,240	$13,600	$16,860	$24,000

• Among family heads younger than 30, only those with a college degree were shielded from very large earnings losses between 1973 and 1986. By 1986 the median earnings of these graduates ($24,000) were four times greater than those of young family heads who were high school dropouts ($6,240), whereas in 1973 they were less than double.

Families' Income Losses Are Taking a High Toll

High poverty rates: Poverty among young families with children almost doubled between 1973 and 1986. Poverty rates rose in every region of the country and among all groups of young families—whether white, black, or Hispanic; whether one- or two-parent. The greatest increases in poverty, however, were for young families headed by those with the least education.

Grim consequences for children have followed the declining incomes of young families. Thirty-five percent of all children living in young families were poor in 1986. If this high poverty rate prevailed among all Americans, 83 million people would have been poor in 1986, rather than the 32 million who actually were.

Lack of health insurance: Children in young families are considerably less likely to have health insurance than other Americans. More than one out of five children in young families had no health insurance in 1986. Their parents are often uninsured as well. Young adults between 18 and 24 years old have been found to be the least likely of any age group to be covered by private health insurance, according to 1984 data from the National Center for Health Statistics. The proportion of births to young women who had received no prenatal care or care late in their pregnancies rose substantially during the decade from 1976 to 1986.

FAMILY POVERTY

Percentages of All Families Living in Poverty by Age of Family Head

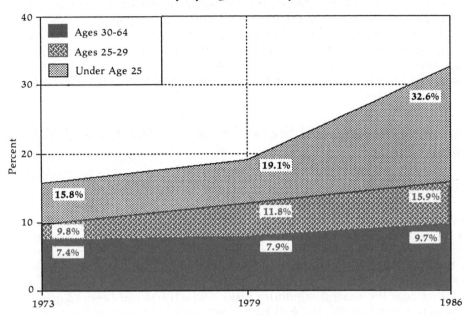

- While poverty rates have risen for all families, poverty among young families has increased dramatically, especially during the 1980s, often rising even when overall economic conditions were improving. The poverty rate for all young families with heads younger than 30 jumped from 12 percent in 1973 to 22 percent in 1986.

POVERTY RATES

Poverty Rates Among Young Families (1973 and 1986)

	1973	1986
All young families	12.3%	21.6%
Families with children	16.1%	30.1%
Families without children	4.9%	4.4%
Married couple	5.4%	9.2%
Female-headed	56.5%	62.6%
White, non-Hispanic	8.0%	15.2%
Black, non-Hispanic	35.0%	45.6%
Hispanic	24.2%	33.6%
High school dropout	28.5%	46.4%
High school graduate	9.3%	20.5%
Some college	6.3%	9.9%
College graduate	1.7%	2.5%

Housing difficulties: Housing has become an ever-greater problem for young families as home purchase costs and rents have skyrocketed and incomes have dropped. The rent burden—median rent as a proportion of median income—for households headed by persons younger than 25 increased by one-half between 1974 and 1987. These increases were especially severe for young families with children. For example, the average rent burden for single parents younger than 25 rose to an alarming 81 percent of their median income.

An important part of the American dream—owning a home—is now out of the question for many young families. In 1973 it took 23 percent of the median income of a young family with children to carry a new mortgage on an average priced house. By 1986 that figure more than doubled to 51 percent.

Sweeping Economic and Social Changes Have Caused Young Families' Plight

The disaster that has afflicted young families is rooted in both economic and social change.

Real wages are declining: Lower hourly wages (rather than increased unemployment) accounted for more than 90 percent of the lost annual earnings between 1979 and 1986 among employed men who headed young married-couple families. Workers took home smaller paychecks as employment shifted from the manufacturing industries to the lower paying service sector. Buying power also eroded with the sharp drop in the earnings of those whose hourly pay is at or near the federal minimum wage—which has not been adjusted since 1981 despite rising living costs. Full-time, year-round employment at the minimum wage now yields earnings that leave a family of three nearly 30 percent below the federal poverty line.

Single-parent families are increasing in numbers: Families headed by single women typically have incomes far less than those of two-parent families, in part because they rarely have a second wage earner to help support the children. In the past two decades the proportion of female-headed young families has increased—a major contributor to rising poverty among young families.

One significant factor driving this demographic shift, however, is economic change. Income declines among America's young workers create a vicious cycle that discourages family formation. Young men who do not earn enough to support at least a small family above the federal poverty line are only one-third to one-fourth as likely to marry in their early twenties as those who do. The earnings of young men fell sharply between 1973 and 1986, and this contributed substantially to their one-third drop in marriage rates in that period. As a result, the proportion of births to young women that were out-of-wedlock nearly doubled, leading to more poverty.

A Federal and State Action Agenda

The task of halting the economic deterioration of young families is complex and requires sustained action on many fronts.

As a first step, in 1989 the federal government should:

- **Enable more young parents to work and reward them more adequately for their efforts.** A three-pronged strategy of helping families find and pay for decent child care, raising wages, and giving income assistance through the tax code would go a long way to ease the plight of young families.

  An increase in the nation's supply of safe, quality, affordable child care will make it possible for more young parents to hold jobs and increase their hours of work, and thus boost their family incomes. Child care help also will free up more of lower income young families' resources for necessities such as food and shelter. The assistance that the Act for Better Child Care would give to lower income families would begin to cushion the shock felt by those with the lowest earnings and growing child care expenses.

Working longer hours and getting child care help will not solve the whole problem, however, unless the work is compensated at levels comparable to those paid to earlier generations of young workers. To do this it is necessary to increase the federal minimum wage, which has lost more than one-fourth of its real value since it was last raised in 1981. Congress should begin by raising the minimum wage from its current $3.35 per hour to $4.55 per hour over three years, with the first step in 1989. From then on, the minimum wage should be adjusted each year to keep pace with average pay levels for all hourly workers.

The third necessary piece is to provide families with children greater income help through the tax code. This can be accomplished through such mechanisms as adjusting the Earned Income Tax Credit for family size and establishing a children's tax credit.

Over the next five years the federal government should:

- **Expand successful programs to help disadvantaged children and youths build skills.** Disadvantaged children and young people need targeted help to become productive, self-sufficient adults and to avert future economic losses. These programs include Head Start, Chapter 1 compensatory education, the Job Corps, and targeted higher education programs such as Pell grants.

- **Repair the safety net for young families.** In addition to improving tax credits for low-income working families, the federal government must extend Medicaid coverage to all pregnant women and children with incomes of less than 200 percent of the federal poverty level and increase basic federal welfare benefits to levels that more adequately reflect the cost of raising a family. Each of these is particularly helpful to struggling young families with small children, which disproportionately rely upon such assistance for survival.

In 1989 state and local governments should:

- **Enter partnerships with the private sector that build stronger bridges from school to work.** The job prospects of noncollege-bound youths can be boosted if programs follow successful models that combine counseling, peer support, and job placement efforts while the youths are in high school. Such programs, already in place in more than a dozen states, cost relatively little and yet have proven effective in raising employment rates and subsequent earnings of high school graduates, particularly among poor and minority youths.

During the next five years each state should:

- **Help boost college enrollments of poor and minority youths.** Programs such as New York State's Liberty Scholarship Program open doors to college attendance for disadvantaged youths who are willing to stay in school and get a high school diploma. These programs provide clear incentives to high school students by guaranteeing tuition payments and providing funds for outreach, recruitment, and counseling efforts.

- **Expand access to essential health care.** To help the disproportionately uninsured population of young adults and their children, states should implement Medicaid options currently available and explore new ways to fill gaps between public and private health insurance coverage.

• **Help assure an adequate income for young families.** Vigorous child support enforcement and an increase in state AFDC benefits are two basic steps that states should take to help meet the basic needs of young families and their children. While preserving an adequate minimum wage is primarily a federal responsibility, states also have the option (already exercised by a dozen states) of raising the wage floor through state law to preserve the earnings of workers until Congress acts.

ESSENTIAL DATA ON AMERICA'S CHILDREN

U.S. CHILDREN IN THE WORLD

Fact Sheet of International Comparisons

Promoting Economic Security

- Sixty-seven industrialized nations, excluding the United States, provide a monthly or weekly cash benefit to families for every child regardless of income and work status of parents. Single mothers often receive additional assistance.

- Many European nations also provide maternity grants at the time of childbearing to assist with the cost of supplies and equipment for the new baby.

- The United States and South Africa are the only major industrialized nations that do not guarantee some form of job-protected maternity leave.

- Of 135 countries providing leave, 125 mandate paid leave. All European nations, and 81 percent of nations in Central America, the Caribbean, and South America, provide cash benefits during maternity leave. Japan provides 12 weeks for mothers at 60 percent of pay; France provides 16 weeks at full pay, and unpaid leave for up to two years for both mothers and fathers; Germany provides 14 weeks for mothers at full pay, and another 10 to 12 months at a reduced rate.

Maternal and Child Health

- The proportion of babies born at low birthweight in European democracies is approximately 4 percent, compared with 6.8 percent in the United States. Even when disaggregrated by race, the rate for U.S. whites (5.6 percent) is still substantially higher.

- Nearly 15 million American women of childbearing age have no private or government health insurance covering maternity. Each year, 555,000 women give birth without health insurance protection. Every year nearly one-fourth of all U.S. women do not receive early prenatal care. Unlike the United States, 10 European nations surveyed in 1987 all set uniform national standards for perinatal care. European nations take extra steps to ensure that pregnant women receive appropriate health care. In Germany, a mother's pass is issued at the first prenatal visit, entitling pregnant women to 10 perinatal visits and one at six weeks postpartum. Ninety-eight percent of pregnant women have a mother's pass at the time of delivery. In Britain, every newborn receives a home visit from a health care provider by the tenth day after birth. Regular visits continue and weekly child health clinics are available for the first five years of life.

- Although higher proportions of U.S. citizens lack access to health care, the United States spends a greater percentage of its gross national product (GNP) on health care. In 1983, the United States spent 10.7 percent of GNP on health care. France spent 8 percent, Ireland 7.4 percent, and Denmark 5.5 percent.

Source: U.S. House of Representatives, Select Committee on Children, Youth, and Families, "Children and Families: Public Policies and Outcomes. A Fact Sheet of International Comparisons," June 1988.

Child Poverty in Industrial Democracies

Of eight industrial democracies studied, the United States had the highest child poverty rate. An Urban Institute study used U.S. definitions of poverty and special methods to account for international exchange rates and varying welfare programs, looking at 1979 and 1982 data. Even though overall family incomes were higher in the United States, child poverty rates were higher and programs for the poor in the United States covered fewer people and provided lower benefits.

Children in Poverty

Country	Percentage of children living below: 75% of Poverty Line	Poverty Line
Switzerland	2.0%	5.1%
Sweden	2.2	5.1
Norway	2.7	7.6
West Germany	2.5	8.2
Canada	4.4	9.6
United Kingdom	3.8	10.7
Australia	7.3	16.9
United States	9.8	17.1

Source: Urban Institute, "Patterns of Income and Poverty: The Economic Status of Children and the Elderly in Eight Countries," by Timothy Smeeding, Barbara Boyle Torrey, and Martin Rein.

Since 1979 child poverty has climbed further in the United States. It was nearly 21 percent in 1987.

Selected List of Countries that Provide Universal Access to Health Care and a Basic Income Support System for Families with Children

Canada	Italy	Finland
France	Spain	Norway
West Germany	Japan	Netherlands
United Kingdom	Australia	Denmark
Sweden	Ireland	New Zealand

Source: U.S. Department of Health and Human Services, Social Security Administration, Office of Policy—Office of Research, Statistics, and International Policy, *Social Security Programs Throughout the World, 1985*. Research Report #60.

Infant Mortality Rates, Selected Countries, 1950-1986

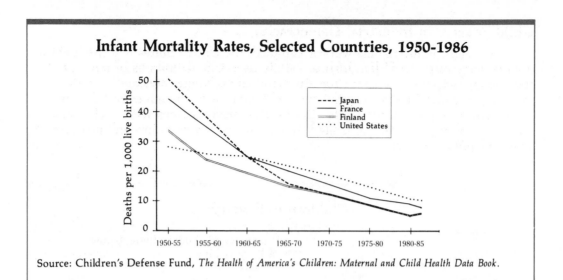

Source: Children's Defense Fund, *The Health of America's Children: Maternal and Child Health Data Book.*

Infant Mortality Rates, Selected Countries, 1986

Rank	Country	Rate*
1	Japan	6
1	Finland	6
1	Sweden	6
4	Denmark	7
4	Switzerland	7
4	Norway	7
7	Netherlands	8
7	France	8
7	Canada	8
10	Hong Kong	9
10	Singapore	9
10	German Dem. Rep.	9
10	Belgium	9
10	Germany Fed. Rep.	9
10	United Kingdom	9
10	Spain	9
10	Ireland	9
	U.S. (White)	*9*
18	Austria	10
18	Australia	10
18	United States	10
21	Italy	11
21	New Zealand	11
23	Greece	12
24	Israel	14
24	Czechoslovakia	14
26	Cuba	15
26	Bulgaria	15
28	Poland	18
28	Hungary	18
28	Portugal	18
28	Costa Rica	18
	U.S. (Black)	*18*

*Deaths per 1,000 live births.
Source: UNICEF.

Percent of Babies Born at Low Birthweight, Selected Countries, 1982

Rank	Country	Percent
1	Norway	3.8
2	Sweden	4.0
2	Netherlands	4.0
4	Finland	4.1
5	Ireland	4.7
6	Switzerland	5.2
6	France	5.2
6	Japan	5.2
9	Germany, Federal Republic	5.5
10	Belgium	5.6
10	Austria	5.6
	U.S. (White)	*5.7*
13	Greece	5.9
14	Canada	6.0
14	Denmark	6.0
16	German Democratic Republic	6.2
17	Italy	6.7
18	U.S. (Total)	6.9
19	United Kingdom	7.0
20	Hong Kong	8.0
21	Costa Rica	8.5
22	Chile	9.0
23	Korea, Republic of	9.2
24	Colombia	10.0
25	Hungary	11.8
	U.S. (Black)	*12.6*

Source: World Health Organization.

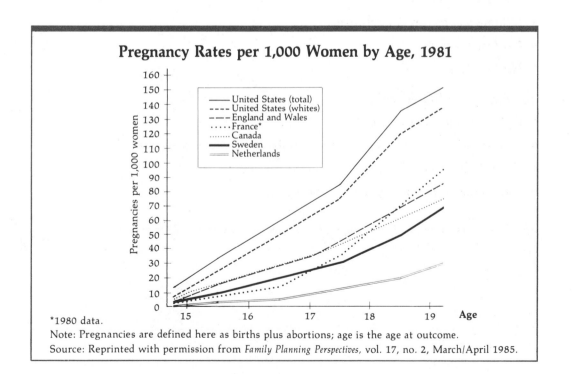

Pregnancy Rates per 1,000 Women by Age, 1981

*1980 data.

Note: Pregnancies are defined here as births plus abortions; age is the age at outcome.

Source: Reprinted with permission from *Family Planning Perspectives*, vol. 17, no. 2, March/April 1985.

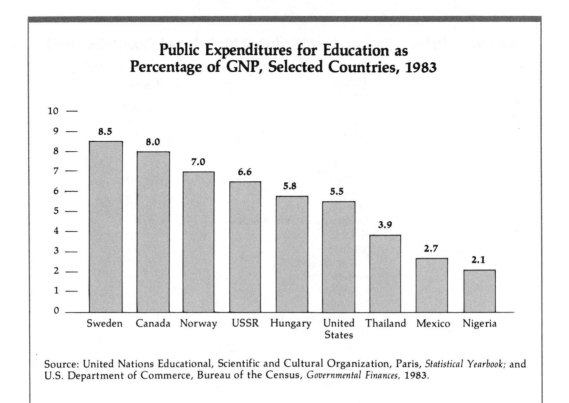

Public Expenditures for Education as Percentage of GNP, Selected Countries, 1983

Source: United Nations Educational, Scientific and Cultural Organization, Paris, *Statistical Yearbook*; and U.S. Department of Commerce, Bureau of the Census, *Governmental Finances*, 1983.

The Nation's Priorities

The United States ranks first among 142 nations in:

• Military expenditures

• Military aid to foreign countries

• Nuclear reactors

• Nuclear tests

But the United States ranks:

• Eighteenth in infant mortality

• Twenty-eighth in infant mortality if only black babies are counted

• Twentieth in school-age population per teacher

• Eighteenth in population per physician

Source: *World Military and Social Expenditures 1987-88*, by Ruth Leger Sivard, World Priorities, 1987.

CHILDREN IN THE NATION

National Trends

Year	Number of Children Under Age 18 Who Are Poor	Child Poverty Rate (%)	Number of Children Under Age 6 Who Are Poor	Under 6 Poverty Rate (%)	Per Capita Amount Poor Children's Income is Below Poverty Level (1987 $)	Unemployment Rates		
						All Ages (%)	Age 16-19 (%)	Age 20-24 (%)
1959	17,552,000	27.3	n/a	n/a	1,109	5.5	14.6	8.5
1960	17,634,000	26.9	n/a	n/a		5.5	14.7	8.7
1961	16,909,000	25.6	n/a	n/a		6.7	16.8	10.4
1962	16,963,000	25.0	n/a	n/a		5.5	14.7	9.0
1963	16,005,000	23.1	n/a	n/a		5.7	17.2	8.8
1964	16,051,000	23.0	n/a	n/a		5.2	16.2	8.3
1965	14,676,000	21.0	n/a	n/a	1,035	4.5	14.8	6.7
1966	12,389,000	17.6	n/a	n/a		3.8	12.8	5.3
1967	11,656,000	16.6	n/a	n/a		3.8	12.9	5.7
1968	10,954,000	15.6	n/a	n/a		3.6	12.7	5.8
1969	9,691,000	14.0	3,298,000	15.3	1,012	3.5	12.2	5.7
1970	10,440,000	15.1	3,561,000	16.6	1,057	4.9	15.3	8.2
1971	10,551,000	15.3	3,499,000	16.9	1,055	5.9	16.9	10.0
1972	10,284,000	15.1	3,276,000	16.1	1,057	5.6	16.2	9.3
1973	9,642,000	14.4	3,097,000	15.7	1,064	4.9	14.5	7.8
1974	10,156,000	15.4	3,294,000	16.9	1,118	5.6	16.0	9.1
1975	11,104,000	17.1	3,460,000	18.2	1,077	8.5	19.9	13.6
1976	10,273,000	16.0	3,270,000	17.7	1,076	7.7	19.0	12.0
1977	10,288,000	16.2	3,326,000	18.1	1,112	7.1	17.8	11.0
1978	9,931,000	15.9	3,184,000	17.2	1,143	6.1	16.4	9.6
1979	10,377,000	16.4	3,415,000	17.8	1,159	5.8	16.1	9.1
1980	11,543,000	18.3	4,030,000	20.5	1,179	7.1	17.8	11.5
1981	12,505,000	20.0	4,422,000	22.0	1,210	7.6	19.6	12.3
1982	13,647,000	21.9	4,821,000	23.3	1,260	9.7	23.2	14.9
1983	13,911,000	22.3	5,122,000	24.6	1,260	9.6	22.4	14.5
1984	13,420,000	21.5	4,938,000	23.4	1,264	7.5	18.9	11.5
1985	13,010,000	20.7	4,832,000	22.6	1,280	7.2	18.6	11.1
1986	12,876,000	20.5	4,619,000	21.6	1,306	7.0	18.3	10.7
1987	13,016,000	20.6	4,818,000	22.3	1,323	6.2	16.9	9.7
Total percent change,								
1965-1980	-21.3	-12.9	n/a	n/a	13.9	57.8	20.3	71.6
1980-1986/7	12.8	12.6	19.6	8.8	12.2	-12.7	-5.1	-15.7
Average annual percent change,								
1965-1980	-1.4	-0.9	n/a	n/a	0.9	3.9	1.4	4.8
1980-1986/7	1.8	1.8	2.8	1.3	1.7	-1.8	-0.7	-2.2

National Trends (Continued)

Year	Infant Mortality Rates[1]			Low Birth-weight (%)	Percent of Babies Born to Mothers Who Received Late or No Prenatal Care			Teen Birth Rate[2]	Teen Out-of-Wedlock Birth Rate[3]
	Total	White	Black		Total	White	Black		
1959	26.4	23.2	44.8	n/a	n/a	n/a	n/a	n/a	n/a
1960	26.0	22.9	44.3	7.7	n/a	n/a	n/a	89.1	15.3
1961	25.3	22.4	41.8	7.8	n/a	n/a	n/a	88.6	16.0
1962	25.3	22.3	42.6	8.0	n/a	n/a	n/a	81.4	14.8
1963	25.2	22.2	42.8	8.2	n/a	n/a	n/a	76.7	15.3
1964	24.8	21.6	42.3	8.2	n/a	n/a	n/a	73.1	15.9
1965	24.7	21.5	41.7	8.3	n/a	n/a	n/a	70.5	16.7
1966	23.7	20.6	40.2	8.3	n/a	n/a	n/a	70.3	17.5
1967	22.4	19.7	37.5	8.2	n/a	n/a	n/a	67.5	18.5
1968	21.8	19.2	36.2	8.2	n/a	n/a	n/a	65.6	19.7
1969	20.9	18.4	34.8	8.1	8.1	6.3	18.2	65.5	20.4
1970	20.0	17.8	32.6	7.9	7.9	6.2	16.6	68.3	22.4
1971	19.1	17.1	30.3	7.7	7.2	5.8	14.6	64.5	22.3
1972	18.5	16.4	29.6	7.7	7.0	5.5	13.2	61.7	22.8
1973	17.7	15.8	28.1	7.6	6.7	5.4	12.4	59.3	22.7
1974	16.7	14.8	26.8	7.4	6.2	5.0	11.4	57.5	23.0
1975	16.1	14.2	26.2	7.4	6.0	5.0	10.5	55.6	23.9
1976	15.2	13.3	25.5	7.3	5.7	4.8	9.9	52.8	23.7
1977	14.1	12.3	23.6	7.1	5.6	4.7	9.6	52.8	25.1
1978	13.8	12.0	23.1	7.1	5.4	4.5	9.3	51.5	24.9
1979	13.1	11.4	21.8	6.9	5.1	4.3	8.9	52.3	26.4
1980	12.6	11.0	21.4	6.8	5.1	4.3	8.8	53.0	27.6
1981	11.9	10.5	20.0	6.8	5.2	4.3	9.1	52.7	28.2
1982	11.5	10.1	19.6	6.8	5.5	4.5	9.6	52.9	28.9
1983	11.2	9.7	19.2	6.8	5.6	4.6	9.7	51.7	29.7
1984	10.8	9.4	18.4	6.7	5.6	4.7	9.6	50.9	30.2
1985	10.6	9.3	18.2	6.8	5.7	4.7	10.0	51.3	31.6
1986	10.4	8.9	18.0	6.8	6.0	5.0	10.6	50.6	32.6
1987	n/a	n/a	n/a	n/a	n/a	n/a	n/a	n/a	n/a
Total percent change,									
1965-1980	-49.0	-48.8	-48.7	-18.1	n/a	n/a	n/a	-24.8	65.3
1980-1986/7	-17.5	-19.1	-15.9	0.0	17.6	16.3	20.5	-4.5	18.1
Average annual percent change,									
1965-1980	-3.3	-3.3	-3.2	-1.2	n/a	n/a	n/a	-1.7	4.4
1980-1986/7	-2.9	-3.2	-2.7	0.0	2.9	2.7	3.4	-0.8	3.0

[1]Per 1,000 live births.

[2]Per 1,000 teen women aged 15-19.

[3]Per 1,000 unmarried teen women aged 15-19.

Note: n/a Data not available.

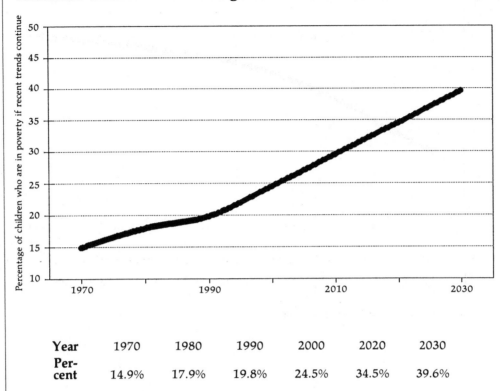

America's Children Are Getting Poorer While the Nation Gets Richer

Year	1970	1980	1990	2000	2020	2030
Per-cent	14.9%	17.9%	19.8%	24.5%	34.5%	39.6%

• In the year 2000, if recent trends continue, there will be 16 million poor children in the United States, 3 million more than in 1987. One in every four children will be poor.

• By the year 2030, there will be 25 million poor children. One in every three children will be poor.

Source: CDF computations based on Census Bureau data.

Children and Young Adults Are Becoming Scarce Resources

Year	Total population (thousands)	Population under age 18 (thousands)	Percent of total population	Population 18-24 years (thousands)	Percent of total population
1985	238,631	62,838	26%	28,739	12%
1995	259,559	67,133	26%	23,702	9%
2000	267,955	67,389	25%	24,601	9%
2030	304,807	65,866	22%	26,226	9%

• The nation's young work force is shrinking. By 1995 there will be 5 million fewer 18- to 24-year-olds than there were in 1985.

• Although the actual number of children under age 18 will increase until the year 2000, the percentage of the population that is under 18 is decreasing. After 2000 the total number of children will begin decreasing as well.

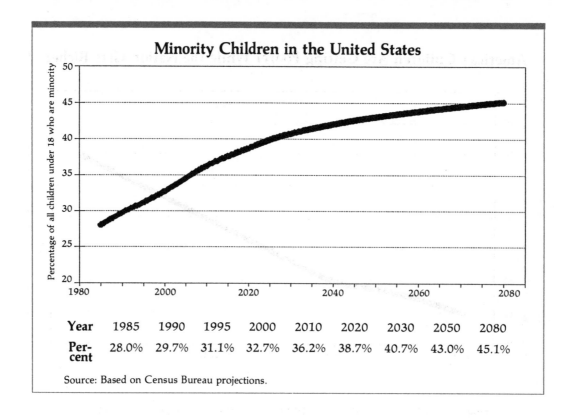

Minority Children in the United States

Year	1985	1990	1995	2000	2010	2020	2030	2050	2080
Per-cent	28.0%	29.7%	31.1%	32.7%	36.2%	38.7%	40.7%	43.0%	45.1%

Source: Based on Census Bureau projections.

America's Future Population: Minorities Are a Growing Share

Compared with 1985, in 2000 there will be:

- 2.4 million more Hispanic children;
- 1.7 million more black children;
- 483,000 more children of other races; and
- 66,000 more white, non-Hispanic children.

The total number of minority children will have increased by 25.5 percent. The proportion of all children who are minority will have increased from 28.0 percent to 32.7 percent.

Compared with 1985, in 2030 there will be:

- 5.5 million more Hispanic children;
- 2.6 million more black children;
- 1.5 million more children of other races; and
- 6.2 million fewer white, non-Hispanic children.

The total number of minority children will have increased by 52.5 percent. The proportion of all children who are minority will have increased from 28.0 percent to 40.7 percent.

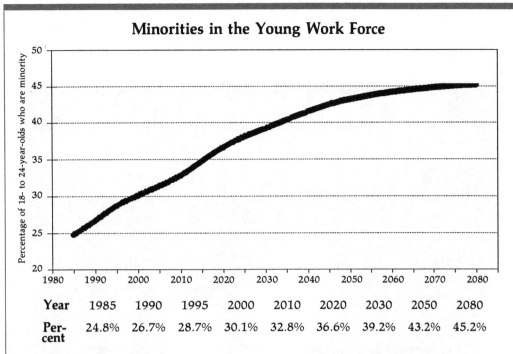

Minorities in the Young Work Force

Year	1985	1990	1995	2000	2010	2020	2030	2050	2080
Percent	24.8%	26.7%	28.7%	30.1%	32.8%	36.6%	39.2%	43.2%	45.2%

• Nearly one-third of the nation's 18- to 24-year-olds will be minorities in 2000, compared with less than one-quarter in 1985.

• There will be 26 percent fewer white, non-Hispanic 18- to 24-year-olds in the year 2030 than there were in 1985.

Source: Based on Census Bureau projections.

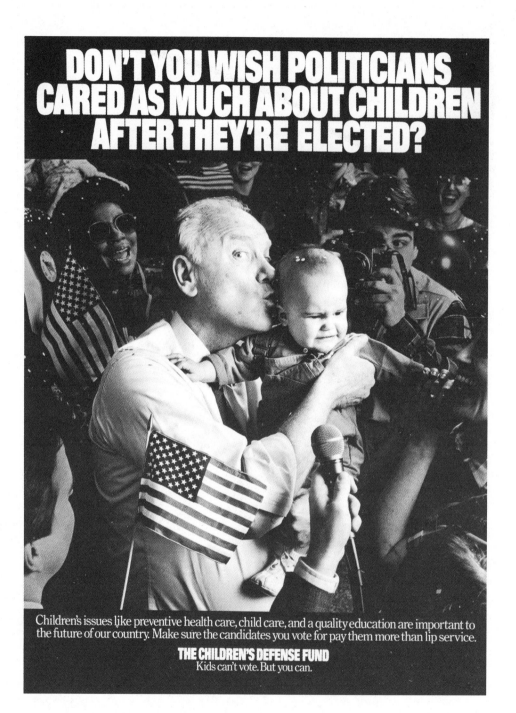

CHILDREN AND CONGRESS

CDF's Nonpartisan Congressional Voting Record of 1988

As parents, grandparents, and others with children in our lives, we work very hard to make sure that the children we love grow up in the safest, healthiest, and most nurturing environment possible.

We try to make good decisions for them about health care, day care, education, and recreation. We carefully monitor both our children's progress and those who can influence their health and well-being: family, teachers, friends, doctors, and others.

All too often, we forget to add elected officials to that list. However, our elected officials at the local, state, and federal levels make hundreds of decisions and cast numerous votes each year that critically affect the lives and futures of our children. A single vote cast by a state legislator may decide whether or not a young person will have the financial resources to attend a state college. A single vote cast by a member of Congress may determine whether or not a child in Chicago or Portland is immunized or can enroll in Head Start or a quality child care program.

Although our children are our country's future, they are the easiest segment of the population for policy makers to neglect. Children are not organized. They cannot vote, and they cannot speak out for the governmental programs and policies they need to grow up safe, healthy, and educated. Unfortunately, elected officials can and do make flowery speeches about the importance of children and family without supporting or voting for the specific programs necessary for their health and well-being.

Our children must rely on each of us to be their voices to their elected officials.

That is why the Children's Defense Fund urges all Americans who are concerned about the nation's children and the future of our country to inform themselves, first, then inform their elected representatives about the significance of their votes to the lives of children. It is equally important for each of us— parents, teachers, religious leaders, and advocates—to review periodically the decisions made and the votes cast by our public servants. Armed with this knowledge, we can thank them when their actions protect and place the interests of children first. And when they do not, we have the responsibility to urge them to do better next time.

To assist you in this effort, every year CDF compiles a record of the most important votes affecting children, adolescents, and families cast by the 100 members of the U.S. Senate and 435 members of the U.S. House of Representatives. We hope others will undertake this task regularly at the state and local levels.

After reviewing all the votes affecting children taken in the U.S. Congress during 1988, CDF selected eight in each house of Congress based on the significance of the program or service involved, the number of children potentially affected, and the importance of the vote to the eventual outcome. Some of the votes we examined deal with specific provisions of complex legislation, such as the welfare reform bill that included some provisions beneficial to poor children and families and others harmful to them.

The votes selected for 1988 include those that determine whether or not additional poor infants and pregnant women have access to essential preventive health care services; whether or not families with children would be protected against housing discrimination; and whether or not senators would even consider new child care legislation or a proposal to raise the minimum wage.

All the votes cast on these bills, motions, and amendments will have a lasting impact on millions of American children and families.

This year, 15 senators and 99 representatives earned a perfect rating of 100. We applaud these members and urge their constituents to contact them and thank them for protecting the needs of children. Similarly, CDF hopes that the constituents of the senators and representatives who received a lower rating will spend whatever time and attention is necessary to educate their representatives about the needs of children in their districts and states.

You and millions of others can send a clear and powerful message to the nation's elected officials that will be reflected in children's lives as well as in CDF's voting record of 1989. Your dedication and concern, coupled with frequent letters, telephone calls, and visits, can convince lawmakers to vote for the crucial investments in programs that work and that children desperately need in order to become successful students and productive adults.

Members may miss a crucial vote for many reasons, some unavoidable. Nevertheless, a missed vote because of an absence may affect the ultimate outcome and thus is taken into account in this rating. An asterisk is placed beside the name of any member whose rating reflects three or more absences.

As a public charity, CDF is permitted under the Tax Reform Act of 1976 to spend a small percentage of its budget on legislative activities.

The compilation of these votes was prepared by Legislate, a computerized legislative service, and is based on Legislate's record of the votes.

©1988 by Children's Defense Fund

Senate Votes: Explanation

Civil Rights Restoration Act (S. 557): Vote to override President's veto of bill to restore broad coverage of four civil rights laws—Title IX of the 1972 Education Act Amendments; Title VI of the 1964 Civil Rights Act; Section 504 of the 1973 Rehabilitation Act; and the 1975 Age Discrimination Act—by making it clear that if one portion of an institution receives federal funds, the entire institution must not discriminate. Override passed 73-24 (two-thirds majority required). Passed on March 22, 1988. CDF Position: **Pass.**

FY 1989 Budget Resolution/Health Care (S. Con. Res. 113): Vote on motion to table amendment to transfer funds to increase spending for childhood immunizations and other health programs. Passed 57-38 on April 14, 1988. CDF Position: **Reject.**

Medicaid Infant Mortality Amendments (H.R. 2470): Vote to adopt Conference Report on the Catastrophic Health Insurance bill, including among its many provisions the Medicaid Infant Mortality Amendments to mandate coverage for all poor pregnant women and infants. Passed 86-11 on June 8, 1988. CDF Position: **Pass.**

Welfare Reform (S. 1511): Vote on motion to table amendment to require unpaid work by at least one parent in two-parent families receiving welfare. Rejected 41-54 on June 16, 1988. CDF Position: **Pass.**

Hunger Prevention (S. 2560): Vote on bill to provide additional benefits under the School Breakfast program, to raise the basic food stamp allowance, and reauthorize various food and nutrition programs. Passed 90-7 on July 26, 1988. CDF Position: **Pass.**

Fair Housing (H.R. 1158): Vote on bill to extend protections against discrimination in the sale or rental of housing to families with children and persons with handicaps, and to provide improved enforcement of laws against housing discrimination on these bases and the bases of race, color, religion, sex, or national origin. Passed 94-3 on August 2, 1988. CDF Position: **Pass.**

Minimum Wage (S. 837): Motion to invoke cloture (thus limiting debate) on bill to raise the minimum wage from $3.35 to $4.55 an hour over three years. Rejected 56-35 (three-fifths majority of the entire Senate required) on September 23, 1988. CDF Position: **Pass.**

Child Care/Parental Leave (S. 2488): Motion to invoke cloture (thus limiting debate) on bill to authorize Act for Better Child Care Services (ABC) and Family and Medical Leave Act. Rejected 50-46 (three-fifths majority of entire Senate required) on October 7, 1988. CDF Position: **Pass.**

House Votes: Explanation

Civil Rights Restoration Act (S. 557): Vote to override President's veto of bill to restore broad coverage of four civil rights laws—Title IX of the 1972 Education Act Amendments; Title VI of the 1964 Civil Rights Act; Section 504 of the 1973 Rehabilitation Act; and the 1975 Age Discrimination Act—by making it clear that if one portion of an institution receives federal funds, the entire institution must not discriminate. Passed 292-133 (two-thirds vote necessary) on March 22, 1988. CDF Position: **Pass.**

FY 1989 Budget Resolution (H. Con. Res. 268): Vote to adopt House-Senate Conference Report on FY 1989 Budget Resolution, with funding allowances for Medicaid Infant Mortality Amendments and Food and Nutrition Assistance and other children's programs. Passed 201-181 on May 26, 1988. CDF Position: **Pass.**

Medicaid Infant Mortality Amendments (H.R. 2470): Vote on rule to allow floor consideration of Conference Report on the Catastrophic Health Insurance bill, including among its many provisions the Medicaid Infant Mortality Amendments to mandate coverage for all poor pregnant women and infants. Passed 269-129 on June 2, 1988. CDF Position: **Pass.**

Funding for Children's Programs (H.R. 4783): Vote on amendment to cut funds from the FY 1989 Labor/Health and Human Services Appropriations bill, including funds from the Low Income Home Energy Assistance Program. Rejected 37-369 on June 15, 1988. CDF Position: **Reject.**

Fair Housing/Discrimination Against Families (H.R. 1158): Vote on amendment to delete from Fair Housing bill a new provision banning discrimination in housing because a family has children. Rejected 116-289 on June 23, 1988. CDF Position: **Reject.**

Welfare Reform (H.R. 1720): Vote on motion to instruct House conferees to keep cost of welfare reform to lower Senate level and include Senate's unpaid work provisions in final bill. Passed 227-168 on July 7, 1988. CDF Position: **Reject.**

Homeless Assistance (H.R. 4352): Vote on bill to reauthorize various programs under the 1987 Stewart McKinney Homeless Assistance Act. Passed 333-80 on August 3, 1988. CDF Position: **Pass.**

Nutrition Monitoring (S. 1081): Vote on bill to develop a nutrition-monitoring plan, to create a nutrition advisory council, and for other purposes. Passed 311-84 on October 12, 1988. CDF Position: **Pass.**

SENATE	Civil Rights Restoration	Budget Resolution/Health Care	Medicaid Infant Mortality	Welfare Reform	Hunger Prevention	Fair Housing	Minimum Wage	Child Care/Parental Leave	% For All Votes
CDF POSITION:	Y	N	Y	Y	Y	Y	Y	Y	
ALABAMA									
Heflin	+	–	+	–	+	+	+	–	63
Shelby	+	–	+	–	+	+	–	–	50
ALASKA									
Murkowski	+	–	+	–	+	+	–	–	50
Stevens	+	+	+	–	?	+	–	–	50
ARIZONA									
DeConcini	+	–	+	–	+	+	+	+	75
McCain	+	–	–	–	+	+	–	–	38
ARKANSAS									
Bumpers	+	+	+	–	+	?	+	+	75
Pryor	+	–	+	+	+	+	+	+	88
CALIFORNIA									
Cranston	+	–	+	+	+	+	+	+	88
Wilson	+	+	+	–	+	+	?	–	63
COLORADO									
Armstrong	–	–	–	–	+	–	–	–	13
Wirth	+	–	+	+	+	+	+	+	88
CONNECTICUT									
Dodd	+	+	+	+	+	+	+	+	100
Weicker	+	+	+	+	?	+	+	+	88
DELAWARE									
Biden*	?	?	?	?	?	?	+	+	25
Roth	+	–	–	–	+	+	+	–	50
FLORIDA									
Chiles	+	–	?	+	+	+	?	+	63
Graham	+	–	+	+	+	+	+	+	88
GEORGIA									
Fowler	+	–	+	+	+	+	+	+	88
Nunn	+	–	+	–	+	+	+	–	63
HAWAII									
Inouye	+	+	+	+	+	+	+	+	100
Matsunaga	+	+	+	+	+	+	+	+	100
IDAHO									
McClure	–	–	–	?	+	+	?	–	25
Symms	–	–	–	–	–	–	–	–	0
ILLINOIS									
Dixon	+	–	+	–	+	+	+	–	63
Simon	+	?	+	+	+	+	+	+	88
INDIANA									
Lugar	–	–	+	–	+	+	–	–	38
Quayle	–	–	+	–	+	+	?	?	38
IOWA									
Grassley	–	–	+	–	+	+	–	–	38
Harkin	+	+	+	+	+	+	+	+	100
KANSAS									
Dole	?	+	+	–	+	+	–	+	50
Kassebaum	+	–	–	–	+	+	–	–	38
KENTUCKY									
Ford	+	–	+	+	+	+	+	+	88
McConnell	–	+	+	–	+	+	–	–	50
LOUISIANA									
Breaux	+	–	+	–	+	+	+	+	75
Johnston	+	–	+	+	+	+	+	+	88
MAINE									
Cohen	+	+	+	–	+	+	–	–	63
Mitchell	+	+	+	+	+	+	+	+	100
MARYLAND									
Mikulski	+	+	+	+	+	+	+	+	100
Sarbanes	+	+	+	+	+	+	+	+	100
MASSACHUSETTS									
Kennedy	+	+	+	+	+	+	+	+	100
Kerry	+	+	+	+	+	+	+	+	100
MICHIGAN									
Levin	+	–	+	?	+	+	+	+	75
Riegle	+	–	+	+	+	+	+	+	88
MINNESOTA									
Boschwitz	+	–	+	–	+	+	–	–	50
Durenberger	+	+	+	?	+	+	–	+	75
MISSISSIPPI									
Cochran	–	–	+	–	+	+	–	–	38
Stennis	?	?	+	+	+	+	+	+	75
MISSOURI									
Bond	–	–	+	–	+	+	–	–	38
Danforth	–	–	+	–	+	+	–	–	38
MONTANA									
Baucus	+	–	+	+	+	+	+	+	88
Melcher	+	–	+	+	+	+	+	–	75
NEBRASKA									
Exon	+	–	+	–	+	+	–	–	50
Karnes	–	+	+	–	+	+	–	?	50
NEVADA									
Hecht	–	+	+	?	+	+	?	–	50
Reid	+	–	+	–	+	?	+	+	63

KEY: Y (yes), N (no) indicates CDF position for (Y) or against (N) vote. + indicates votes in support of CDF position; – indicates votes in opposition to CDF position; ? = was not present for vote; % = number of times voted for CDF position/total votes—absences during voting are computed as a negative vote; * indicates missed three or more votes. Republicans in italics.

SENATE	Civil Rights Restoration	Budget Resolution/Health Care	Medicaid Infant Mortality	Welfare Reform	Hunger Prevention	Fair Housing	Minimum Wage	Child Care/Parental Leave	% For All Votes
CDF POSITION:	Y	N	Y	Y	Y	Y	Y	Y	
NEW HAMPSHIRE									
Humphrey	–	–	–	–,	+	–	–	–	13
Rudman	+	+	+	–	+	+	–	–	63
NEW JERSEY									
Bradley	+	+	+	+	+	+	?	+	88
Lautenberg	+	?	+	+	+	+	+	+	88
NEW MEXICO									
Bingaman	+	–	+	+	+	+	+	+	88
Domenici	+	–	+	–	+	+	–	–	50
NEW YORK									
D'Amato	+	+	+	–	+	–	–	–	63
Moynihan	+	+	+	+	+	+	+	+	100
NORTH CAROLINA									
Helms	–	–	–	–	–	–	–	–	0
Sanford	+	–	+	+	+	+	+	+	88
NORTH DAKOTA									
Burdick	+	+	+	+	+	+	+	+	100
Conrad	+	+	+	+	+	+	+	+	100
OHIO									
Glenn	+	–	+	+	+	+	+	+	88
Metzenbaum	+	–	+	+	+	+	+	+	88
OKLAHOMA									
Boren	+	–	+	–	+	+	–	–	50
Nickles	–	–	–	–	+	+	–	–	25
OREGON									
Hatfield	+	+	+	–	+	+	+	–	75
Packwood	+	+	+	–	+	+	+	–	75
PENNSYLVANIA									
Heinz	+	+	+	–	+	+	+	–	75
Specter	+	+	?	–	+	+	+	+	75
RHODE ISLAND									
Chafee	+	+	+	+	+	+	+	+	100
Pell	+	+	+	+	+	+	+	+	100

SENATE	Civil Rights Restoration	Budget Resolution/Health Care	Medicaid Infant Mortality	Welfare Reform	Hunger Prevention	Fair Housing	Minimum Wage	Child Care/Parental Leave	% For All Votes
CDF POSITION:	Y	N	Y	Y	Y	Y	Y	Y	
SOUTH CAROLINA									
Hollings	+	–	+	+	+	+	+	+	88
Thurmond	–	–	+	–	+	+	–	–	38
SOUTH DAKOTA									
Daschle	+	–	+	+	+	+	+	+	88
Pressler	–	–	+	–	+	+	–	–	38
TENNESSEE									
Gore	+	?	+	–	+	+	+	+	75
Sasser	+	–	+	+	+	+	+	+	88
TEXAS									
Bentsen	+	–	+	–	+	+	?	?	50
Gramm	–	–	–	–	+	+	?	–	13
UTAH									
Garn	–	–	–	–	–	+	–	–	13
Hatch	–	–	+	–	–	+	–	–	25
VERMONT									
Leahy	+	+	+	+	+	+	+	+	100
Stafford	+	+	+	–	+	+	+	+	88
VIRGINIA									
Trible	–	+	–	–	+	+	–	–	50
Warner	–	–	+	–	+	–	–	–	38
WASHINGTON									
Adams	+	–	+	+	+	+	+	+	88
Evans	+	–	+	+	+	+	–	–	63
WEST VIRGINIA									
Byrd	+	+	+	–	+	+	+	+	88
Rockefeller	+	+	+	–	+	+	+	+	88
WISCONSIN									
Kasten	+	–	+	–	+	+	–	–	50
Proxmire	+	+	+	–	–	+	+	+	75
WYOMING									
Simpson	–	+	+	–	+	+	–	–	50
Wallop	–	–	+	–	+	+	?	?	38

HOUSE	Civil Rights Restoration	Budget Resolution	Medicaid Infant Mortality	Children's Programs	Fair Housing	Welfare Reform	Homeless Assistance	Nutrition Monitoring	% For All Votes
CDF POSITION:	Y	Y	Y	N	N	N	Y	Y	
ALABAMA									
1 *Callahan*	–	–	–	–	–	–	–	–	0
2 *Dickinson*	–	–	–	+	–	–	+	–	25
3 Nichols	+	?	+	+	+	–	+	+	75
4 Bevill	+	–	+	+	+	–	+	+	75
5 Flippo	+	–	+	+	+	–	+	+	75
6 Erdreich	+	–	+	+	+	–	+	+	75
7 Harris	+	–	+	+	+	–	+	+	75
ALASKA									
1 *Young, D.*	+	+	?	+	+	–	+	–	63
ARIZONA									
1 *Rhodes*	–	–	–	+	–	–	–	–	13
2 Udall	+	+	?	+	+	+	?	+	75
3 *Stump*	–	–	–	–	–	–	–	–	0
4 *Kyl*	–	–	–	–	–	–	–	–	0
5 *Kolbe*	+	–	–	+	–	–	–	+	38
ARKANSAS									
1 Alexander	+	+	+	+	+	+	+	+	100
2 Robinson	+	+	+	+	+	+	+	–	88
3 *Hammerschmidt*	–	–	+	+	–	–	–	–	25
4 Anthony	+	+	+	+	+	+	+	+	100
CALIFORNIA									
1 Bosco	+	+	+	+	+	?	+	+	88
2 *Herger*	–	–	–	+	–	–	+	+	38
3 Matsui	+	+	+	+	+	+	+	+	100
4 Fazio	+	+	+	+	+	+	+	+	100
5 Pelosi	+	+	+	+	+	+	+	+	100
6 Boxer	+	+	+	+	+	+	+	+	100
7 Miller, G.	+	+	+	+	+	+	+	+	100
8 Dellums	+	?	+	+	?	+	+	+	75
9 Stark	+	+	+	+	+	+	+	+	100
10 Edwards, D.	+	+	+	+	+	+	+	+	100
11 Lantos	+	+	+	+	+	+	+	+	100
12 *Konnyu**	–	?	?	–	?	–	–	+	13
13 Mineta	+	+	+	+	+	+	+	+	100
14 *Shumway*	–	–	–	+	–	–	–	–	13
15 Coelho	+	+	+	+	+	+	+	?	88
16 Panetta	+	+	+	+	+	+	+	+	100
17 *Pashayan*	+	–	–	+	+	–	+	–	50
18 Lehman, R.	+	+	+	+	+	?	+	+	88
19 *Lagomarsino*	–	+	+	+	+	–	+	–	63
20 *Thomas, Wm.*	–	+	+	+	+	–	–	–	38
21 *Gallegly*	–	–	–	+	–	–	–	–	13
22 *Moorhead*	–	–	–	+	–	–	–	–	13
23 Beilenson	+	+	+	+	+	+	+	+	100
24 Waxman	+	+	+	+	+	+	+	+	100
25 Roybal	+	–	+	+	+	+	+	+	88
26 Berman	+	+	+	+	+	+	+	+	100
27 Levine	+	+	+	+	+	+	+	+	100
28 Dixon	+	+	?	+	+	?	+	+	75
29 Hawkins	+	+	+	+	+	+	+	?	88
30 Martinez	?	+	+	+	+	+	+	+	88
31 Dymally	+	+	+	+	+	+	+	+	100
32 Anderson	+	+	+	+	+	?	+	+	88
33 *Dreier*	–	–	–	+	–	–	–	–	13
34 Torres	+	+	+	+	+	+	+	?	88
35 *Lewis, J.*	–	?	?	+	+	–	–	–	25
36 Brown, G.	+	?	+	+	?	+	+	+	75
37 *McCandless*	–	–	–	+	–	–	–	–	13
38 *Dornan*	–	–	–	–	–	–	–	–	0
39 *Dannemeyer*	–	–	–	?	–	–	–	–	0
40 *Badham*	–	?	–	–	?	–	–	–	0
41 *Lowery*	–	–	?	+	–	–	–	+	25
42 *Lungren*	+	–	–	+	–	?	–	–	25
43 *Packard*	–	+	–	?	–	–	–	?	13
44 Bates	+	–	+	+	+	+	+	+	88
45 *Hunter*	–	–	–	–	–	–	–	–	0
COLORADO									
1 Schroeder	+	+	+	+	+	+	+	+	100
2 Skaggs	+	+	+	+	+	–	+	+	88
3 Campbell	+	–	?	+	+	+	+	+	63
4 *Brown, H.*	+	–	–	+	–	–	–	–	25
5 *Hefley*	–	–	–	+	–	–	–	–	13
6 *Schaefer*	–	–	–	+	–	–	–	–	13
CONNECTICUT									
1 Kennelly	+	+	+	+	+	+	+	+	100
2 Gejdenson	+	+	+	+	+	+	+	+	100
3 Morrison, B.	+	+	+	+	+	+	+	+	100
4 *Shays*	+	–	+	+	+	+	+	+	88
5 *Rowland, J.*	+	–	+	+	+	–	+	+	75
6 *Johnson, N.*	+	+	–	+	+	–	+	+	75
DELAWARE									
1 Carper	+	–	+	+	+	–	+	+	75
FLORIDA									
1 Hutto	–	?	+	+	+	–	+	+	63
2 Grant	+	+	+	+	+	–	+	+	88
3 Bennett	+	+	+	+	+	–	+	+	88
4 Chappell	+	+	+	+	–	–	+	+	75
5 *McCollum*	–	?	–	+	–	–	–	–	13
6 MacKay*	+	?	+	?	?	?	?	?	25
7 Gibbons	+	+	+	+	+	+	+	+	100
8 *Young, B.*	–	–	–	+	–	–	+	–	25
9 *Bilirakis*	–	+	–	+	–	–	–	+	38
10 *Ireland*	–	–	–	+	–	–	+	–	25

KEY: Y (yes), N (no) indicates CDF position for (Y) or against (N) vote. + indicates votes in support of CDF position; – indicates vote in opposition to CDF position; ? = was not present for vote; 0 = not a member at time of vote; % = number of times voted for CDF position/total number of votes—absences during voting are computed as negative votes; * indicates missed three or more votes; ** indicates Speaker of the House (votes only in a tie). Republicans in italics.

HOUSE	Civil Rights Restoration	Budget Resolution	Medicaid Infant Mortality	Children's Programs	Fair Housing	Welfare Reform	Homeless Assistance	Nutrition Monitoring	% For All Votes
CDF POSITION:	Y	Y	Y	N	N	N	Y	Y	
11 Nelson	+	+	+	+	+	+	+	+	100
12 Lewis, T.	-	-	-	+	-	-	-	+	25
13 Mack*	-	?	?	?	-	-	-	?	0
14 Mica*	+	?	?	?	?	?	?	?	13
15 Shaw	-	-	-	+	-	-	-	+	25
16 Smith, L.	+	+	+	+	-	+	+	+	88
17 Lehman, Wm.	+	+	+	+	+	+	+	+	88
18 Pepper	+	+	+	+	+	+	+	+	100
19 Fascell	+	+	+	+	+	+	+	+	100
GEORGIA									
1 Thomas, L.	+	+	+	+	+	-	+	+	75
2 Hatcher	+	?	+	+	+	?	+	+	75
3 Ray*	-	+	?	?	?	?	+	+	38
4 Swindall	-	-	-	+	-	-	-	?	13
5 Lewis, J.	+	+	+	+	+	+	+	+	100
6 Gingrich	-	-	-	+	-	-	-	-	13
7 Darden	+	+	+	+	-	-	+	+	75
8 Rowland, R.	-	+	+	+	+	+	+	+	75
9 Jenkins	+	?	+	+	+	+	+	+	75
10 Barnard	-	-	-	+	-	-	+	+	38
HAWAII									
1 Saiki	+	+	+	+	-	+	+	+	88
2 Akaka	+	+	+	+	+	+	+	+	100
IDAHO									
1 Craig	-	?	+	+	-	-	-	-	13
2 Stallings	+	+	+	+	-	+	?		75
ILLINOIS									
1 Hayes, C.	+	+	+	?	+	+	+	+	88
2 Savage	+	+	+	+	+	+	+	+	100
3 Russo	-	+	+	?	-	+	+	+	63
4 Davis, J.	-	-	-	+	-	+	+	-	25
5 Lipinski	+	+	+	+	-	+	+	+	88
6 Hyde	-	+	-	+	?	-	+	-	38
7 Collins	+	+	+	+	+	+	+	+	100
8 Rostenkowski	+	+	+	+	+	+	+	+	100
9 Yates	+	-	+	+	+	+	+	+	88
10 Porter	+	-	+	+	+	+	-	-	50
11 Annunzio	+	+	+	+	+	?	+	+	88
12 Crane	-	-	-	-	-	-	-	-	0
13 Fawell	-	-	-	+	-	-	+	+	25
14 Hastert	-	-	-	+	-	+	-	-	13
15 Madigan	?	-	-	+	-	-	+	-	25
16 Martin, L.	+	-	-	+	-	-	-	-	38
17 Evans	+	+	+	+	+	+	+	+	100
18 Michel	-	-	-	+	-	-	-	-	13
19 Bruce	+	-	+	+	+	-	+	+	75
20 Durbin	+	-	+	+	+	+	+	+	88
21 Costello	0	0	0	0	0	0	0	+	100
21 Price, M.	?	0	0	0	0	0	0	0	0
22 Gray, K.	?	?	+	+	+	+	+	+	75
INDIANA									
1 Visclosky	+	-	+	+	+	+	+	+	88
2 Sharp	+	-	+	+	-	+	+	+	75
3 Hiler	-	?	-	+	-	-	+	?	25
4 Coats	-	-	-	+	+	-	+	-	38
5 Jontz	+	+	+	+	+	+	+	+	100
6 Burton	-	-	-	-	-	-	-	-	0
7 Myers	-	-	-	+	+	?	+	-	38
8 McCloskey	+	+	+	+	+	+	+	+	100
9 Hamilton	+	-	+	+	+	+	+	+	88
10 Jacobs	+	-	+	?	+	+	+	+	75
IOWA									
1 Leach	+	?	-	+	+	-	+	+	63
2 Tauke	-	-	-	+	+	-	+	?	38
3 Nagle	+	+	+	+	+	+	+	+	88
4 Smith, N.	+	-	+	+	+	+	+	+	88
5 Lightfoot	?	-	-	+	-	-	-	+	25
6 Grandy	-	-	-	+	-	+	+	+	50
KANSAS									
1 Roberts	-	-	?	+	-	-	-	+	25
2 Slattery	+	+	-	+	+	-	+	+	75
3 Meyers	+	-	-	+	-	-	+	+	50
4 Glickman	+	-	+	+	+	-	?	+	63
5 Whittaker	-	-	-	+	-	-	-	+	25
KENTUCKY									
1 Hubbard	-	-	-	+	+	-	+	+	63
2 Natcher	+	+	+	+	+	+	+	+	100
3 Mazzoli	+	+	+	+	+	+	+	+	100
4 Bunning	-	-	-	+	+	-	-	+	38
5 Rogers	-	-	-	+	+	-	-	+	50
6 Hopkins	+	-	-	+	-	-	-	-	25
7 Perkins	+	+	+	+	+	+	+	+	100
LOUISIANA									
1 Livingston	-	-	-	+	-	-	-	+	13
2 Boggs	+	-	+	+	?	+	+	+	75
3 Tauzin	+	-	+	+	+	-	-	+	63
4 McCrery	0	-	-	+	+	-	+	+	43
5 Huckaby	+	-	+	+	+	-	-	+	63
6 Baker	-	-	-	+	-	-	-	+	25
7 Hayes, J.	+	-	+	+	+	-	+	+	75
8 Holloway	-	-	-	-	-	-	+	+	25
MAINE									
1 Brennan	+	+	+	+	+	+	+	+	100
2 Snowe	+	-	+	+	+	-	+	+	75
MARYLAND									
1 Dyson	+	+	+	+	+	?	+	?	75
2 Bentley	-	+	-	+	-	-	+	+	50
3 Cardin	+	+	+	+	+	+	+	+	100
4 McMillen, T.	+	+	+	+	+	-	+	+	88
5 Hoyer	+	+	+	+	+	+	+	+	100
6 Byron	+	+	+	+	+	-	+	+	75
7 Mfume	+	+	+	+	+	+	+	+	100
8 Morella	+	+	+	+	+	+	+	+	100
MASSACHUSETTS									
1 Conte	+	+	+	+	+	+	+	+	100
2 Boland	+	?	+	+	+	+	+	+	88
3 Early	+	+	+	+	+	+	+	+	100

HOUSE	Civil Rights Restoration	Budget Resolution	Medicaid Infant Mortality	Children's Programs	Fair Housing	Welfare Reform	Homeless Assistance	Nutrition Monitoring	% For All Votes
CDF POSITION:	Y	Y	Y	N	N	N	Y	Y	
4 Frank	+	+	+	+	+	+	+	+	100
5 Atkins	+	+	+	+	+	+	+	+	100
6 Mavroules	+	+	+	+	+	+	+	+	100
7 Markey	+	+	+	+	+	+	+	+	100
8 Kennedy	+	+	+	+	+	+	+	+	100
9 Moakley	+	?	+	+	+	+	+	+	88
10 Studds	+	–	+	+	+	+	+	+	88
11 Donnelly	+	+	+	+	+	+	+	+	100
MICHIGAN									
1 Conyers	+	+	+	+	+	+	+	+	100
2 *Pursell*	–	–	+	+	+	–	+	+	63
3 Wolpe	+	?	+	+	+	+	+	+	88
4 *Upton*	–	–	–	+	–	+	+	+	38
5 *Henry*	–	–	+	+	+	–	+	+	63
6 Carr	+	–	+	+	+	+	+	+	88
7 Kildee	+	+	+	+	+	+	+	+	100
8 Traxler	+	+	+	+	+	+	+	?	88
9 *Vander Jagt*	–	–	–	+	–	–	+	+	38
10 *Schuette*	+	–	+	+	+	–	+	+	75
11 *Davis, R.*	+	+	+	–	+	+	+	+	88
12 Bonior	+	+	+	+	+	+	+	+	100
13 Crockett	+	+	+	+	+	+	+	+	100
14 Hertel	+	+	+	+	+	+	+	+	100
15 Ford, Wm.	+	+	+	+	+	+	+	+	100
16 Dingell	+	+	+	+	+	+	+	+	100
17 Levin	+	+	+	+	+	+	+	+	100
18 *Broomfield*	–	–	+	+	+	–	+	?	50
MINNESOTA									
1 Penny	+	+	+	+	+	–	+	+	88
2 *Weber*	–	–	–	+	+	–	–	+	38
3 *Frenzel*	+	–	–	+	?	?	–	–	25
4 Vento	+	+	+	+	+	+	+	+	100
5 Sabo	+	+	+	+	+	+	+	+	100
6 Sikorski	+	+	+	+	+	+	+	+	100
7 *Stangeland*	–	–	–	+	–	–	–	+	25
8 Oberstar	+	+	+	+	?	+	+	+	88
MISSISSIPPI									
1 Whitten	+	–	+	+	?	+	+	?	63
2 Espy	+	?	+	+	+	+	?	+	75
3 Montgomery	+	+	+	+	+	–	+	+	88
4 Dowdy*	+	+	+	+	?	+	?	?	63
5 *Lott*	–	–	–	–	–	–	?	?	0
MISSOURI									
1 Clay	+	+	+	+	+	+	+	+	100
2 *Buechner*	–	–	–	+	+	–	+	+	50
3 Gephardt*	?	+	?	+	+	+	?	+	63
4 Skelton	+	+	+	+	+	+	+	–	75
5 Wheat	+	+	+	+	+	+	+	+	100
6 *Coleman, T.*	–	+	–	+	+	–	+	?	50
7 *Taylor*	–	–	?	+	–	–	?	+	25
8 *Emerson*	–	–	+	+	+	–	+	+	63
9 Volkmer	+	+	+	+	+	–	+	+	88

HOUSE	Civil Rights Restoration	Budget Resolution	Medicaid Infant Mortality	Children's Programs	Fair Housing	Welfare Reform	Homeless Assistance	Nutrition Monitoring	% For All Votes
CDF POSITION:	Y	Y	Y	N	N	N	Y	Y	
MONTANA									
1 Williams	+	+	+	+	+	+	+	+	100
2 *Marlenee*	–	–	–	+	–	–	–	–	13
NEBRASKA									
1 *Bereuter*	+	–	–	+	+	–	–	+	50
2 *Daub*	–	–	?	–	–	?	–	–	0
3 *Smith, V.*	–	–	+	+	+	–	+	+	63
NEVADA									
1 Bilbray	+	–	–	+	+	–	+	+	75
2 *Vucanovich*	–	–	–	+	–	–	+	+	38
NEW HAMPSHIRE									
1 *Smith, R.C.*	–	–	–	+	–	–	–	–	13
2 *Gregg**	–	–	–	+	?	?	–	?	13
NEW JERSEY									
1 Florio	+	?	+	+	+	+	+	+	88
2 Hughes	+	–	–	+	+	–	+	+	63
3 Howard	+	0	0	0	0	0	0	0	100
4 *Smith, C.*	+	+	+	+	+	–	+	+	88
5 *Roukema*	+	?	–	+	+	–	+	+	63
6 *Dwyer*	+	?	+	+	+	?	+	+	75
7 *Rinaldo*	+	+	+	+	+	–	+	+	88
8 Roe	+	+	+	+	+	+	+	+	100
9 Torricelli	+	+	+	+	+	+	+	?	88
10 Rodino	+	+	+	+	+	+	+	+	100
11 *Gallo*	+	?	–	+	+	–	+	+	63
12 *Courter*	+	–	+	–	–	–	+	?	38
13 *Saxton*	+	–	+	+	–	–	+	+	63
14 Guarini	+	+	+	+	+	+	+	+	100
NEW MEXICO									
1 *Lujan*	–	?	–	–	–	–	+	–	25
2 *Skeen*	–	–	–	+	–	–	+	+	38
3 Richardson	+	+	+	+	+	?	+	+	88
NEW YORK									
1 Hochbrueckner	+	+	+	+	+	+	+	+	100
2 Downey	+	+	+	+	+	+	+	+	100
3 Mrazek	+	?	+	+	+	?	+	+	75
4 *Lent*	+	–	+	+	+	–	+	–	50
5 *McGrath*	+	–	?	+	+	–	+	+	63
6 Flake	+	+	+	+	+	?	+	+	88
7 Ackerman	+	+	+	+	+	?	+	?	75
8 Scheuer	+	+	+	+	+	?	+	+	88
9 Manton	+	+	?	+	+	+	+	+	88
10 Schumer	+	+	+	+	?	+	+	+	88
11 Towns	+	+	+	+	+	+	+	+	100
12 Owens	+	+	+	+	+	+	?	?	75
13 Solarz	+	+	+	+	+	?	+	+	88
14 *Molinari*	+	–	+	+	+	–	+	+	50
15 *Green*	+	+	+	+	+	–	+	+	88
16 Rangel	+	+	+	+	+	+	+	+	100
17 Weiss	+	?	?	+	+	+	+	+	75
18 Garcia*	+	?	?	+	?	+	+	+	63
19 Biaggi*	?	?	?	?	?	?	?	0	0
20 *DioGuardi*	+	–	–	+	+	–	+	+	63

HOUSE	Civil Rights Restoration	Budget Resolution	Medicaid Infant Mortality	Children's Programs	Fair Housing	Welfare Reform	Homeless Assistance	Nutrition Monitoring	% For All Votes
CDF POSITION:	Y	Y	Y	N	N	N	Y	Y	
21 Fish	+	–	+	+	+	–	+	+	75
22 Gilman	+	–	+	+	+	–	+	+	75
23 Stratton	+	+	+	+	+	+	+	?	88
24 Solomon	–	–	–	–	–	–	–	+	25
25 Boehlert	+	+	+	+	+	–	+	+	88
26 Martin, D.	+	?	+	+	+	–	+	+	75
27 Wortley	–	?	–	+	–	?	+	+	38
28 McHugh	+	–	+	+	+	+	+	+	88
29 Horton	+	+	+	+	+	–	+	+	88
30 Slaughter, L.	+	–	+	+	+	–	+	+	75
31 Kemp*	–	–	?	?	?	?	?	–	0
32 LaFalce	+	–	+	+	?	+	+	+	75
33 Nowak	+	+	+	+	+	+	+	+	100
34 Houghton	+	+	+	+	+	–	+	+	88
NORTH CAROLINA									
1 Jones, W.	+	+	+	+	+	+	+	?	88
2 Valentine	+	+	+	+	+	–	+	?	75
3 Lancaster	+	?	+	+	+	–	+	+	75
4 Price, D.	+	+	+	+	+	–	+	+	88
5 Neal	+	+	+	+	+	–	+	+	88
6 Coble	–	–	–	+	+	–	+	+	38
7 Rose	+	?	+	+	+	+	+	+	88
8 Hefner	+	+	+	?	+	–	+	+	75
9 McMillan, A.	–	–	–	+	–	–	+	–	25
10 Ballenger	–	–	–	–	–	–	–	–	0
11 Clarke	+	+	+	+	+	–	+	+	88
NORTH DAKOTA									
1 Dorgan	+	–	+	+	+	+	+	+	88
OHIO									
1 Luken, T.	+	+	+	+	+	–	+	+	88
2 Gradison	+	–	+	+	+	–	+	–	63
3 Hall, T.	+	+	+	+	+	+	+	+	100
4 Oxley	–	?	?	+	+	–	–	–	25
5 Latta	–	–	?	+	+	–	–	–	25
6 McEwen	–	–	–	+	+	–	–	–	25
7 DeWine	–	+	?	+	+	–	+	+	63
8 Lukens, D.	–	–	?	–	–	–	–	–	0
9 Kaptur	+	+	+	+	+	–	+	+	88
10 Miller, C.	–	–	+	–	+	–	+	–	25
11 Eckart	+	–	+	+	+	–	+	+	88
12 Kasich	–	–	–	+	+	–	+	–	38
13 Pease	+	+	+	?	–	+	+	+	75
14 Sawyer	+	+	+	+	+	+	+	+	100
15 Wylie	–	–	–	+	+	–	+	–	38
16 Regula	–	–	+	+	+	–	+	–	50
17 Traficant	+	+	+	+	+	+	+	+	100
18 Applegate	+	–	+	+	+	+	+	+	75
19 Feighan	+	+	+	+	+	+	+	+	100
20 Oakar	+	?	+	+	+	+	+	+	88
21 Stokes	+	+	+	+	+	+	+	+	100
OKLAHOMA									
1 Inhofe	–	–	–	–	–	–	–	+	13
2 Synar	+	+	+	+	+	+	+	+	100
3 Watkins	+	–	+	+	+	–	+	+	75
4 McCurdy	+	+	+	+	+	–	+	+	88
5 Edwards, M.	–	–	–	–	+	–	+	+	50
6 English	–	–	+	+	+	–	+	+	63
OREGON									
1 AuCoin	+	+	+	+	+	+	+	+	100
2 Smith, R.F.	–	–	–	+	+	–	+	–	38
3 Wyden	+	+	+	+	+	+	+	+	100
4 DeFazio	+	+	+	+	+	?	+	?	75
5 Smith, D.	–	–	–	–	–	–	–	–	0
PENNSYLVANIA									
1 Foglietta	+	+	+	+	+	+	+	+	100
2 Gray, Wm.	+	+	+	?	?	+	+	+	75
3 Borski	+	+	+	+	+	+	+	+	100
4 Kolter	+	+	+	+	–	?	+	+	75
5 Schulze	+	–	?	+	–	–	+	+	50
6 Yatron	+	–	+	+	+	–	+	+	63
7 Weldon	+	–	+	+	+	–	+	+	75
8 Kostmayer	+	+	+	+	+	–	+	+	88
9 Shuster	–	–	–	–	–	–	–	–	0
10 McDade	–	+	+	+	+	–	+	?	63
11 Kanjorski	+	+	+	+	–	+	+	+	88
12 Murtha	+	+	+	?	+	–	+	+	88
13 Coughlin	+	–	+	+	+	–	+	?	50
14 Coyne	+	+	+	+	+	?	+	+	88
15 Ritter	–	–	–	+	+	–	–	+	38
16 Walker	–	–	–	–	–	–	+	–	13
17 Gekas	–	–	–	–	–	–	+	–	13
18 Walgren	+	+	+	+	+	+	+	+	100
19 Goodling	+	+	–	+	–	–	+	+	50
20 Gaydos	+	+	+	?	–	–	+	+	63
21 Ridge	+	–	+	+	–	–	+	+	63
22 Murphy	+	–	+	+	+	–	+	+	88
23 Clinger	–	–	–	+	–	–	+	+	38
RHODE ISLAND									
1 St. Germain	+	?	+	+	+	+	+	+	88
2 Schneider	+	–	–	+	+	–	+	?	50
SOUTH CAROLINA									
1 Ravenel	–	–	–	+	+	–	+	+	50
2 Spence *	–	?	?	?	?	?	?	+	13
3 Derrick	+	+	+	+	+	+	+	+	100
4 Patterson	+	–	+	+	+	–	+	+	75
5 Spratt	+	+	+	?	+	–	+	+	75
6 Tallon	+	–	+	+	+	–	+	+	75
SOUTH DAKOTA									
1 Johnson, T.	+	–	+	+	–	–	+	+	63
TENNESSEE									
1 Quillen	–	?	+	+	–	–	+	–	38
2 Duncan*	+	?	?	?	0	0	0	0	25
3 Lloyd	+	–	+	+	+	–	+	+	75
4 Cooper	+	+	–	+	+	+	+	+	88
5 Clement	+	+	+	?	+	+	+	+	88
6 Gordon	+	+	+	+	+	+	+	+	100
7 Sundquist	–	–	–	+	?	–	+	–	25

HOUSE	Civil Rights Restoration	Budget Resolution	Medicaid Infant Mortality	Children's Programs	Fair Housing	Welfare Reform	Homeless Assistance	Nutrition Monitoring	% For All Votes
CDF POSITION:	Y	Y	Y	N	N	N	Y	Y	
8 Jones, E.*	+	?	?	+	+	?	+	?	50
9 Ford, H.*	+	+	+	+	?	?	?	+	63
TEXAS									
1 Chapman	+	?	+	+	+	−	+	+	75
2 Wilson*	+	?	?	?	+	+	+	+	63
3 Bartlett	−	−	−	−	−	−	−	+	13
4 Hall, R.	−	−	+	−	−	−	+	+	38
5 Bryant	+	?	+	+	+	?	+	+	75
6 Barton	−	+	−	−	−	−	−	−	13
7 Archer	−	−	−	−	−	−	−	−	0
8 Fields	−	−	−	−	−	?	−	−	0
9 Brooks	+	+	+	+	+	+	+	?	88
10 Pickle	+	+	+	+	+	+	+	?	88
11 Leath	−	+	−	+	−	−	+	−	38
12 Wright**									
13 Boulter*	−	?	?	?	?	?	?	?	0
14 Sweeney	−	−	−	−	+	−	−	−	13
15 de la Garza	+	+	+	+	+	+	?	+	88
16 Coleman, R.	+	?	+	+	+	+	+	+	88
17 Stenholm	−	−	−	+	−	−	+	+	38
18 Leland	+	+	+	?	+	+	+	+	88
19 Combest	−	−	−	−	−	−	−	+	13
20 Gonzalez	+	+	+	+	+	+	+	+	100
21 Smith, L.	−	−	−	−	−	−	−	?	0
22 DeLay	−	−	−	−	−	−	−	−	0
23 Bustamante	+	?	?	+	+	+	+	+	75
24 Frost	+	+	+	+	+	+	+	+	100
25 Andrews	+	+	+	+	+	+	+	+	100
26 Armey	−	−	−	−	−	−	−	−	0
27 Ortiz	+	+	?	+	?	+	+	+	75
UTAH									
1 Hansen	−	?	?	+	−	−	−	−	13
2 Owens, W.	+	+	+	+	+	+	+	+	100
3 Nielson	−	−	−	+	−	−	−	−	13
VERMONT									
1 Jeffords	+	+	?	+	+	−	+	+	75
CDF POSITION:	Y	Y	Y	N	N	N	Y	Y	
VIRGINIA									
1 Bateman	−	+	−	+	−	−	+	−	38
2 Pickett	+	+	+	+	+	−	+	+	88
3 Bliley	−	−	−	+	+	−	+	−	38
4 Sisisky	+	+	+	+	+	−	+	+	88
5 Payne	0	0	0	0	+	−	+	+	75
6 Olin	+	−	−	+	+	−	+	+	63
7 Slaughter, D.	−	−	−	−	−	−	+	−	13
8 Parris	−	−	+	?	−	−	+	−	25
9 Boucher	+	+	+	+	+	−	+	+	88
10 Wolf	−	+	−	+	+	−	+	+	63
WASHINGTON									
1 Miller, J.	+	−	+	+	+	−	+	+	75
2 Swift	+	+	+	+	+	+	+	+	100
3 Bonker	+	+	+	+	+	+	+	+	100
4 Morrison, S.	+	−	+	+	+	−	+	+	75
5 Foley	+	+	+	+	+	+	+	+	100
6 Dicks	+	?	+	+	+	+	+	+	88
7 Lowry	+	+	+	+	+	+	+	+	100
8 Chandler	+	−	−	+	+	−	+	+	63
WEST VIRGINIA									
1 Mollohan	+	+	+	+	−	−	+	+	75
2 Staggers	+	+	+	+	+	+	+	+	100
3 Wise	+	+	+	+	+	−	+	+	88
4 Rahall	+	+	+	+	+	+	+	+	100
WISCONSIN									
1 Aspin	+	?	+	+	+	?	+	+	75
2 Kastenmeier	+	+	+	+	+	+	+	+	100
3 Gunderson	+	−	+	+	−	−	+	+	63
4 Kleczka	+	+	+	+	+	+	+	+	100
5 Moody*	+	+	+	?	?	+	+	?	63
6 Petri	+	−	−	+	−	−	−	−	25
7 Obey	+	+	+	+	+	+	+	+	100
8 Roth	−	−	−	+	−	−	−	−	13
9 Sensenbrenner	−	−	−	+	−	−	−	−	13
WYOMING									
1 Cheney	−	−	−	−	−	?	−	−	0

1989 Congressional Recess Schedule

Senate
Convenes January 3

House
Convenes January 3

Not in session:

District work periods:

January 5-20
February 13-17
March 20-31
April 24-28
May 22-30
June 26-July 7
August 7-September 5

January 5-18
February 11-20
March 24-April 2
May 26-29
July 1-9
August 5-September 5

Senators and representatives are often in their home states and districts during recesses. You can visit them in their district offices at these times and tell them your opinions of budget cuts that hurt children. District offices are listed in the phone book.

How to Contact Your Representatives in Congress

Letters to your senators may be sent to:
The Honorable _____
U.S. Senate
Washington, D.C. 20510

Letters to your representatives may be sent to:
The Honorable _____
U.S. House of Representatives
Washington, D.C. 20515

By telephone, senators and representatives can be reached by calling the U.S. Capitol Switchboard at (202) 224-3121.

CHILDREN IN THE STATES

Child Population and Child Poverty

	Number of Children Under 5 (1987)	Number of Children Age 5-17 (1987)	Total Children Under 18 (1987)	Total State Population (1987)	Children as Percent of State Population (1987)
Alabama	295,000	822,000	1,117,000	4,083,000	27.36
Alaska	60,000	112,000	171,000	525,000	32.57
Arizona	287,000	632,000	919,000	3,386,000	27.14
Arkansas	173,000	475,000	647,000	2,388,000	27.09
California	2,302,000	5,000,000	7,301,000	27,663,000	26.39
Colorado	268,000	605,000	874,000	3,296,000	26.52
Connecticut	214,000	543,000	757,000	3,211,000	23.58
Delaware	47,000	115,000	162,000	644,000	25.16
D.C.	46,000	90,000	136,000	622,000	21.86
Florida	812,000	1,892,000	2,704,000	12,023,000	22.49
Georgia	477,000	1,259,000	1,736,000	6,222,000	27.90
Hawaii	89,000	197,000	286,000	1,083,000	26.41
Idaho	84,000	222,000	305,000	998,000	30.56
Illinois	861,000	2,174,000	3,035,000	11,582,000	26.20
Indiana	390,000	1,080,000	1,470,000	5,531,000	26.58
Iowa	196,000	536,000	732,000	2,834,000	25.83
Kansas	192,000	458,000	651,000	2,476,000	26.29
Kentucky	258,000	738,000	996,000	3,727,000	26.72
Louisiana	385,000	930,000	1,316,000	4,461,000	29.50
Maine	83,000	220,000	303,000	1,187,000	25.53
Maryland	333,000	792,000	1,125,000	4,535,000	24.81
Massachusetts	389,000	947,000	1,336,000	5,855,000	22.82
Michigan	665,000	1,795,000	2,460,000	9,200,000	26.74
Minnesota	323,000	788,000	1,111,000	4,246,000	26.17
Mississippi	211,000	580,000	792,000	2,625,000	30.17
Missouri	369,000	940,000	1,309,000	5,103,000	25.65
Montana	64,000	160,000	224,000	809,000	27.69
Nebraska	122,000	302,000	423,000	1,594,000	26.54
Nevada	77,000	176,000	252,000	1,007,000	25.02
New Hampshire	76,000	190,000	266,000	1,057,000	25.17
New Jersey	513,000	1,318,000	1,831,000	7,672,000	23.87
New Mexico	134,000	312,000	447,000	1,500,000	29.80
New York	1,248,000	3,113,000	4,361,000	17,825,000	24.47
North Carolina	438,000	1,189,000	1,627,000	6,413,000	25.37
North Dakota	55,000	132,000	187,000	672,000	27.83
Ohio	773,000	2,063,000	2,837,000	10,784,000	26.31
Oklahoma	258,000	635,000	893,000	3,272,000	27.29
Oregon	190,000	496,000	686,000	2,724,000	25.18
Pennsylvania	783,000	2,068,000	2,851,000	11,936,000	23.89
Rhode Island	65,000	164,000	229,000	986,000	23.23
South Carolina	256,000	685,000	941,000	3,425,000	27.47
South Dakota	58,000	138,000	196,000	709,000	27.64
Tennessee	328,000	923,000	1,251,000	4,855,000	25.77
Texas	1,502,000	3,482,000	4,984,000	16,789,000	29.69
Utah	184,000	445,000	629,000	1,680,000	37.44
Vermont	40,000	101,000	140,000	548,000	25.55
Virginia	421,000	1,038,000	1,460,000	5,904,000	24.73
Washington	342,000	827,000	1,169,000	4,538,000	25.76
West Virginia	117,000	373,000	490,000	1,897,000	25.83
Wisconsin	356,000	913,000	1,270,000	4,807,000	26.42
Wyoming	43,000	105,000	148,000	490,000	30.20
U.S. Total	18,252,000	45,290,000	63,542,000	243,400,000	26.11

Child Population and Child Poverty (Continued)

	Estimated Average Number of Poor Children, 1983-1987	Estimated Average Child Poverty Rate, 1983-1987	Rank of Average Child Poverty Rate 1983-1987	Change in Child Poverty Rate from 1979 to 1983-1987	Estimated State Median Income of 4-Person Families (1989)	Estimated State Median Income Rank (1989)
Alabama	348,000	31.7	50	8.1	29,799	38
Alaska	21,000	12.7	3	0.6	41,292	5
Arizona	183,000	21.2	32	4.7	33,477	23
Arkansas	192,000	29.0	46	5.6	27,157	47
California	1,512,000	21.4	35	6.2	36,026	14
Colorado	131,000	16.2	16	4.7	36,026	14
Connecticut	86,000	11.8	2	0.4	44,330	2
Delaware	24,000	15.3	10	-0.3	35,766	16
D.C.	39,000	31.3	49	4.3	35,424	17
Florida	575,000	21.1	31	2.6	33,368	24
Georgia	381,000	24.2	43	3.1	34,602	19
Hawaii	46,000	16.7	19	3.7	36,618	11
Idaho	67,000	21.7	36	7.4	27,075	49
Illinois	730,000	22.8	38	7.9	36,163	12
Indiana	259,000	18.4	23	6.5	32,026	30
Iowa	170,000	21.3	33	9.8	30,556	37
Kansas	96,000	14.5	7	3.1	32,512	27
Kentucky	238,000	23.6	42	2.0	28,464	45
Louisiana	390,000	30.6	48	7.1	29,614	39
Maine	48,000	16.0	14	0.2	31,297	34
Maryland	133,000	13.0	4	0.5	42,250	4
Massachusetts	204,000	14.1	6	1.0	42,295	3
Michigan	564,000	22.7	37	9.4	36,088	13
Minnesota	186,000	16.3	17	6.1	36,746	10
Mississippi	257,000	34.3	51	3.9	26,763	51
Missouri	268,000	20.5	29	5.9	33,149	25
Montana	48,000	20.1	27	6.3	29,190	42
Nebraska	86,000	18.7	25	6.6	31,484	32
Nevada	39,000	15.2	9	5.2	33,604	22
New Hampshire	15,000	6.2	1	-3.2	39,503	6
New Jersey	288,000	15.5	12	1.4	44,591	1
New Mexico	117,000	27.5	45	5.4	27,474	46
New York	1,031,000	23.6	41	4.6	36,796	9
North Carolina	294,000	19.5	26	1.2	31,787	31
North Dakota	33,000	16.4	18	2.1	29,424	41
Ohio	581,000	20.2	28	7.0	34,038	20
Oklahoma	188,000	21.0	30	5.3	29,071	43
Oregon	121,000	17.7	22	5.7	31,392	33
Pennsylvania	516,000	18.4	24	4.5	32,700	26
Rhode Island	38,000	16.7	20	3.1	35,837	15
South Carolina	215,000	23.5	40	2.5	31,025	35
South Dakota	43,000	21.3	34	1.3	27,008	50
Tennessee	293,000	25.2	44	4.6	29,568	40
Texas	1,079,000	23.3	39	4.6	32,442	29
Utah	81,000	13.2	5	2.5	30,635	36
Vermont	22,000	16.1	15	2.2	32,490	28
Virginia	207,000	14.9	8	0.0	37,885	7
Washington	194,000	16.9	21	5.4	35,071	18
West Virginia	155,000	30.4	47	11.9	27,094	48
Wisconsin	199,000	15.8	13	5.4	33,739	21
Wyoming	23,000	15.5	11	7.8	28,742	44
U.S. Total	13,055,000	20.9		4.9	34,716	

Family Income and Supports

	Total Unemployment Rate (1987)	Total Unemployment Rank (1987)	Black Unemployment Rate (1987)	Percent of Unemployed Receiving Unemployment Insurance (1987)	Percent of Child Support Enforcement Cases with at Least One Payment (1987)	Child Support Enforcement Cases with Payment, Rank (1987)	Monthly AFDC Benefit for a 3-Person Family (July 1988)
Alabama	7.8	40	14.2	25.4	12.7	30	118
Alaska	10.8	49	17.4	57.5	18.3	19	779
Arizona	6.2	26	n/a	27.0	5.8	49	293
Arkansas	8.1	42	19.5	30.2	16.8	22	204
California	5.8	24	10.8	43.8	18.8	18	663
Colorado	7.7	39	15.6	25.3	6.3	45	356
Connecticut	3.3	4	6.7	34.8	30.5	4	623
Delaware	3.2	2	6.6	35.7	35.7	2	319
D.C.	6.3	28	8.4	41.7	5.9	48	379
Florida	5.3	18	10.7	17.1	11.8	33	275
Georgia	5.5	20	10.3	24.6	10.1	40	270
Hawaii	3.8	6	n/a	36.4	13.0	29	557
Idaho	8.0	41	n/a	39.4	17.2	20	304
Illinois	7.4	35	18.1	29.2	7.4	43	342
Indiana	6.4	31	17.0	21.3	11.0	36	288
Iowa	5.5	21	n/a	27.4	17.2	21	394
Kansas	4.9	14	11.8	39.6	11.1	35	427
Kentucky	8.8	46	21.4	20.1	12.7	31	218
Louisiana	12.0	51	20.6	28.7	10.8	37	190
Maine	4.4	12	n/a	39.5	26.1	10	416
Maryland	4.2	9	8.6	30.2	15.4	27	377
Massachusetts	3.2	3	6.0	53.4	37.6	1	539
Michigan	8.2	43	21.1	33.2	27.6	7	436
Minnesota	5.4	19	n/a	31.9	25.7	11	532
Mississippi	10.2	48	18.1	21.8	6.4	44	120
Missouri	6.3	29	15.7	30.1	15.5	26	282
Montana	7.4	36	n/a	31.2	6.3	46	359
Nebraska	4.9	15	n/a	27.0	27.2	8	364
Nevada	6.3	30	13.3	30.9	22.3	14	330
New Hampshire	2.5	1	n/a	17.3	29.8	5	496
New Jersey	4.0	8	8.5	44.9	23.7	13	424
New Mexico	8.9	47	n/a	23.8	5.8	50	264
New York	4.9	16	9.3	41.5	20.1	16	539
North Carolina	4.5	13	8.7	28.4	15.6	25	266
North Dakota	5.2	17	n/a	37.7	16.0	24	371
Ohio	7.0	34	15.4	28.7	12.6	32	309
Oklahoma	7.4	37	15.6	21.4	4.1	51	310
Oregon	6.2	27	n/a	42.5	19.4	17	412
Pennsylvania	5.7	23	10.9	41.5	24.3	12	402
Rhode Island	3.8	7	11.8	58.5	15.3	28	517
South Carolina	5.6	22	12.3	24.6	11.3	34	201
South Dakota	4.2	10	n/a	19.9	28.0	6	366
Tennessee	6.6	33	14.2	25.4	10.4	38	173
Texas	8.4	44	15.9	21.6	8.7	42	184
Utah	6.4	32	n/a	27.8	22.3	15	376
Vermont	3.6	5	n/a	39.5	27.2	9	629
Virginia	4.2	11	8.4	16.6	10.3	39	354
Washington	7.6	38	16.1	37.6	16.4	23	492
West Virginia	10.8	50	26.6	25.5	6.1	47	249
Wisconsin	6.1	25	21.6	33.0	33.0	3	517
Wyoming	8.6	45	n/a	30.9	9.6	41	360
U.S. Total	6.2		13.0	31.5	16.5		n/a

Family Income and Supports (Continued)

	1988 AFDC Benefits as Percent of 1987 Federal Poverty Level for 3-Person Families	AFDC Benefits as Percent of Federal Poverty Level, Rank	Monthly Combined AFDC and Food Stamps for 3 Persons (July 1988)	Monthly Combined AFDC and Food Stamps (July 1988) as Percent of Federal (1987) Poverty Level	Percent of AFDC Households Receiving Food Stamps (1986)	HUD-Determined Fair Market Rent in Lowest Cost Metropolitan Area in State (1987)	HUD Fair Market Rent as Percent of AFDC Grant for 3 Persons (July 1988)	State Income Tax on a $10,000 Annual Income (1988)
Alabama	15.6	51	346	45.8	83.3	306	259.3	156
Alaska	82.6	3	980	103.8	65.4	576	73.9	*
Arizona	38.8	36	512	67.8	80.5	529	180.5	32
Arkansas	27.0	45	432	57.2	84.2	349	171.1	130
California	87.8	1	771	102.1	71.8	407	61.4	0
Colorado	47.2	28	557	73.8	86.0	435	122.2	0
Connecticut	82.5	4	743	98.4	80.6	503	80.7	*
Delaware	42.3	32	531	70.3	78.6	541	169.6	45
D.C.	50.2	20	573	75.9	n/a	671	177.0	0
Florida	36.4	39	500	66.2	77.1	335	121.8	*
Georgia	35.8	40	496	65.7	78.3	368	136.3	10
Hawaii	64.2	12	853	98.3	88.6	619	111.1	116
Idaho	40.3	35	520	68.9	88.3	510	167.8	0
Illinois	45.3	30	552	73.1	88.5	420	122.8	150
Indiana	38.1	37	509	67.4	81.7	346	120.1	204
Iowa	52.2	19	583	77.2	87.7	408	103.6	144
Kansas	56.6	14	622	82.4	78.8	413	96.7	0
Kentucky	28.9	44	446	59.1	86.5	335	153.7	281
Louisiana	25.2	47	418	55.4	n/a	359	188.9	0
Maine	55.1	16	599	79.3	86.2	443	106.5	0
Maryland	49.9	21	589	78.0	81.3	365	96.8	0
Massachusetts	71.4	5	685	90.7	79.8	496	92.0	0
Michigan	57.7	13	613	81.2	93.3	371	85.1	129
Minnesota	70.5	7	680	90.1	78.1	415	78.0	0
Mississippi	15.9	50	348	46.1	87.6	358	298.3	0
Missouri	37.4	38	505	66.9	82.2	320	113.5	31
Montana	47.5	27	559	74.0	90.6	424	118.1	109
Nebraska	48.2	25	562	74.4	85.4	408	112.1	0
Nevada	43.7	31	538	71.3	72.2	596	180.6	*
New Hampshire	65.7	10	655	86.8	80.5	569	114.7	*
New Jersey	56.2	15	612	81.1	85.9	450	106.1	120
New Mexico	35.0	42	492	65.2	88.1	391	148.1	0
New York	71.4	6	701	92.8	92.9	400	74.2	252
North Carolina	35.2	41	494	65.4	72.2	337	126.7	0
North Dakota	49.1	23	567	75.1	74.2	404	108.9	0
Ohio	40.9	34	528	69.9	89.3	352	113.9	0
Oklahoma	41.1	33	524	69.4	78.9	353	113.9	33
Oregon	54.6	17	631	83.6	90.2	468	113.6	50
Pennsylvania	53.2	18	589	78.0	88.4	369	91.8	211
Rhode Island	68.5	8	674	89.3	90.3	506	97.9	0
South Carolina	26.6	46	429	56.8	79.5	333	165.7	0
South Dakota	48.5	24	564	74.7	72.8	379	103.6	*
Tennessee	22.9	49	401	53.1	85.2	346	200.0	*
Texas	24.4	48	412	54.6	87.3	349	189.7	*
Utah	49.8	22	571	75.6	81.1	402	106.9	0
Vermont	83.3	2	748	99.1	84.2	579	92.1	93
Virginia	46.9	29	555	73.5	58.9	417	84.8	*
Washington	65.2	11	666	88.2	84.0	365	146.6	60
West Virginia	33.0	43	477	63.2	92.8	365	73.9	0
Wisconsin	68.5	9	669	88.6	84.8	382	73.9	*
Wyoming	47.7	26	559	74.0	85.4	467	129.7	*
U.S. Total	n/a	n/a	n/a	n/a	83.4	n/a	n/a	n/a

*No broad-based individual income tax.

Note: Unemployment insurance, percent of AFDC families receiving food stamps, and income tax data from the Center on Budget and Policy Priorities.

Maternal and Child Health

	Percent of Babies Born to Mothers Receiving Early Prenatal Care (1st Trimester) (1986)	Early Prenatal Care Rank (1986)	Percent of Babies Born to Mothers Receiving No Care or Late (3rd Trimester) Care (1986)	Late Or No Prenatal Care Rank (1986)
Alabama	73.2	41	6.5	40
Alaska	77.2	31	4.3	21
Arizona	71.6	43	8.2	46
Arkansas	69.5	46	6.9	43
California	75.4	35	5.7	36
Colorado	77.6	26	5.2	31
Connecticut	85.8	1	3.3	11
Delaware	78.2	23	3.9	15
D.C.	59.3	50	11.4	49
Florida	68.4	47	8.6	47
Georgia	73.5	40	6.4	39
Hawaii	77.5	27	5.1	30
Idaho	76.1	32	5.3	33
Illinois	78.4	22	4.6	23
Indiana	77.3	29	5.3	32
Iowa	85.7	2	2.2	1
Kansas	81.2	13	3.9	14
Kentucky	75.6	34	4.9	27
Louisiana	78.6	21	4.7	25
Maine	83.1	6	2.2	2
Maryland	80.3	15	4.0	17
Massachusetts	84.0	4	2.8	6
Michigan	80.4	14	3.4	12
Minnesota	80.0	17	3.8	13
Mississippi	76.0	33	4.1	19
Missouri	80.0	18	4.3	22
Montana	77.3	30	4.7	26
Nebraska	81.6	11	3.2	8
Nevada	73.7	39	6.5	41
New Hampshire	83.7	5	2.6	3
New Jersey	81.3	12	5.0	29
New Mexico	58.4	51	13.3	51
New York	71.7	42	10.2	48
North Carolina	77.7	25	4.6	24
North Dakota	82.1	9	2.7	5
Ohio	82.2	8	3.3	10
Oklahoma	71.5	44	7.3	44
Oregon	73.9	38	6.4	38
Pennsylvania	78.0	24	5.3	34
Rhode Island	85.4	3	2.6	4
South Carolina	67.3	48	8.1	45
South Dakota	74.1	37	5.7	37
Tennessee	75.2	36	5.5	35
Texas	66.8	49	11.5	50
Utah	82.0	10	3.1	7
Vermont	78.9	20	4.2	20
Virginia	80.1	16	4.0	18
Washington	77.4	28	4.9	28
West Virginia	70.6	45	6.9	42
Wisconsin	82.8	7	3.2	9
Wyoming	80.0	19	3.9	16
United States	n/a		n/a	

Maternal and Child Health (Continued)

	Infant Mortality Rate (1986)	Infant Mortality Rank (1986)	Black Infant Mortality Rate (1986)	Number of Low-Birthweight Births (1986)	Percent of All Births that are Low Birthweight (1986)	Low Birthweight Rank (1986)
Alabama	13.3	49	20.0	4,760	8.0	46
Alaska	10.8	33	n/a	558	4.6	1
Arizona	9.4	16	14.7	3,764	6.2	18
Arkansas	10.3	28	15.3	2,614	7.6	41
California	8.9	8	16.2	28,769	6.0	17
Colorado	8.6	5	17.2	4,254	7.7	43
Connecticut	9.1	9	18.4	2,944	6.6	23
Delaware	11.5	41	17.6	722	7.4	37
D.C.	21.1	51	24.0	1,224	12.2	51
Florida	11.0	35	18.2	12,718	7.6	40
Georgia	12.5	47	18.4	7,946	8.1	47
Hawaii	9.3	14	n/a	1,253	6.9	29
Idaho	11.3	39	n/a	852	5.2	7
Illinois	12.1	45	22.3	13,141	7.4	39
Indiana	11.3	38	21.5	5,047	6.4	20
Iowa	8.5	3	n/a	2,031	5.2	10
Kansas	8.9	7	15.0	2,433	6.2	19
Kentucky	9.8	23	12.7	3,673	7.1	35
Louisiana	11.9	44	17.0	6,734	8.6	49
Maine	8.8	6	n/a	858	5.1	5
Maryland	11.7	43	17.3	5,348	7.7	42
Massachusetts	8.5	2	18.5	4,716	5.8	15
Michigan	11.4	40	22.8	9,493	6.9	31
Minnesota	9.2	12	16.4	3,315	5.1	3
Mississippi	12.4	46	16.2	3,621	8.7	50
Missouri	10.7	32	18.5	5,124	6.8	25
Montana	9.6	20	n/a	748	5.9	16
Nebraska	10.1	25	n/a	1,343	5.5	14
Nevada	9.1	11	n/a	1,182	7.4	38
New Hampshire	9.1	10	n/a	824	5.2	9
New Jersey	9.8	21	18.5	7,413	6.8	26
New Mexico	9.5	19	n/a	1,906	7.1	34
New York	10.7	31	16.7	19,271	7.3	36
North Carolina	11.5	42	17.4	7,132	7.9	44
North Dakota	8.4	1	n/a	532	4.9	2
Ohio	10.6	30	17.4	10,550	6.7	24
Oklahoma	10.4	29	17.3	3,290	6.5	22
Oregon	9.4	17	n/a	1,990	5.1	4
Pennsylvania	10.2	26	19.8	11,046	6.9	30
Rhode Island	9.4	15	n/a	862	6.4	21
South Carolina	13.2	48	18.1	4,435	8.6	48
South Dakota	13.3	50	n/a	616	5.3	11
Tennessee	11.0	36	18.6	5,240	7.9	45
Texas	9.5	18	15.9	20,984	6.8	28
Utah	8.6	4	n/a	1,974	5.4	13
Vermont	10.0	24	n/a	419	5.2	6
Virginia	11.1	37	18.0	6,127	7.0	33
Washington	9.8	22	13.5	3,596	5.2	8
West Virginia	10.2	27	n/a	1,628	7.0	32
Wisconsin	9.2	13	17.3	3,891	5.4	12
Wyoming	10.9	34	n/a	589	6.8	27
United States	n/a		n/a	255,500	n/a	

State Medicaid Eligibility Characteristics for Children and Pregnant Women, October 1988

State	Expanded Financial Eligibility				Other Eligibility and Benefit Options		
	Up to 100% of Federal Poverty Level		Above 100% of Federal Poverty Level	Current Maximum Age for Children Under 100% Poverty[1]		Continuous Eligibility for Pregnant Women	
	Pregnant Women and Infants	Children Over Age One	Pregnant Women and Infants		Waives Asset Test		Presumptive Eligibility
Alabama	Yes	No	No	—	Yes	Yes	Yes
Alaska	Yes	No	No	—	No	No	No
Arizona	Yes	Yes	No	5	Yes	Yes	No
Arkansas	Yes	Yes	No	5	No	Yes	Yes
California	Yes	No	Yes	—	No	No	No
Colorado	No	No	No	—	No	No	No
Connecticut	Yes	No	Yes	—	Yes	Yes	No
Delaware	Yes	No	No	—	Yes	Yes	No
District of Columbia	Yes	Yes	No	2	Yes	Yes	No
Florida	Yes	Yes	No	5	Yes	Yes	Yes
Georgia	Yes	Yes	No	2(5)	Yes	No	Yes
Hawaii	Yes	No	No	—	Yes	Yes	Yes
Idaho	Yes	No	No	—	Yes	No	No
Illinois	Yes	No	No	—	Yes	Yes	Yes
Indiana	Yes	No	No	—	Yes	Yes	Yes
Iowa	Yes	Yes	Yes	2(5)	No	No	No
Kansas	Yes	Yes	No	2	Yes	No	No
Kentucky	Yes	Yes	Yes	2	No	Yes	No
Louisiana	Yes	Yes	No	5(8)	Yes	Yes	Yes
Maine	Yes	Yes	Yes	5	Yes	Yes	Yes
Maryland	Yes	Yes	No	2	Yes	Yes	Yes
Massachusetts	Yes	Yes	Yes	5	Yes	Yes	Yes
Michigan	Yes	Yes	Yes	3(5)	Yes	Yes	No
Minnesota	Yes	No	Yes	—	Yes	Yes	No
Mississippi	Yes	Yes	Yes	2(5)	No	Yes	No
Missouri	Yes	Yes	No	3(5)	No	Yes	No
Montana	No	No	No	—	No	No	No
Nebraska	Yes	Yes	No	2(5)	Yes	Yes	Yes
Nevada	No	No	No	—	No	No	No
New Hampshire	No	No	No	—	No	No	No
New Jersey	Yes	Yes	No	2	Yes	Yes	Yes
New Mexico	Yes	Yes	No	3(5)	No	Yes	Yes
New York	No	No	No	—	No	No	No
North Carolina	Yes	Yes	No	3(5)	Yes	Yes	Yes
North Dakota	No	No	No	—	No	No	No
Ohio	Yes	No	No	—	Yes	Yes	No
Oklahoma	Yes	Yes	No	2	Yes	Yes	No
Oregon	Yes	Yes	No	3	Yes	Yes	No
Pennsylvania	Yes	Yes	No	3(5)	Yes	No	Yes
Rhode Island	Yes	Yes	Yes	5(8)	Yes	Yes	No
South Carolina	Yes	No	No	—	Yes	Yes	No
South Dakota	Yes	No	No	—	Yes	Yes	No
Tennessee	Yes	Yes	No	5	Yes	Yes	Yes
Texas	Yes	Yes	No	2(5)	No	Yes	Yes
Utah	Yes	No	No	—	Yes	Yes	Yes
Vermont	Yes	Yes	Yes	5(8)	No	Yes	No
Virginia	Yes	No	No	—	Yes	Yes	No
Washington	Yes	Yes	No	3	No	Yes	No
West Virginia	Yes	Yes	Yes	5(8)	Yes	Yes	No
Wisconsin	Yes[2]	No	Yes[2]	—	No	No	Yes
Wyoming	Yes	No	No	—	Yes	Yes	No
Total	45	28	13		33	37	20

[1]Number in parentheses indicates authorized age limit in states phasing in coverage of children below poverty.

State Medicaid Eligibility Levels for Children and Pregnant Women, October 1988

Maximum Medicaid Income Eligibility Levels as a Percentage of the Federal Poverty Level for a Family of Three

State	Pregnant Women and Infants	Young Children[1]	Older Children	Medically Needy Income Level	Maximum AFDC Payment Level[2]
Alabama	100.0	14.6	14.6	—	14.6
Alaska	100.0	77.2	77.2	—	77.2
Arizona	100.0	100.0(5)	36.3	—	36.3
Arkansas	100.0	100.0(5)	25.3	34.1	25.3
California	185.0	82.1	82.1	110.5	82.1
Colorado	52.1	52.1	52.1	—	44.1(52.1)
Connecticut	185.0	77.2	77.2	87.9	77.2
Delaware	100.0	39.5	39.5	—	39.5
District of Columbia	100.0	100.0(2)	46.9	60.1	46.9
Florida	100.0	100.0(5)	34.1	45.4	34.1
Georgia	100.0	100.0(5)	33.4	45.4	33.4
Hawaii	100.0	59.9	59.9	59.9	59.9
Idaho	68.0	37.6	37.6	—	37.6
Illinois	100.0	42.4	42.4	56.7	42.4
Indiana	50.0	35.7	35.7	—	35.7
Iowa	150.0	100.0(5)	48.8	65.0	48.8
Kansas	100.0	100.0(2)	52.9	59.4	52.9
Kentucky	125.0	100.0(2)	27.0	36.2	27.0
Louisiana	100.0	100.0(8)	23.5	32.0	23.5
Maine	185.0	100.0(5)	71.0	69.1	51.5(71.0)
Maryland	100.0	100.0(2)	46.7	54.7	46.7
Massachusetts	185.0	100.0(5)	66.7	90.8	66.7
Michigan	185.0	100.0(5)	74.8	68.0	57.7(74.8)
Minnesota	185.0	65.9	65.9	87.8	65.9
Mississippi	185.0	100.0(5)	45.6	—	14.9(45.6)
Missouri	100.0	100.0(5)	34.9	—	34.9
Montana	50.5	44.5	44.5	50.5	44.5
Nebraska	100.0	100.0(5)	45.1	60.9	45.1
Nevada	40.9	40.9	40.9	—	40.9
New Hampshire	69.0	61.4	61.4	69.0	61.4
New Jersey	100.0	100.0(2)	52.5	70.1	52.5
New Mexico	100.0	100.0(5)	32.7	—	32.7
New York	82.4	82.4	82.4	78.5	82.4
North Carolina	100.0	100.0(5)	32.9	44.3	32.9
North Dakota	53.9	45.9	45.9	53.9	45.9
Ohio	100.0	38.3	38.3	—	38.3
Oklahoma	100.0	100.0(2)	58.3	53.6	38.4(58.3)
Oregon	100.0	100.0(3)	51.0	69.2	51.0
Pennsylvania	100.0	100.0(5)	49.8	55.7	49.8
Rhode Island	185.0	100.0(8)	64.0	85.7	64.0
South Carolina	100.0	49.9	49.9	—	24.9(49.9)
South Dakota	100.0	45.3	45.3	—	45.3
Tennessee	100.0	100.0(5)	45.2	28.9	21.4(45.2)
Texas	100.0	100.0(5)	22.8	33.1	22.8
Utah	100.0	62.2	62.2	62.0	46.6(62.2)
Vermont	185.0	100.0(8)	77.9	104.1	77.9
Virginia	100.0	43.8	43.8	44.3	43.8
Washington	90.0	90.0(3)	60.9	74.2	60.9
West Virginia	150.0	100.0(8)	30.8	35.9	30.8
Wisconsin	120.0[3]	64.0	64.0	85.3	64.0
Wyoming	100.0	44.6	44.6	—	44.6

[1]States have the option of covering children older than one born after September 30, 1983, with incomes above the AFDC payment level and up to the federal poverty level until their eighth birthday. The number in parentheses indicates the age limit chosen by states for eventual coverage if more than the current age limit.

[2]Most states use the AFDC payment level as the Medicaid income eligibility threshhold. Eight states have chosen to use the higher AFDC standard of need level to determine Medicaid eligibility. The AFDC standard of need level is included in parentheses for those states.

[3]100 percent state-funded.

Out-of-Wedlock Births and Births to Adolescent Mothers

	Total Number of Births (1986)	Percent Born Out-of-Wedlock (1986)	Out-of-Wedlock Rank (1986)	Number of Babies Born to Teens (1986)
Alabama	59,465	25.9	39	10,362
Alaska	12,167	20.8	28	1,057
Arizona	60,874	25.6	38	8,384
Arkansas	34,393	24.0	35	6,547
California	482,236	26.5	40	52,776
Colorado	55,151	18.0	15	5,645
Connecticut	44,850	19.0	17	3,940
Delaware	9,718	27.0	42	1,280
D.C.	10,045	57.7	51	1,711
Florida	167,601	26.7	41	23,081
Georgia	98,183	27.2	44	16,708
Hawaii	18,297	20.3	26	1,750
Idaho	16,448	11.8	2	1,780
Illinois	176,717	27.1	43	22,086
Indiana	79,322	21.0	29	11,122
Iowa	38,771	15.0	6	3,569
Kansas	39,265	16.7	11	4,497
Kentucky	51,794	20.0	25	9,033
Louisiana	77,955	30.2	48	13,120
Maine	16,709	19.0	18	1,939
Maryland	69,538	30.5	49	8,156
Massachusetts	82,190	19.3	19	6,855
Michigan	137,631	19.3	20	16,874
Minnesota	65,784	16.3	8	4,808
Mississippi	41,871	34.0	50	8,599
Missouri	75,259	22.5	31	10,119
Montana	12,734	17.8	14	1,280
Nebraska	24,426	15.5	7	2,164
Nevada	15,897	16.6	9	1,895
New Hampshire	15,895	13.9	4	1,227
New Jersey	108,812	22.9	32	10,242
New Mexico	27,392	27.9	46	4,194
New York	264,027	29.4	47	25,664
North Carolina	90,254	23.6	34	14,354
North Dakota	10,819	12.9	3	868
Ohio	158,026	23.4	33	21,078
Oklahoma	50,640	18.6	16	7,906
Oregon	38,871	20.6	27	4,228
Pennsylvania	160,970	24.4	36	18,197
Rhode Island	13,444	19.8	23	1,383
South Carolina	51,800	27.6	45	8,595
South Dakota	11,615	17.5	12	1,131
Tennessee	66,249	25.3	37	11,265
Texas	307,066	17.7	13	46,672
Utah	36,412	9.8	1	3,404
Vermont	8,139	16.7	10	751
Virginia	87,183	22.4	30	10,482
Washington	69,440	19.8	24	7,252
West Virginia	23,236	19.5	21	3,979
Wisconsin	72,333	19.6	22	7,146
Wyoming	8,633	13.9	5	926
United States	3,756,547	23.4		472,081

Out-of-Wedlock Births and Births to Adolescent Mothers (Continued)

	Percent of All Births that Were to Teens (1986)	Percent of All Births to Teens, Rank (1986)	Number of Out-of-Wedlock Births to Teens (1986)	Percent of All Births to Teens That Were Out-of-Wedlock (1986)	Teen Out-of-Wedlock Birth Rank (1986)	Percent of Births to Teenage Mothers who Received Early Prenatal Care (1986)
Alabama	17.4	48	6,034	58.2	15	50.4
Alaska	8.7	5	613	58.0	14	58.4
Arizona	13.8	36	5,187	61.9	31	53.0
Arkansas	19.0	50	3,438	52.5	9	50.6
California	10.9	23	32,561	61.7	30	55.4
Colorado	10.2	17	3,392	60.1	22	50.6
Connecticut	8.8	6	2,458	62.4	32	58.2
Delaware	13.2	32	908	70.9	43	57.4
D.C.	17.0	46	1,587	92.8	51	37.5
Florida	13.8	35	14,624	63.4	34	41.4
Georgia	17.0	45	9,922	59.4	20	53.4
Hawaii	9.6	12	1,115	63.7	36	57.9
Idaho	10.8	21	730	41.0	2	57.7
Illinois	12.5	31	16,479	74.6	47	54.5
Indiana	14.0	37	6,585	59.2	19	54.9
Iowa	9.2	8	2,142	60.0	21	66.1
Kansas	11.5	25	2,419	53.8	11	60.3
Kentucky	17.4	49	3,951	43.7	3	57.8
Louisiana	16.8	43	8,576	65.4	39	62.7
Maine	11.6	26	1,195	61.6	28	66.1
Maryland	11.7	27	6,318	77.5	49	57.2
Massachusetts	8.3	4	5,050	73.7	46	60.5
Michigan	12.3	30	9,905	58.7	17	57.8
Minnesota	7.3	1	3,415	71.0	44	54.3
Mississippi	20.5	51	5,831	67.8	40	60.0
Missouri	13.4	34	6,110	60.4	25	56.1
Montana	10.1	16	753	58.8	18	55.1
Nebraska	8.9	7	1,352	62.5	33	56.8
Nevada	11.9	28	895	47.2	8	49.4
New Hampshire	7.7	2	752	61.3	26	58.9
New Jersey	9.4	11	8,032	78.4	50	52.8
New Mexico	15.3	39	2,527	60.3	24	39.7
New York	9.7	13	19,637	76.5	48	45.1
North Carolina	15.9	41	8,404	58.5	16	55.4
North Dakota	8.0	3	487	56.1	12	59.6
Ohio	13.3	33	13,608	64.6	37	61.0
Oklahoma	15.6	40	3,688	46.6	7	50.2
Oregon	10.9	22	2,545	60.2	23	49.4
Pennsylvania	11.3	24	12,948	71.2	45	52.7
Rhode Island	10.3	18	942	68.1	41	65.8
South Carolina	16.6	42	5,557	64.7	38	41.6
South Dakota	9.7	14	653	57.7	13	52.0
Tennessee	17.0	44	5,995	53.2	10	54.9
Texas	15.2	38	20,769	44.5	4	43.6
Utah	9.3	10	1,351	39.7	1	64.6
Vermont	9.2	9	477	63.5	35	57.1
Virginia	12.0	29	6,442	61.5	27	57.9
Washington	10.4	19	4,474	61.7	29	53.9
West Virginia	17.1	47	1,823	45.8	5	47.7
Wisconsin	9.9	15	5,048	70.6	42	59.5
Wyoming	10.7	20	431	46.5	6	61.8
United States	n/a		290,135	61.5		53.0

Working Mothers, Single Mothers, and Child Care

	Percent of Children in Single-Parent Families (1980)	Number of Mothers of Children Under 6 Who Are in the Labor Force (1980)	Percent of Mothers of Children Under 6 Who Are in the Labor Force (1980)	Number of Mothers of Children 6-17 Who Are in the Labor Force (1980)	Percent of Mothers of Children Age 6-17 Who Are in the Labor Force (1980)
Alabama	27.0	121,144	48.97	185,976	60.74
Alaska	20.1	14,815	47.37	19,010	65.29
Arizona	22.4	74,582	44.54	116,676	61.40
Arkansas	24.4	74,852	50.99	109,235	62.59
California	26.1	643,658	46.34	1,084,702	65.16
Colorado	20.2	84,877	46.37	143,495	66.14
Connecticut	21.4	65,531	40.85	165,479	66.68
Delaware	25.0	16,777	48.76	30,835	64.96
D.C.	58.4	16,814	62.13	28,153	72.15
Florida	28.5	239,124	50.70	438,971	64.86
Georgia	28.5	187,672	53.94	290,484	66.56
Hawaii	21.9	32,215	51.46	45,523	69.65
Idaho	16.0	30,658	43.47	42,557	64.53
Illinois	24.2	299,384	43.35	533,822	63.19
Indiana	20.2	166,157	47.10	276,698	64.05
Iowa	14.8	90,190	49.13	140,500	65.80
Kansas	17.5	72,676	48.31	114,595	67.31
Kentucky	20.8	103,395	41.95	159,815	55.82
Louisiana	28.6	128,005	43.98	173,225	55.54
Maine	19.4	30,097	45.34	56,765	63.62
Maryland	27.0	117,155	50.85	233,397	66.86
Massachusetts	21.6	121,355	41.82	281,921	65.45
Michigan	23.6	238,178	41.58	437,667	59.59
Minnesota	14.6	127,727	50.38	205,757	66.97
Mississippi	30.9	92,586	54.40	117,569	62.78
Missouri	21.7	151,162	50.53	235,719	64.36
Montana	17.0	23,679	44.65	36,461	63.35
Nebraska	15.8	50,622	49.36	74,200	67.18
Nevada	26.0	24,364	54.13	41,651	71.13
New Hampshire	17.3	26,858	49.73	50,486	70.02
New Jersey	23.8	155,381	39.11	360,544	62.21
New Mexico	23.0	39,715	42.50	55,396	57.21
New York	26.9	359,593	37.50	776,996	59.28
North Carolina	26.0	203,233	58.32	335,633	70.34
North Dakota	12.3	21,173	47.23	26,499	58.99
Ohio	20.6	280,855	42.17	498,759	59.28
Oklahoma	20.9	93,784	47.20	143,290	63.21
Oregon	21.6	69,430	43.14	123,183	64.54
Pennsylvania	20.8	237,285	37.39	514,559	57.44
Rhode Island	21.6	22,026	45.01	48,863	68.02
South Carolina	28.3	114,638	58.12	167,117	67.94
South Dakota	16.5	24,227	50.90	30,524	64.55
Tennessee	25.2	143,252	50.96	231,926	63.41
Texas	22.1	468,649	48.10	661,620	63.02
Utah	13.3	49,346	37.44	55,339	64.46
Vermont	18.8	14,469	48.10	26,246	67.59
Virginia	24.1	155,359	49.80	275,923	64.93
Washington	20.7	107,403	42.71	193,407	63.71
West Virginia	17.8	39,780	31.62	68,158	45.94
Wisconsin	16.9	139,824	48.59	239,384	67.34
Wyoming	15.6	14,794	41.53	21,415	66.57
U.S. Total	23.3	6,220,525	45.68	10,726,125	63.03

Working Mothers, Single Mothers, and Child Care (Continued)

	Number of Working Women (1987)	Percent Change in Number of Working Women Since 1977	Title XX Funded Child Care Slots (1988)	Change in Title XX Funded Slots 1981-1988
Alabama	848,000	40.4	6,500	-50.0
Alaska	114,000	58.3	6,093	164.9
Arizona	714,000	81.2	14,945	-.7
Arkansas	483,000	27.4	2,191	.6
California	5,990,000	42.0	112,500	n/a
Colorado	771,000	51.5	8,191	17.9
Connecticut	815,000	27.1	12,000	20.0
Delaware	154,000	35.1	1,976	-5.9
D.C.	170,000	8.3	6,739	24.0
Florida	2,693,000	79.9	34,534	110.8
Georgia	1,411,000	48.5	7,999	-2.5
Hawaii	244,000	36.3	1,188	-80.0
Idaho	201,000	30.5	1,057	n/a
Illinois	2,557,000	20.7	20,528	-26.9
Indiana	1,290,000	28.9	7,000	-37.5
Iowa	645,000	16.6	1,673	-3.2
Kansas	569,000	22.9	5,458	-9.0
Kentucky	731,000	20.2	7,714	10.4
Louisiana	836,000	34.8	6,500	-13.9
Maine	262,000	36.5	2,400	-17.8
Maryland	1,108,000	38.2	8,745	28.0
Massachusetts	1,443,000	22.5	18,451	53.8
Michigan	2,021,000	24.4	7,539	-78.9
Minnesota	1,029,000	33.3	n/a	n/a
Mississippi	508,000	23.0	2,712	-43.5
Missouri	1,166,000	22.6	8,969	n/a
Montana	179,000	38.8	455	-58.6
Nebraska	375,000	19.8	14,784	55.5
Nevada	255,000	93.2	280	-68.1
New Hampshire	265,000	52.3	6,500	62.5
New Jersey	1,757,000	25.5	13,500	19.4
New Mexico	295,000	41.1	3,400	130.5
New York	3,784,000	19.2	6,200	n/a
North Carolina	1,525,000	32.4	15,300	2.0
North Dakota	146,000	33.9	190	90.0
Ohio	2,324,000	20.9	15,800	-60.2
Oklahoma	699,000	42.9	15,500	-6.1
Oregon	632,000	39.5	4,981	84.7
Pennsylvania	2,489,000	21.3	26,823	14.5
Rhode Island	245,000	28.9	1,861	-11.9
South Carolina	743,000	32.4	4,500	-9.4
South Dakota	161,000	26.8	64	-96.9
Tennessee	1,062,000	32.1	12,349	-5.0
Texas	3,605,000	53.3	14,900	30.5
Utah	333,000	61.7	7,503	72.4
Vermont	137,000	47.3	2,200	69.2
Virginia	1,347,000	35.2	4,502	-13.4
Washington	1,022,000	50.7	8,690	113.1
West Virginia	312,000	30.5	4,700	-9.6
Wisconsin	1,107,000	22.6	12,690	63.2
Wyoming	105,000	43.8	1,336	n/a
U.S. Total	53,677,000	33.9	n/a	n/a

Education and Youth Employment

	16- to 24-Year-Olds Not in School and Not High School Graduates (1980)	As a Percent of All 16- to 24-Year-Olds (1980)	Rank	Per Pupil Expenditures (1984-1985)	Rank
Alabama	129,000	19.3	45	$2,325	50
Alaska	10,000	13.2	20	7,843	1
Arizona	83,000	17.8	38	3,009	36
Arkansas	69,000	19.2	44	2,482	45
California	704,000	17.4	36	3,256	28
Colorado	69,000	13.3	21	3,697	17
Connecticut	60,000	12.0	13	4,738	5
Delaware	13,000	12.7	15	4,184	9
D.C.	19,000	16.0	32	5,103	3
Florida	257,000	17.7	37	3,241	30
Georgia	195,000	20.9	49	2,657	43
Hawaii	17,000	10.0	6	3,465	24
Idaho	26,000	16.1	33	2,362	48
Illinois	296,000	15.5	29	3,538	21
Indiana	143,000	15.2	27	3,051	34
Iowa	48,000	9.7	4	3,467	23
Kansas	52,000	12.7	16	3,560	20
Kentucky	150,000	24.0	51	2,390	46
Louisiana	148,000	19.5	47	2,990	37
Maine	22,000	12.0	12	3,024	35
Maryland	102,000	14.4	25	4,102	10
Massachusetts	97,000	9.9	5	4,026	11
Michigan	217,000	13.5	23	3,848	13
Minnesota	56,000	8.0	1	3,674	18
Mississippi	94,000	21.2	50	2,350	49
Missouri	128,000	15.7	31	2,958	38
Montana	14,000	10.7	8	3,847	14
Nebraska	24,000	8.8	3	3,471	22
Nevada	24,000	18.4	41	2,829	41
New Hampshire	19,000	13.0	17	3,271	27
New Jersey	139,000	12.3	14	4,504	6
New Mexico	43,000	18.3	40	3,153	32
New York	363,000	13.1	19	5,492	2
North Carolina	195,000	18.9	42	2,625	44
North Dakota	11,000	8.7	2	3,339	25
Ohio	239,000	13.3	22	3,285	26
Oklahoma	83,000	16.4	34	2,850	40
Oregon	65,000	15.6	30	3,889	12
Pennsylvania	217,000	11.3	11	4,237	8
Rhode Island	24,000	15.1	26	4,287	7
South Carolina	103,000	18.0	39	2,783	42
South Dakota	13,000	11.1	10	2,892	39
Tennessee	148,000	19.4	46	2,385	47
Texas	497,000	19.9	48	3,124	33
Utah	34,000	13.0	18	2,220	51
Vermont	9,000	10.1	7	3,651	19
Virginia	154,000	16.7	35	3,155	31
Washington	97,000	13.8	24	3,725	16
West Virginia	58,000	19.0	43	3,244	29
Wisconsin	89,000	10.8	9	3,815	15
Wyoming	13,000	15.4	28	4,799	4
U.S. Total	5,883,000	15.4		3,470	

Education and Youth Employment (Continued)

	Real Percent Change, 1980-1 to 1984-5	Chapter 1 Participants (1985-1986)	Chapter 1 Participants Per 100 Poor Children Aged 5-17 (1983-1987 Average)	Rank	Annual Unemployment Rate, Age 16-19 (1987)	Rank
Alabama	-11.7	117,655	49.6	23	21.1	39
Alaska	4.0	4,301	30.1	49	16.7	26
Arizona	.5	62,826	50.4	20	18.6	34
Arkansas	10.1	65,728	50.3	21	24.8	46
California	-.8	444,099	43.1	34	16.9	27
Colorado	3.5	39,096	43.8	33	20.6	38
Connecticut	24.3	53,890	92.0	2	11.1	9
Delaware	4.5	9,667	59.1	13	9.3	4
D.C.	11.9	16,213	61.0	10	22.0	43
Florida	1.8	151,599	38.7	42	16.1	24
Georgia	17.3	122,604	47.2	28	17.7	31
Hawaii	.3	14,158	45.2	29	13.1	16
Idaho	-4.0	16,829	36.9	43	18.2	33
Illinois	-1.3	162,615	32.7	47	18.0	32
Indiana	14.5	106,993	60.6	12	18.8	36
Iowa	-2.0	25,460	22.0	51	10.0	5
Kansas	4.9	35,506	54.3	15	10.7	8
Kentucky	1.1	101,492	62.6	7	24.1	45
Louisiana	-8.7	108,265	40.7	37	30.8	50
Maine	17.9	21,753	66.5	5	7.9	3
Maryland	6.2	70,852	78.2	4	14.4	18
Massachusetts	3.3	84,822	61.0	11	7.7	2
Michigan	-4.4	155,743	40.5	38	18.7	35
Minnesota	3.7	56,378	44.5	30	12.0	12
Mississippi	10.4	92,960	53.1	16	35.9	51
Missouri	2.7	74,027	40.5	39	14.7	20
Montana	8.2	13,342	40.8	36	15.0	22
Nebraska	9.8	24,971	42.6	35	14.7	21
Nevada	2.7	9,392	35.4	45	19.8	37
New Hampshire	8.9	11,840	115.9	1	5.8	1
New Jersey	4.4	166,206	84.7	3	10.1	6
New Mexico	2.1	31,715	39.8	41	24.8	47
New York	10.7	342,638	48.8	26	12.1	13
North Carolina	-1.1	125,355	62.6	8	13.5	17
North Dakota	10.7	9,042	40.2	40	11.6	10
Ohio	7.6	136,661	34.5	46	17.1	29
Oklahoma	-2.3	62,081	48.5	27	21.7	42
Oregon	-5.4	42,686	51.8	17	16.9	28
Pennsylvania	13.2	217,594	61.9	9	14.5	19
Rhode Island	10.5	12,805	49.5	24	12.3	14
South Carolina	21.1	52,685	36.0	44	16.1	25
South Dakota	9.5	13,002	44.4	31	10.2	7
Tennessee	.3	103,328	51.8	18	21.6	41
Texas	17.4	365,578	49.7	22	23.0	44
Utah	-8.0	24,494	44.4	32	15.2	23
Vermont	11.2	9,841	65.7	6	11.8	11
Virginia	9.2	77,303	54.8	14	17.4	30
Washington	10.5	65,267	49.4	25	21.2	40
West Virginia	14.0	33,614	31.8	48	28.1	49
Wisconsin	5.1	69,408	51.2	19	12.7	15
Wyoming	22.0	4,123	26.3	50	24.9	48
U.S. Total	4.6	4,240,502	49.6		16.9	

CHILDREN IN THE CITIES

City	Number of Children Under 18 (1980)	Rank (1980)	Percent of Child Population that is Black (1980)	Percent of Child Population that is Hispanic (1980)	Child Poverty Rate (%) (1980)	Rank (1980)	Percent of Teens (16-19) Who Are Dropouts (1980)	AFDC Grant, Family of Three ($) (1988)	HUD-Determined Fair Market Rent ($) (1988)	AFDC Grant as Percentage of Fair Market Rent (1988)
Baltimore	211,943	10	66.77	1.12	32.5	24	20.3	377	508	74.21
Boston	121,683	22	35.89	11.83	30.9	19	9.7	539	803	67.12
Chicago	852,876	2	50.70	19.92	30.8	18	20.1	342	580	58.97
Cleveland	159,444	17	50.83	4.70	31.3	20	18.4	309	395	78.23
Columbus	145,867	20	29.76	1.00	21.3	11	14.1	309	418	73.92
Dallas	243,792	8	40.32	18.21	20.4	10	20.5	184	421	43.71
Denver	110,877	24	17.73	32.27	20.2	9	21.0	356	502	70.92
Detroit	364,618	6	74.03	3.14	31.5	21	21.2	436	514	84.82
El Paso	148,812	19	3.04	72.02	28.7	16	13.0	184	382	48.17
Houston	452,255	4	34.19	23.88	17.0	7	22.2	184	388	47.42
Indianapolis	200,447	12	27.36	1.18	15.6	5	18.6	288	410	70.24
Jacksonville	155,581	18	31.93	2.12	22.2	12	18.1	275	426	64.55
Los Angeles	745,738	3	20.51	39.97	23.7	14	19.5	663	684	96.93
Memphis	188,018	14	61.23	1.01	31.6	22	12.1	173	405	42.72
Milwaukee	171,866	15	36.48	6.75	22.5	13	17.8	517	455	113.63
New Orleans	160,332	16	70.99	3.24	38.7	25	14.8	190	499	38.08
New York	1,765,467	1	32.98	28.52	31.8	23	15.8	539	566	95.23
Philadelphia	437,158	5	46.87	6.17	30.0	17	15.0	402	511	78.67
Phoenix	228,752	9	6.25	21.74	13.7	3	21.9	293	554	52.89
San Antonio	253,238	7	7.30	65.68	14.4	4	19.0	184	420	43.81
San Diego	211,432	11	11.99	23.37	16.6	6	11.8	663	647	102.47
San Francisco	116,611	23	20.41	19.57	19.4	8	10.8	663	848	78.18
San Jose	195,285	13	5.57	29.34	10.0	1	15.7	663	840	78.93
Seattle	86,963	25	17.52	4.26	13.4	2	11.5	492	481	102.29
Washington, D.C.	143,491	21	85.99	2.59	27.0	15	12.7	379	671	56.48

City	Number of Births to All Teens (1986)	Number of Births to Black Teens (1986)	Number of Births to Unmarried Teens (1986)	Percentage of Teen Births That were Out-of-Wedlock (1986)	Teen Out-of-Wedlock Rank (1986)	Percentage of All Births That Are to Teens (1986)
Baltimore	2,880	2,320	2,639	91.63	21	21.69
Boston	1,166	603	1,012	86.79	18	12.76
Chicago	9,955	6,892	8,560	85.99	16	18.47
Cleveland	2,031	1,269	1,697	83.55	13	19.99
Columbus	1,585	729	1,184	74.70	11	14.74
Dallas	4,001	1,947	2,684	67.08	7	19.22
Denver	1,310	314	n.a.	n.a.	n.a.	14.25
Detroit	3,991	3,343	3,395	85.07	14	21.00
El Paso	1,459	65	n.a.	n.a.	n.a.	13.87
Houston	5,585	2,262	3,395	60.79	2	15.40
Indianapolis	2,206	952	1,622	73.53	10	16.62
Jacksonville	1,716	891	1,058	61.66	3	15.51
Los Angeles	8,877	2,419	6,353	71.57	9	12.45
Memphis	2,151	1,805	1,843	85.68	15	18.82
Milwaukee	2,227	1,499	1,921	86.26	17	18.36
New Orleans	1,834	1,685	1,648	89.86	20	18.24
New York	13,129	6,890	10,857	82.69	12	11.14
Philadelphia	5,035	3,410	4,507	89.51	19	17.92
Phoenix	2,700	336	1,780	65.93	6	15.59
San Antonio	3,278	262	1,457	44.45	1	18.68
San Diego	1,634	434	1,048	64.14	4	9.42
San Francisco	757	342	533	70.41	8	7.81
San Jose	1,440	120	939	65.21	5	9.50
Seattle	593	231	n.a.	n.a.	n.a.	8.60
Washington, D.C.	1,711	1,584	1,587	92.75	22	17.03

City	Percentage of Black Births That Are to Teens (1986)	Infant Mortality Rate[1] (1986)	Infant Mortality Rank (1986)	Infant Mortality Rate, Black[1] (1986)	Low-birthweight Rate (%) (1986)	Low-birthweight Rank (1986)	Low-birthweight Rate, Black (%) (1986)
Baltimore	25.88	16.2	18	18.2	12.2	20	14.6
Boston	17.15	13.9	13	23.0	8.7	12	12.1
Chicago	26.60	16.6	20	22.9	10.6	17	15.1
Cleveland	24.08	16.3	19	20.3	10.5	16	13.4
Columbus	24.62	12.3	10	13.8	7.5	7	11.1
Dallas	28.01	11.8	8	16.0	9.1	14	14.5
Denver	21.67	n.a.	n.a.	n.a.	n.a.	n.a.	n.a.
Detroit	23.45	20.3	21	24.0	12.7	22	14.5
El Paso	14.74	n.a.	n.a.	n.a.	n.a.	n.a.	n.a.
Houston	21.87	11.3	7	17.2	7.7	8	12.1
Indianapolis	28.17	14.2	14	24.6	8.1	10	13.1
Jacksonville	24.40	13.1	12	19.7	8.1	9	12.2
Los Angeles	18.94	10.1	4	21.2	6.8	5	13.6
Memphis	24.72	15.8	17	18.4	10.3	15	12.8
Milwaukee	30.28	12.2	9	17.2	8.2	11	12.3
New Orleans	22.81	15.5	15	16.8	11.0	19	13.0
New York	15.20	12.4	11	15.5	9.0	13	12.7
Philadelphia	24.11	15.5	16	21.8	10.7	18	14.7
Phoenix	25.75	11.0	6	—	6.8	3	12.7
San Antonio	20.57	10.2	5	—	7.1	6	9.7
San Diego	17.21	9.4	3	14.3	5.9	2	11.0
San Francisco	19.76	8.8	2	—	6.8	4	11.3
San Jose	13.00	7.3	1	—	5.3	1	9.4
Seattle	20.85	n.a.	n.a.	n.a.	n.a.	n.a.	n.a.
Washington, D.C.	20.11	21.1	22	24.0	12.2	21	14.2

[1] Per 1,000 live births.
Note: n.a. Data not available.

— Number too small to calculate a reliable rate.

INDEX

147